D1192306

Southern Christian University Library
1200 Taylor Rd
Montgomery, AL 36117

AMRIDGE UNIVERSITY
LIBRARY

ANCIENT EDUCATION

68-59

ANCIENT EDUCATION

by

WILLIAM A. SMITH

University of California

370.93
S664
57090

LA   00046217
31   Smith, William Anton, 1880-1954.
.S63   Ancient education.

PHILOSOPHICAL LIBRARY
New York

Copyright, 1955, by
PHILOSOPHICAL LIBRARY, INC.
15 East 40th Street, New York 16, N.Y.

All rights reserved

PRINTED IN THE UNITED STATES OF AMERICA

Preface

IN *Ancient Education* I have endeavored to trace the cultural and educational development of seven early peoples —the Mesopotamians, the Egyptians, the Indians, the Chinese, the Greeks, the Romans, and the Hebrews. Basically, my concern has of course been their educational ventures and achievements. But due to the fact that education is itself a part of culture and has no meaning or significance apart from the total cultural setting in any given case, it has been necessary to use the cultures themselves as the points of departure. The traditional history of education, focussed largely upon the characterization of a succession of events, moments, and practices apart from the factors that condition them, is a passing phenomenon. Social science has no sanctions for it.

Since education is a broad concept—a concept the connotation of which ranges all the way from the total socialization process operative in a society to formally organized institutional programs—its scope for historical treatment must of necessity be delimited. For a variety of reasons it seems desirable—apart from a final chapter on Education in Nonliterate Societies—in a survey treatise of this type to concentrate upon the foundations of what ultimately come to be the organized institutional programs. Briefly, this demands some account of the origin and nature of systems of writing, numeral notation, and standardized weights and measures; an identification of the situations and problems—economic, political, religious—that impelled recourse to education; an enumeration of the agencies that defined the aims of education and directed its course; a ferreting out of the varying aims and purposes as such; a characterization of curricular and methodological ventures; and some notion of the beginnings of deliberate speculation about education.

While education in ancient societies revolved about matters of fundamental concern to the societies, one would scarcely turn to the history of education as the source of principles for the solution of contemporary problems. Some decades ago the pedagogically minded were so intent upon doing this that the subject was in danger of falling into complete disrepute. History does not solve problems, and it does not technically repeat itself.

And yet, the history of education is of inestimable value in social engineering. Within limits the farther back it goes the more valuable it becomes. Its value and significance lie of course in the light which it sheds upon the possibilities and limitations of man under varying conditions. Basically, it throws into perspective man's conquest of himself and nature—in the latest stage of which he discovered that he could lift himself by his own boot straps.

What man has accomplished, along with the errors that he succumbed to, show him to be a creature of marked potential and of great vulnerability. All this is abundantly documented in the story of ancient man. This story should be of great interest to contemporary man, especially to that segment of him that exercises leadership. However, as yet Western society has—apart from the Greeks, the Romans, and the Hebrews—been strangely apathetic toward him. It has accepted him as an ethnological curiosity but scarcely as a *bona fide* cultural ancestor. All this points to a venerable provincialism that needs to be sloughed off. To this end, the history of ancient education, as a chapter in the history of human culture, should make a significant contribution.

Contents

AMRIDGE UNIVERSITY LIBRARY

CHAPTER I

The Rise of Old World Cultures

The Grand Divisions of Culture History

IT has long been customary to divide the total span of culture history into four Grand Divisions—the Paleolithic, or Old Stone Age; the Neolithic, or New Stone Age; the Bronze Age; and the Iron Age (11:394). In this scheme the stone ages correspond roughly to prehistory, and the metal ages to the historic period (11:142). The Paleolithic is further commonly divided into at least two stages—the Lower and the Upper. The Neolithic likewise falls into two stages—the initial or Mesolithic, and the full Neolithic. Finally, the Lower and Upper Paleolithic have subsumed under them, in chronological sequence, series of culture epochs, frequently referred to as *industries*. These derive their names from the localities where artifacts characteristic of them were first discovered. The main epochs of the Lower Paleolithic are the Pre-Chellean, Chellean, Acheulian, and Mousterian; those of the Upper Paleolithic in turn are the Aurignacian, Solutrian, and Magdalenian.

It should be noted further that the Paleolithic corresponds roughly to the geologic epoch known as the Pleistocene, and extends therefore over approximately one million years. The Neolithic and the metal ages in turn correspond to the Holocene or recent epoch which began about 14,000 years ago. Finally, it must be borne in mind that the culture epochs associated with the Paleolithic were established in western and northern Europe where the archeological discoveries

3

relating to Old Stone Age Man originated. It is now known
that similar cultural developments and sequences were characteristic of the other regions of the Old World. Indeed, in
many cases they occurred there much earlier than in Europe.
This suggests among other things that European developments may have been appreciably influenced by the cultures
of successive invaders. And it means of course that the European Paleolithic culture epoch nomenclature is local and at
best only indirectly applicable to other Old World regions
(16:23). Nevertheless, it is clear that man everywhere passed
through a stage corresponding to the Old Stone Age in Europe and in due time reached the Neolithic in one form or
other.

Lower Paleolithic Culture Epochs

During nineteen twentieths of his first million years—the
time taken up by the Lower Paleolithic—man made very
little headway. Nevertheless, although primarily a hunter
and food-gatherer, he laid the foundations for toolmaking
and he discovered how to produce fire artificially. During
the Pre-Chellean epoch he hit upon the idea of shattering
flint nodules to secure tools. This, as Nelson puts it, resulted
in "three important inventions: namely, the *hammer*, the
core, and the *flake*" (14:153). The flakes, constituting the primary objective at this stage, served as crude knives, scrapers,
and perforators. There are as yet no indications of attempts
to improve their quality by sharpening or retouching (13:
140).

During the succeeding Chellean epoch man discovered
that he could use the flint core as a first-axe. This, now
commonly known as the *coup-de-poing,* was pointed at one
end and crudely chipped on both faces, and could be held in
the hand and used as a more or less all-purpose tool. It is "the
first designedly dressed and fashioned implement on record"
(14:154). During much of the succeeding Acheulian epoch

this basic tool underwent marked improvement. Toward the end of the epoch, however, it was gradually abandoned. Man had by this time discovered that "a chance flake, properly selected, might serve various special purposes far better" (14: 155). Hence, he began to split it into two—a departure that was to have far-reaching effects in succeeding epochs. Although the tool-makers of these early epochs plied their trade over an enormous time interval in various parts of Europe, Africa, and Asia, and were roughly contemporary with the fossil men antedating Neanderthal man, there are no known fossil remains of them. The cultures have been thoroughly established, but the men that carried them are yet to be discovered.

The last culture epoch of the Lower Paleolithic—the Mousterian—is definitely associated with Neanderthal man, although not necessarily restricted to him. For the first time, then, we not only know the culture but also the men who carried it. The *coup-de-poing* or first-axe disappears at the beginning of this epoch, and flakes designed for a variety of purposes—cutting, chopping, sawing, scraping, and perforating—take its place. The hammer stone also appears in recognizable form. The supreme contribution of this epoch was, however, the invention of pressure chipping—a process that gave the artisan much greater control over flake production. This did not supplant the original percussion method, but rather supplemented it since it was peculiarly suitable for the production of delicate tools and for retouching.

This epoch also furnished the first evidence of artificial fire production, though fire had of course been in use earlier. And the Mousterians buried their dead in ceremonial fashion. This, as Hooton observes, "implies the existence of a whole complex of ideas about death, the future life, the existence of the soul, as well as the development of affection and social solidarity" (10:334). Beyond this, they have left no tangible clues regarding their non-material culture. Their artifacts are not embellished, and there are no decorations in their caves.

Upper Paleolithic Culture Epochs

On the Upper Paleolithic we encounter the Aurignacian, the Solutrian, and the Magdalenian cultures—cultures that are clearly the creations of men of our own species. However, we must bear in mind that these men did not begin *de novo.* They took up where the others left off, and began to make their own contributions—for the most part at an increasingly rapid pace. Relatively, that had of course been true all along the line.

The foundations of Upper Paleolithic culture were, as Kroeber observes, laid during the Aurignacian epoch (11:396). Subsequent developments centered largely around differentiation and enrichment. In the matter of flaking, for example, the flint knapper had near the beginning of this epoch succeeded in preparing a core of roughly conical shape with flattened end which enabled him to remove several flakes from the same form. This was to remain the chief source of long slender flakes to the end of the Neolithic (14:157). The Aurignacians also laid the foundation for bone implements, body ornaments, and certain of the arts—notably, carving, etching, and painting. The utilization of bone and horn called for new processes—chopping, cutting, scraping, and boring—and it gave rise to new tools, among them awls, pins, spear-heads, polishers, and engraving instruments. Some implements were carved and engraved. Body ornaments included paint, and necklaces and anklets made of perforated shells and teeth. Sculpture was directed chiefly toward human figurines and statuettes which appear to have been associated in one way or another with magic or religious cults (14:164–165). In the end of course the greatest achievements of the Aurignacians are generally conceded to have been the realistic paintings and engravings with which they had begun to redecorate the walls of some of their caves toward the close of the epoch.

During the Solutrian epoch, which was brief and localized, flint work reached its highest development, resulting in the famous *laurel leaf* blades both sides of which were equally retouched, and in other tools of marked excellence. The eyed bone needle, which in turn implied thread and the art of sewing, also appeared at this time. Sculpture, involving both human and animal forms, and making use of ivory, reached a new level of excellence.

During the Magdalenian epoch progress in stone work ceased, although stone implements remained in use. Two factors appear to account for this. In the first place, flaking from prepared cores, initiated during the Aurignacian epoch, had come to yield implements that required little retouching. In the second place, the Magdalenians shifted to bone and horn as basic materials (11:162–164). In implements made of these materials—barbed harpoons, javelin and spear points, spear throwers, and duplicates of previously existing tools— they reached the acme of perfection, so much so, that the epoch might well be characterized as the age of bone (14: 165). In addition to their technical excellences, many of the implements were elaborately carved and ornamented.

Two Magdalenian weapons—the spear thrower and the bow and arrow—deserve particular consideration. As Turner observes, these not only greatly extended man's control over certain aspects of his environment, but they involved the first instance of the mechanical manipulation of physical power. The spear thrower, embodying the principle of the lever, appreciably lengthened the range of the spear. The bow and arrow, in which transverse stresses were transformed into horizontal motion, was even more revolutionary, representing in essence the transition from throwing to shooting (16:31).

However, it was in the cave wall paintings and engravings, so auspiciously begun by the Aurignacians, that the Magdalenians reached the height of their achievement. Representation, centering mainly around animal and human forms, came to be strikingly realistic and true. Although never wholly achieved, there seemed to be attempts at composition. Marked skill was displayed in the blending and use of several colors (11:174). Further evidence of the artistic talent of the Magdalenians is supplied by the excellence of their miniature animal and human sculpture. Having reached its climax late in the epoch, Magdalenian art began to shift toward conventionalization and inevitable decline.

This brings us to the close of the Paleolithic. Our primary concern has been man's material progress in West Central Europe. He was of course, as implied earlier, advancing in other regions as well. The first over-all impression that we get is that his conquest of nature and himself was exceedingly slow and halting. At the end of nearly a million years he was still a parasite in the sense that he made no attempt to cultivate his own food supply. However, in the matter of devising ways and means of obtaining what nature offered he had become strikingly ingenious and resourceful as attested by numerous tools and implements that have in improved form become a part of the social heritage. The same thing is true of his art ventures, especially when we bear in mind that there was no tradition to guide him.

In long range perspective, we have reason to assume that man's most significant achievement by the Close of the Paleolithic was the progress which he had made toward the conquest of himself. An abundance of indirect evidence tends to show that he had come to be much more than a roaming animal. He was clearly a keen observer of the things about him, and showed marked capacity to concentrate and to adapt means to ends. The construction and use of some of his more complicated weapons would have been out of the question without appreciable degrees of manual dexterity and motor skill. Thus, the spear thrower, as Kroeber aptly observes, could not have been invented by a person unskilled in bodily movements, nor could it have been used effectively in hunting by individuals who were unwilling to submit to practice (11:167). We have reason to believe, further, that man must by this time have achieved a measure of inter-group cooperation. As Childe stresses, hunting the mammoth and the bison would have been out of the question without it (5:60).

The non-material cultural status of Upper Paleolithic man has to be largely inferred, and inferences are in this case at best hazardous. Primitive contemporary peoples on some-what comparable levels of material development have for the most part well-developed non-material cultures. How-ever, these cultures have long antecedents, and we have no right to assume that the lag in material development was necessarily accompanied by a corresponding lag in the elabo-ration of non-material culture (5:44–47). We are, neverthe-less,—quite apart from the cultural status of the contemporary primitive—justified in assuming that the universal culture pattern was already a going concern among Upper Paleo-lithic peoples. Indeed, some of its categories—art, religion, material traits—stand out clearly. And it would of course be rather preposterous to deny them speech, social organization, and mythology. We know that these must have been present in some degree. What we do not know is the nature of their content, except within limits in the case of art, religion, and material traits.

The Neolithic Revolution

The Upper Paleolithic came to a close some 14,000 years ago. The great hunting cultures, which had reached their climax in the Magdalenian, disappeared with it, for the most part because drastic climatic changes deprived them of their chief means of livelihood—the bison, the mammoth, and the reindeer (6:36). During the succeeding Mesolithic, which represents the transition to the Neolithic, man had to cope with more precious natural resources—forests and small game. Accordingly, this age is characterized by a succession of cultures, all of them relatively meager. While tools generally decreased in size, some at least were clearly being adapted to the conquest of timber. There are indications, further, that man had begun to solve the transportation problem by building sledges. And the dog appropriately enough appears for the first time as a close ally of man (6:36–37).

The time-setting of the Neolithic varied from region to region. As Turner points out, there were in post-glacial times at least six Old World regions between the twenty-fifth and the forty-sixth parallels which in varying degrees met the conditions essential for the development of unified cultures, namely: the Mediterranean Basin, the Fertile Crescent, Iran, central Asia, India, and the north China plain (16:43). In each of these regions a distinctive and enduring culture arose in due time, and each one emerged from a Neolithic base the onset and duration of which varied. The earliest Neolithic innovations were confined to the Fertile Crescent and Iran regions. The time-setting for these cannot at present be extended beyond the sixth millennium B.C. (5:43). Compared to the preceding ages, the duration of the Neolithic was generally short. In Egypt and Mesopotamia, for example, it came to a close during the fourth millennium B.C., before it had actually gotten under way in Europe (16:51). In western and central Europe it began of course later than in the Mediterranean Basin—about the middle of the third millennium B.C. (5:43). Finally, it should be borne in mind that the transition from the Mesolithic to the Neolithic was probably rarely abrupt. As a result, the two types of culture frequently co-existed in given regions for considerable periods of time. However, as we shall note presently, wherever the Neolithic really got under way it tended to advance at an unprecedented pace.

Originally, polished stone was presumed to be the trait most characteristic of the Neolithic. While stone implements, along with the mill to produce them, did appear for the first time in this age, we now realize that two other innovations—agriculture and domesticated animals—were of vastly greater significance, and therefore, far more characteristic of the age. Basically, the Neolithic involved of course the transition from food-gathering and hunting to food production. The long range consequences of this were so momentous that Childe characterizes it as the first revolution in man's control over his environment (5:66). It made him potentially once for always the master of his own food supply. While most of Man's previous advances had come by slow process of accretion, the transition from a food-gathering to a food-producing economy was revolutionary. It called for a new orientation and new attitudes toward life. The change did not of course occur abruptly. Food-gathering and hunting continued to supplement food-production, and they decreased in importance only as the latter became firmly entrenched (5:82). We shall make no attempt to enumerate the plants and animals that were domesticated during the Neolithic. Viewed in world-wide perspective, there is very little in either the plant or the animal kingdom that Neolithic man overlooked. Says Childe: "Every single cultivated food plant of any importance has been discovered by some nameless barbarian society" (6:49). And Turner adds: "No important species of animal—has been brought under human management since ancient times;—modern Western man has failed in efforts to domesticate new species" (16:60).

Among the material traits peculiarly characteristic of the Neolithic were clay pottery, the bow and arrow, bone and horn implements, stone axes, whorls, looms, dwellings, and granaries. While the original molds for pottery appear to have been gourds and baskets, the ring method which lent itself admirably for the elaboration of varied designs, early came into widespread use (5:92). Clay pottery made possible real cooking and thus greatly extended the range of items which could be used for food. The bow and arrow, although of earlier origin as evidenced by Magdalenian cave paintings, now came into general use as an efficient hunting weapon (16:31; 5:57). Bone and horn, likewise in use among earlier men, now gave rise to the first genuinely smooth tools, and may in turn have suggested subsequent polished stone implements. The hewn stone ax was at first a crude chipped implement serving primarily as a wedge. Its highly polished and hafted successor in due time became a tool of unsurpassed excellence. Whorls and looms, which made possible spinning and weaving, were prevalent in early Neolithic times in both Egypt and Mesopotamia, and by degrees gave rise to an extensive textile industry (5:94). Man-made dwellings, varying from region to region, became a constant feature among the Neolithic, as did granaries for the storage of grain.

In respect to mode of subsistence, the Neolithic gave rise to three distinct patterns—the hoe, the nomadic, and the peasant-village economies. The hoe peoples, usually found in close proximity to forest areas, relied upon simple agriculture supplemented by hunting. The nomadic peoples, more often found in highland regions, depended primarily upon domesticated animals which were moved about with the seasons. The peasant-village peoples, more or less universal in their distribution, combined agriculture with animal husbandry, and in addition, because of their settled mode of life, were able to develop the arts and crafts on a large scale (16:63–65).

Nomadism, although it played a conspicuous role during the Neolithic, failed to supply the foundation for subsequent cultural elaboration. The peasant-village system suffered from no such limitations. It represented an essentially sound reaction to the demands of life under the ensuing conditions. Upon the groundwork which it laid were to be built the social structures of succeeding millennia.

Actually, peasant-villages appeared rather abruptly wherever the Neolithic got under way. By 5000 B.C. they had spread over the region extending from the Nile valley to the Caspian Basin and the Iranian Plateau, and they were about as conspicuous in the Indus valley (16:174; 247). In China they did not appear until after the opening of the third millennium B.C. (16:407). In eastern and southern Europe they began to appear with the third millennium B.C. During the second millennium they spread over the whole continent, and the opening of the first millennium saw them firmly established everywhere (16:442–451). Among primitive contemporary peoples peasant-village life has of course persisted to the present, and the peasants in some of our more complex societies are not far removed from it.

Peasant-village life thus appeared at different times in different parts of the world. It represented a natural response to given conditions. Wherever and whenever these began to prevail, the peasant-village appeared. If and when in the normal course of events new conditions ensued, peasant-village life became an integral part of a new and more complex mode of life—the urban. The conditioning factors underlying peasant-village life were of course agriculture, animal husbandry, and craftsmanship. Wherever it was possible to combine these three processes into a unified mode of life, peasant-village cultures arose (16:64).

The groups comprising the peasant-village societies were small, rarely exceeding three or four dozen householders (6: 52). Apart from the different roles assigned men and women, division of labor seems to have been limited. There is evidence of close integration, and of mutual cooperation for collective purposes (6:52). Otherwise economic activities appear to have been centered in the household (16:69). At base each village was essentially self-sufficient. However, in time the increase of luxury goods gave rise to exchange over large areas. This in turn facilitated the spread of non-material traits.

There are no indications of class stratification. Each village appears to have been a democratic self-governing community. Archaeological findings furnished little evidence of warfare during the earlier stages of peasant-village life. Later, when competition for favored locations had gotten under way and the villages had spread far and wide, the picture reverses itself (6:59–60).

The Urban Revolution

The Neolithic revolution left the whole region from the Nile to the Indus scattered with small farming communities. A second revolution—the Urban—was to transform some of these "into populous cities, nourished by secondary industries and foreign trade" (5:105). However, before this could materialize epoch-making inventions had to be made. Childe enumerates the following: "artificial irrigation using canals and ditches; the harnessing of animal motive-power; the sailing boat; wheeled vehicles; orchard husbandry; fermentation; the production and use of copper; bricks; the arch; glazing; the seal; and—in the earlier stages of the revolution—a solar calendar, writing, numeral notation, and bronze" (5:227). As Childe stresses, not until the days of Galileo was progress in knowledge and significant discoveries to be so phenomenal as it was immediately preceding the urban revolution (5:105). Indeed, the two thousand years following the revolution have only four comparable achievements to their credit, namely: "the 'decimal notation' of Babylonia (about 2000 B.C.); an economical method for smelting iron on an industrial scale (1400 B.C.); a truly alphabetic script (1300 B.C.); aqueducts supplying water to cities (700 B.C.)" (5:227).

The urban revolution, although it occurred rapidly compared with the cultural developments during the preceding epochs, did not take place over night. In the Ancient-Oriental lands—Mesopotamia, India, Egypt, and Crete—it required approximately 1500 years to establish the new mode of life. The

Mesopotamian and Egyptian developments, extending from about 5000 to 3500 B.C., paralleled each other so closely that authorities are not agreed as to which deserves precedence (16:174). In India and Crete the revolution occurred somewhat later (16:168–214).

In advance of any attempt to characterize developments in these lands, it should be noted that the transition from village to urban life was conditioned by the capacity of human groups to produce more than they needed for subsistence. Such an excess of production is technically known as an *economic surplus*. The foundations for this were of course laid with the domestication of plants and animals. However, the latter alone could not have assured a sufficient surplus to condition urban developments. As implied above, large-scale technological innovations were required in addition. Once a sizable and fairly stable surplus was achieved in any given case, a portion of the population could be released for activities other than primary production. Without such a release cultures could not have advanced beyond the village level. As a rule the proportion thus released was small, probably not in excess of ten or fifteen per cent.

Mesopotamia

Mesopotamia supplies the most complete archeological records of the transition from the peasant-village to the full-fledged urban community. At Tepe Gawra, alone, twenty-six successive occupational levels testify to every important phase of this process (16:126). The Sumerians, a non-Semitic people, developed the first urban culture in the lower Tigris-Euphrates valley. By the beginning of the third millennium B.C. such cities as Ur, Lagash, and Nippur were already old. The Sumerian city-states were basically independent. However, due to clashing interests, they were almost constantly at war.

Sometime before the middle of the third millennium B.C.

the Sumerians were conquered by the Semitic Akkadians under the leadership of Sargon, and remained under their domination for approximately two centuries. During this time Sumerian culture spread throughout Mesopotamia. Then the valley was invaded by the Gutians and the Amorites. The former took over the Sumerian cities and administered them under native governors; the latter gained control over the region immediately to the north. Under the leadership of one of the native governors Sumerian culture was revived, and, after the Gutians had been driven out, it reached its golden age. By 2250 B.C. Ur had achieved a splendor that was unprecedented. However, its triumph was to be shortlived. By 2100 B.C. a new line of Semitic kings, of which Hammurabi was to be the most famous, had emerged at Babylon. This was to assimilate Sumerian culture and rule the cities, along with an extended area, until the conquest of Babylon by the Kassites about 1750 B.C.

Sumerian culture rested upon an economic base that represented a natural elaboration and extension of Neolithic foundations. Agriculture and animal husbandry were basic, and remarkable ingenuity was displayed in their pursuit. The ox-drawn plow came into use during the fourth millennium B.C., and the next millennium witnessed an elaborate system of dikes and canals designed to control the flow of the rivers and to provide irrigation. Crops—including grains, fruits, and vegetables—became highly diversified, and they were cultivated systematically. Domesticated animals were put to new uses—donkeys drawing wheeled carts and chariots, cattle and goats supplying milk, and sheep furnishing wool.

The Neolithic crafts in turn were elaborated into extensive industries. The shift from stone to copper and bronze came gradually. The potter's wheel came into use early, as did dyes. In the manipulation of metals, the transition from pounding to smelting appears to have been made by about 3000 B.C. (5:118). There is abundant evidence of the early acquisition of great skill in metal-work, sculpture, and engraving. In spite of the fact that their basic building material was limited to sun-dried and baked brick, the Sumerians succeeded in constructing magnificent palaces and temples. They displayed remarkable ingenuity in the use of the vault, the arch, the dome, and the column (15:26).

Partly at least because of the scarcity of essential materials—metals, timber, and stone—the Sumerians early began to develop an extensive system of commerce. During the third millennium B.C. this assumed tremendous proportions. The records of their commercial transactions, which have come down to us on clay tablets, show that business was highly organized and systematically pursued.

The Sumerian city-state of the fourth millennium B.C. appears to have been basically democratic. Political power was in the hands of a general assembly of all freemen. In normal times community affairs were administered by a council of elders. When danger threatened, the assembly had the power to appoint a king who held office only during the emergency (8:128–129). The city-state of the next millennium stands in marked contrast to this. The king was now the tenant of the god of the city and administered the affairs of the community in the interests of the God and his coterie of related deities. The kingship, although nominally renewed each year, was now hereditary. The king, the priestly class, and the soldiers controlled most of the land. As a result, the bulk of the population eked out its existence as share-croppers, serfs, and slaves (8:186). The lot of the freeman, to the extent that he still existed, was not enviable. Craftsmen and tradesmen may have fared somewhat better.

Even so, the king and the priestly class were anything but parasites. The king was technically in charge of all governmental enterprises—the temples, the army, commerce, the irrigation system, taxation, weights and measures. Since the temples served as centers of all important cultural activities—

commercial, industrial, technical, educational, religious—the priestly class rendered a multitude of indispensable services.

Religion pervaded every aspect of Sumerian life. For them, as for primitive man, the universe was peopled with spirits and deities, and these had to be reckoned with at every turn. The supernatural world of the Sumerians was, however, more orderly and more predictable than that of primitive man. The long array of some four thousand deities was headed by a pantheon of six great gods—the god of the sky, the god of the storm, the god of the earth, the goddess of fertility, the god of the moon, and the god of the sun. These constituted an assembly of the ruling powers of the universe conceived of as a super-state. Within this framework the various city-states, owned and ruled by their respective gods, were minor structures. Just as the universe was the abode of the major gods, so the city-states were the estates of the minor gods. They existed for their benefit, and man had to accommodate himself to their desires (8:185). In the same way, every other human situation—every family, every enterprise, every individual—had in charge of it some deity.

While these deities were at base non-malevolent, they were in no way obligated to man. He had to gain from them whatever he wanted through rigid observance of their wishes. Hence, the large-scale recourse to divination, dream interpretation, and star reading. The religion of the Sumerians was thus a strictly practical mundane affair. Their notion of the hereafter was at best vague and played no appreciable role in their lives.

The Sumerians, along with the Babylonians, laid the foundation for a learned tradition embodying science and literature. They were the first people to devise means of measuring time, distance, areas, and quantities. Although they had no sign for the zero, the Sumerians achieved respectable competence in arithmetical processes, including fractions. An embryonic system of geometry was in the making, and there were indications pointing to the beginning of abstract mathematics. Although they do not appear to have recognized them as physical objects, their observations of the heavenly bodies were remarkably accurate. The discovery that the movements of these bodies could be predicted led to what Turner characterizes as the "most profound philosophical achievement of early urban cultures, namely, the principle of universal causation" (16:165). However, due to the fact that they conceived of such causation in terms of the will of the gods, they developed an astrological, rather than an astronomical, view of the universe.

Among the practical outcomes of their study of the heavenly bodies was a calendar of twelve lunar months together with provision for the correction of discrepancies at intervals. Beyond this, they divided the day into twelve double hours, and devised water clocks and sundials for the measurement of such time intervals (6:101). Furthermore, the basic unit of 60 (in place of our 100) in their numerical system appears subsequently to have led to the division of the circle into 360 degrees, with hours, minutes, and seconds (15:28).

One of the most significant Sumerian achievements was the development of the *cuneiform* writing system. In this the characters were impressed upon moist clay tablets by means of the wedge-like point of a reed stylus. With the impressions completed, the tablets were sun dried or baked and thus became highly imperishable. This, together with the fact that it subsequently became possible to decipher the inscriptions, accounts for most of our knowledge of Mesopotamian culture. Although there are indications of earlier beginnings, the development of the Sumerian writing system appears to have extended from about 3500 to 2700 B.C. (16:145). When it was finally completed, the script consisted of several hundred signs representing words, syllables, and determinatives. The syllable signs made it possible to form new words, many of them denoting abstract concepts. The determinatives in turn were used as classifiers to denote categories of things. Although there were special signs for some letters, the Sumerians failed to take the final step in the development of an alphabet—the reduction of the syllable signs to letter signs. The Sumerian script was adopted by the Semites and reached the height of its development under Hammurabi (16:145–148).

Although the Sumerian writing system arose originally as a practical device to record temple transactions, it was destined in time to become the vehicle of a remarkable literature centering mainly upon religious and cosmological themes. Taking the form of ritual hymns, legends, and epics, this literature has come down to us primarily through Assyrian recordings of Babylonian versions. Outstanding among these are the epics of Creation and the Flood which appear to have appreciably influenced subsequent Hebrew renditions, and the epic of Gilgamesh, the central theme of which is the futile quest for immortality (15:30–32).

As noted above, about 2100 B.C. the Sumerian cities passed under the control of the Semitic Babylonians. The latter assimilated Sumerian culture and elaborated certain phases of it. This process reached its climax under Hammurabi whose rule extended from about 1947–1905 B.C. (15:33). His most notable achievement was the famous code that bears his name. The code represents an attempt to harmonize and systematize existing laws and to bring them up to date. Its most important provisions have to do with property, wages and fees, slavery, domestic relations, and crime (16:141). In drawing it up, Hammurabi made large use of earlier Sumerian codes. As may be inferred from the fact that trial by ordeal existed along with an elaborate system of justice administered by the state, the code reflects a strange combination of primitive and advanced standards.[1]

In concluding our review of Mesopotamian culture developments, we must bear in mind, as Turner aptly puts it, that "the Semitic rendering of Sumerian culture influenced the development of civilization in southwestern Asia during the next twenty-five centuries, quite as Greek culture has influenced the development of Western civilization in a more recent twenty-five centuries" (16:148).

The Indus Valley

The Indus valley cities appear to have been founded about the beginning of the third millennium B.C. By 2500 B.C. they were rich and prosperous. Then, for reasons which are not clear at present, they began to decline and disappear. Archaeological evidence shows that they were the product of essentially the same factors as the cities of Mesopotamia. And, during the earlier stages at least, there are indications of close contact between the two regions. The Indus valley people subsisted on agriculture, animal husbandry, and trade. In addition, they were skilled craftsmen. Wheel-turned pottery was common, and spindle whorls point to an extensive textile industry. Metallurgy—including smelting in brick furnaces, casting in molds, soldering, and riveting—had reached a high level of development. The production of bronze was understood, and bronze tools were in use. River and seagoing craft were being produced on a large scale.

The major cities—Mohenjo-Daro, Harrapa, and Chandhu-Daro—were remarkably well planned, and this warrants the assumption that they were well governed. The chief building material was oven-baked brick. Art objects, ranging from the relatively crude to the skillfully executed, point to a class

1. Concerning the Chronology of Hammurabi, consult J. W. Swain, *The Ancient World*, Vol. I, page 168. New York: Harper and Brothers, 1950.

structure. Since the Indus script, consisting of several hundred symbols, has not been deciphered, little is known regarding the intellectual outlook of the people. However, there are indications of a well-developed system of measurement, and certain archaeological evidence points to the existence of a priestly class. The causes responsible for the decline and disappearance of these urban cultures are almost wholly conjectural. Nor is it known to what extent Indus valley cultural elements may have found their way into the subsequent Hindu cultural tradition. However, certain cues suggest that the Indus valley people may have been in fairly close contact with the people of India before the Indo-European invaders arrived (16:168–173; 4:Chapter VIII).

Egypt

Cultural developments in Egypt followed essentially the same pattern as in Mesopotamia, but for a variety of reasons the details of the pattern do not stand out as clearly. There is, however, abundant evidence of Paleolithic cultures, followed in due time by Neolithic peasant-village communities thriving on agriculture, animal husbandry, and the crafts. In the course of the fifth millennium B.C. some of these began to evolve into cities. The precise manner in which this occurred is not known. However, the first urban centers—Heliopolis, Coptos, Abydos, Butos, and Sais—arose in regions that were favorably located for trade (16:180). Then there was of course the pressing problem of developing and controlling irrigation dikes and canals. This seems to have forced communities into close cooperative relationships in very early times, giving rise by degrees to *nomes* or administrative districts headed by the chieftains of the strongest towns.

Near the beginning of the fifth millennium B.C. rivalry among the chieftains of the strongest districts led to the organization of two kingdoms—Lower Egypt comprising the Delta region, and Upper Egypt including the Nile valley from the southern apex of the Delta to the First Cataract. Much later, probably sometime during the forty-third century B.C., a king of Lower Egypt seized control of Upper Egypt and effected what Breasted characterizes as the First Union with its capital at Heliopolis (3:51–52). After some centuries the two kingdoms drifted apart and were not reunited until about 3200 B.C. when Menes, the legendary king of Upper Egypt, effected the Second Union. This marks the beginning of dynastic times. The thirty-one dynasties which followed extended down to 332 B.C.

Historians have found it convenient to divide this long interval into periods corresponding to certain developmental sequences. Our concern at this point is with the two main periods preceding the Empire—the Old Kingdom and the Middle Kingdom. The former embraces the first six dynasties, and extends roughly from 3200 to 2270 B.C.; the latter includes the next six dynasties, and extends from 2270 to about 1800 B.C.

During the Old Kingdom copper came into widespread use, a powerful centralized government arose, trade and commerce expanded, cities grew apace, and it was of course during this time that the pyramids were built. During the sixth dynasty social disintegration set in. As a result, the Middle Kingdom ushered in a feudalistic regime dominated by an oligarchy of priests and nobles. Sometime thereafter, the masses revolted—the first instance of its kind in the annals of mankind. The net outcome was a very fundamental reorientation in social outlook, and as might be expected great disillusionment on the part of the nobility. After a protracted period of confusion, a strong central government emerged once more with the Twelfth Dynasty. This bore in some respects a close resemblance to the secular monarchy set up by Hammurabi in Mesopotamia (16:187). Once more peace and prosperity returned, but not for long, for the invading Hyksos were in the offing.

As in the case of Mesopotamia, Egyptian culture rested upon an economic base that represented a natural elaboration and extension of Neolithic foundations. In this, agriculture, animal husbandry, and the crafts were basic. Commerce played an important role, although Egypt was always much more self-contained than Mesopotamia. With the introduction of metals, mining came into prominence. Near the beginning of the third millennium B.C. an elaborate craft industry, organized around households and temples, had come into being. As in Mesopotamia, success in agriculture depended upon irrigation dikes and canals. The Egyptians appear to have placed the control of the latter in the hands of the king's officials in the course of the First Union. They had also very early effected the transition from hoe culture to ox-drawn plow-culture (3:52–54).

Under the Old Kingdom, government became more centralized than in Mesopotamia. The pharaoh was not a tenant of a god, but a god—the falcon god Horus. He was also the son of the sun-god Re, and the chief priest of all other gods. As high priest he performed the sacred rituals, and as political ruler he was head of the irrigation system, the administrative machinery of the nomes, and the set-up for national defense. His chief administrative assistant, the vizier, known as the *man*, in contrast to the *god*, served in the multiple capacity of prime minister, chief justice, chief engineer, and chief architect (16:182). The land, owned by the pharaoh, was divided into large estates held by priestly landlords. The agricultural workers were mainly serfs who eked out a meager existence. Below them were the slaves (15:46). The pharaoh was of course surrounded by an elaborate court of nobles. The priestly class, as a caste, appears to have developed rather late (15:50).

The Egyptians, like the Mesopotamians, looked upon the universe as peopled with spirits and deities. Hence, in Egypt as in Mesopotamia, every aspect of life was governed by supernatural beings. In spite of these similarities in basic outlook, religion played different roles in the two cultures. It completely dominated the former, and merely exerted a powerful influence upon the latter. As a result, the Egyptians cannot be understood apart from their religion; the Mesopotamians can. Beyond this, the religions of the two peoples differed strikingly in their orientations. The supreme goal of the Egyptian religion was the achievement of immortality. Mesopotamian religion on the other hand was oriented almost wholly toward success in life.

In part at least because of their extreme absorption in it, the Egyptians made little attempt to systematize their religion. They developed no formal pantheon, no systematic theology, and no coherent doctrine of immortality (16:195–197). Although new concepts and new deities appeared from time to time, the Egyptians rarely abandoned the old, preferring instead to tie the new in with it. The result was a religious system that was at best incoherent. Nevertheless, certain features of it stand out rather clearly. To begin with, there was at least the semblance of unity among the innumerable gods since two of them—Re, the god of the living and the creator of all things; and Osiris, the god of the dead and the bestower of immortality,—stood out supreme (3:71). The former symbolized the sun, and the latter the Nile. All other gods were tied in with these, and the divine pharaoh represented the incarnation of all of them (15:50).

In contrast to most other peoples, the Egyptians did not look upon immortality as a natural sequence to life, but rather as something to be achieved (2:47–48). Although they had come to distinguish various aspects of the individual: the body (khat), its surviving guardian spirit or double (ka), and the soul (ba), they could not conceive of survival in the future apart from the body. Hence they took great pains to preserve the latter and to make the grave a fitting abode for the ka during the time that it was guiding the deceased in his quest of immortality (2:50). This explains the practice of embalming, the material equipment found in graves, and the elaborate tombs which reached their climax in the great pyramids. It also gave rise by degrees to an extensive priestly class whose primary function was to administer an elaborate system of sympathetic magic as a means to physical immortality and subsistence after death (15:55).

Despite its conservative character, there is evidence of significant changes in Egyptian religion from one period to another. Originally, for instance, only the pharaohs enjoyed the right to immortality. In the course of the Old Kingdom the nobles by degrees acquired such prerogatives. And by 2000 B.C. the masses had come to enjoy substantially the same religious rights as the pharaoh and the nobles. There are also indications about this time of the emergence of ethical elements. Immortality, hitherto achieved in a purely formal manner, became now in part at least dependent upon righteous living. There were of course as yet no lofty ideals of right and duty as worthy ends in themselves. Nevertheless, the fact that an individual's moral conduct had become subject to review by his fellowmen and by Osiris shows that the Egyptians had begun to develop an initial sense of moral responsibility—for the first time in the history of mankind (15: 53–55).

The development of Egyptian architecture and art was motivated almost wholly by religion. This, as Trever aptly puts it, "furnished its purpose, determined its form, and gave it symbolic significance" (15:47). The supreme achievements in architecture were of course the great pyramids, the construction of which began with the Third Dynasty, reached its height during the Fourth, and then declined. For a time thereafter, the emphasis shifted to smaller structures—temples and palaces. The decentralized conditions of the Middle Kingdom were not conducive to architectural advancement. Hence, little was accomplished until the Twelfth Dynasty when magnificently pillared cliff-tombs began to displace the pyramids as royal burial structures, and Thebes entered upon a developmental era that was to crown her as the greatest monumental city of Egypt (16:204).

While art permeated every aspect of Egyptian life, the fact that perspective and shading had not been adequately mastered precluded notable achievements in some areas. On the other hand, the religious importance of the human statue as an essential abode of the ka gave a tremendous impetus to portrait sculpture, and it was in this that Egypt early achieved its highest perfection. Notable examples are of course the two representations of the Pharaoh Khafre—the Diorite Head, and the Great Sphinx. Almost as unique were the achievements in painted reliefs and hieroglyphic inscriptions in the chapel tombs of the nobles. The minor arts, extending over a wide range, were of such fine caliber that Will Durant characterizes them as "the major art of Egypt" (7:191).

The Egyptians early began to lay the foundations for a learned tradition embodying science and literature. Compared with the Sumerians, their mathematical ventures were clumsy and crude. They had difficulty with the fundamental operations, and failed to master fractions adequately. Their geometry likewise was decidedly rudimentary. They showed little inclination to systematize and generalize. By way of compensation, however, they were good observers and exceedingly practical in their approach to the solution of problems. This would seem to explain why they succeeded in developing a relatively accurate solar calendar as early as 4226 B.C. The calendar provided for a year of 360 days plus five days for correction. The year was divided into 12 months of 30 days each, and day and night into 12 hours each. In place of the seven-day week, there was a provision for a ten-day decad (16:207).

As might be expected, Egyptian science had difficulty extricating itself from magic and religion. The greatest advance in this respect appears to have been achieved in medicine. There are indications that medical schools had been established in temples before the end of the Old Kingdom. At least one surgical treatise, apparently written at this time, has come down to us. The description and classification of the cases, together with the treatments recommended, show that they were based upon direct observation of injuries. Other treatises, concerned mainly with medical knowledge, point to the first known attempts to explain health and disease in terms of natural facts (16:209–212).

Since the Egyptian system of writing was already well developed at the beginning of the Old Kingdom it may have gotten under way appreciably earlier than that of the Sumerians. That it began with the customary pictographic stage is attested by the character of the symbols. However, there are indications that most signs early lost their pictorial values and came to represent linguistic forms—words and syllables. This means that the signs were now phonograms that could be combined to form new words—many of them denoting abstract concepts that could not have been pictorially represented. In actual practice, however, some of the original signs continued to serve primarily as signs for specific words, and others were used as classifiers to denote categories. As a result, there were really three types of signs—word signs, syllable signs, and classifiers.

So far the Egyptian writing system differed in no essential respect from the Sumerian. At this point, however, the Egyptians made a unique departure. They went beyond the syllable principle and developed twenty-four pure letter signs. These were all consonants since vowels were not written. They now had an alphabet—the first one to be developed—which would have enabled them to write their own language phonetically as we do ours. However, they failed to supplant the old with the new and continued to write in traditional fashion. Much later—sometime before 1500 B.C.—a Semitic speaking people borrowed this alphabet and put it into use (1:288–289). Subsequently, after undergoing various modifications, it came down to us (7:172–173).

At an early date the Egyptians also devised a varied equipment for writing, including reed pens, ink, and papyrus. Their script became by degrees differentiated into three varieties—the hieroglyphic, the hieratic, and the demotic—used primarily for religious, secular, and popular purposes, respectively.

The written records that have come down to us from the ancient Egyptians are limited and fragmentary. Under these circumstances it is difficult to make an accurate appraisal of their literary achievements. The famous Pyramid Texts, written in hieroglyphics on the walls of five pyramids in the course of a century and a half—roughly between 2625 and 2475 B.C.—review religious and historical events almost from the beginning of the Old Kingdom. However, apart from certain religious hymns, the form of which was subsequently to influence the Hebrew psalmists, there is little in them that could be classed as literature (2:65–72). The same thing is true of the Coffin Texts which appeared several centuries later. These consisted of magic spells written on the inside of coffins. They drew heavily upon the Pyramid Texts, and subsequently gave rise to the so-called Book of the Dead (2:235–237).

Egyptian literature, as Kroeber points out, appears rather abruptly with the Twelfth Dynasty, 2000–1788 B.C. Its most distinctive feature was a simple narrative prose told for its own sake—a prose that was not to be equalled elsewhere for a thousand years (12:483–487). Especially notable among these short stories were the adventures of Sinuhe, an Egyptian Odysseus in Asia, and the tale of the Shipwrecked Sailor, strongly suggestive of Sindbad the Sailor (3:88–89).

In contrast with the Mesopotamians, the early Egyptians failed to develop an astrological interpretation of heavenly phenomena. Instead, they hit by degrees upon the notion of a universe embodying a moral order. Under the Old Kingdom morality was largely an individual matter. After the social revolution of the Middle Kingdom it was gradually extended to include social justice as well. However, the concept of social justice was as yet a very rudimentary one. There was no hint of social equality. Poverty, misery, and inequality were accepted without question. In fact, as Turner observes, it never occurred to an Egyptian that "the circumstances of worldly existence could or should be altered" (16:213–214).

Crete

In Crete the transition from Neolithic to Urban culture began about 3000 B.C. Excavations on a hill at Cnossos revealed more than twenty-four feet of Neolithic deposits accumulated during the preceding millennium (15:122). Cretan or Minoan urban culture began with the introduction of copper and ended with the appearance of iron. Three general developmental periods stand out—the Early Minoan, 3000–2200 B.C.; the Middle Minoan, 2200–1600 B.C.; and the Late Minoan, 1600–1100 B.C. Throughout these periods there are indications of close contact with Egypt (3:239–249). And as a maritime people the Cretans were of course in touch with Asia Minor and other Mediterranean regions.

The Minoan cities rose along the coast on sites that were convenient for shipping. The economic surplus that made them possible was drawn largely from the profits of trade (16:216). In the inland regions agriculture and animal husbandry were carried on. Phaistos appears to have been the earliest city to gain prominence. Subsequently, Cnossos surpassed it by degrees. The cities also served as centers of elaborate industries—epecially, metal and woodworking, textiles, and ceramics (15:132–133).

Since the Minoan script has not been deciphered, the political and social organization of the cities has to be largely inferred from archaeological remains. Real political unity among the cities does not appear to have been achieved until the Minos Dynasty came into power as sea kings. The enormous palace at Cnossos, along with the elaborate equipment which it features, points to a complex and highly centralized government (15:132). The general layout of the city, which may have comprised a population of some eighty thousand, points to the customary social stratification of early urban communities. The palace was surrounded by the elegant homes of the nobles. Beyond these lay the meager dwellings of the traders and craftsmen (3:244).

The Cretans appear to have taken religion much less seriously than the Egyptians. The chief deity was a mother goddess symbolized by the dove and the serpent, the former connoting divine inspiration and the latter fertility. She was served by priestesses. There were no elaborate temples, and no large statues of deities. Although there was a cult of the dead, it played a minor role in contrast with Egyptian practices (15:135).

The Cretan's supreme achievements were in art. Their splendid palaces with colonnaded halls, elegant stairways, and impressive open areas represented, as Breasted observes, the first real architecture in the northern Mediterranean (3:243). Although the use of perspective and shading was not understood, their fresco painting was masterly. The same thing holds true of their painting on pottery. They were adept in the use of colors and in the selection of decorative motifs. About as notable, if not more so, were their achievements in carving, modeling, and ceramics (16:220).

Since the Minoan script has not been deciphered, little is known regarding their learned tradition. The early writing system consisted of pictographs on beads and seals. In Middle Minoan times this system was replaced by a linear script. Most of the documents are clay tablets (16:218). Compared with other early peoples, the Minoans stand out as a remarkably balanced people—a people with a secular outlook and a feeling for life as a whole (16:221).

The First Imperial Age

The rise of urban cultures in the ancient-oriental lands was followed in due time by the emergence of empires. "Just as the cities rose out of the villages," says Turner, "so the empires rose out of the cities" (16:222). Altogether, there were six of them—the Empire of the Hurri, 1800–1400 B.C., confined to the upper Tigris-Euphrates valley and border lands; the Egyptian Empire, 1600–1350 B.C., extending from the Euphrates in Asia to the Fourth Cataract of the Nile in Africa; the Minoan Sea Empire, 1600–1400 B.C., extending throughout the Aegean Basin; the Hittite Empire, 1400–1200 B.C., reaching from Asia Minor into northern Syria; the Assyrian Empire, 1400–600 B.C., including the entire Fertile Crescent, much of the northern mountain country, and the lower Nile valley; and the Chaldean Empire, early sixth century B.C., embracing the entire Fertile Crescent (16:227–244).

The distinctive achievement of this age was, as Turner stresses, "the preservation and transmission of ancient materials that could be used by new peoples in the development of new cultural traditions" (16:268).

BIBLIOGRAPHY

1. Bloomfield, Leonard, Language. New York: Henry Holt and Company, 1933.
2. Breasted, James H., The Dawn of Conscience. New York: Charles Scribner's Sons, 1933.
3. Breasted, James H., The Conquest of Civilization. New York: Harper and Brothers, 1938.
4. Childe, V. Gordon, New Light on the Ancient East. London: Kegan, Paul, Trench, Truber and Company, 1935.
5. Childe, V. Gordon, Man Makes Himself, London: Watts and Company, 1941.
6. Childe, V. Gordon, What Happened in History. New York: Penguin Books, 1946.
7. Durant, Will, The Story of Civilization—Our Oriental Heritage. New York: Simon and Schuster, 1935.

8. Frankfort, H. and H. A., John A. Wilson, Thorkild Jacobson, and William A. Irwin, The Intellectual Adventure of Ancient Man. Chicago: The University of Chicago Press, 1946.

9. Gillin, John, The Ways of Men. New York: D. Appleton–Century Company, 1948.

10. Hooton, E. A., Up From the Ape. New York: The Macmillan Company, 1931.

11. Kroeber, A. L., Anthropology. New York: Harcourt, Brace and Company, 1923.

12. Kroeber, A. L., Configurations of Culture Growth. Berkeley and Los Angeles: University of California Press, 1944.

13. Murray, R. W., Man's Unknown Ancestors. Milwaukee: Bruce Publishing Company, 1943.

14. Nelson, S. C., "Prehistoric Archaeology." Pages 146–237 in General Anthropology edited by Franz Boas. Boston: D. C. Heath and Company, 1933.

15. Trever, Albert A., History of Ancient Civilization, Volume I. New York: Harcourt, Brace and Company, 1936.

16. Turner, Ralph, The Great Cultural Traditions, Volume I, The Ancient Cities. New York: McGraw-Hill Book Co., 1941.

CHAPTER II

Education in Mesopotamia and Ancient Egypt

The Rise of Formal Education

FORMAL education arose initially to prepare specialists. The need for trained specialists grew out of the conditions induced by the urban revolution. The revolution itself was conditioned by the capacity of societies in certain regions to produce more than they needed for subsistence. Such an excess of production is technically known as an *economic surplus*. Its immediate effect, whenever it occurred, was to release a small proportion of the population for activities other than primary production. This made possible a degree of cultural elaboration that would have been impossible under peasant-village conditions. The segment of the population thus released from primary production not only lived upon the economic surplus, but it devolved upon it to administer it.

The centers of administration were usually the great temples and the courts, and the technical administrators were priestly and royal officials. The administration of the surplus demanded, as might be expected, elaborate records and accounting techniques. As a result, systems of writing and numerical notation emerged by degrees. "The beginnings of writing and of mathematics and the standardization of weights and measures," as Childe says, "coincide in time with the revolution. The synchronism is not accidental. The

34

practical needs of the new economy had, in fact, evoked the innovations" (5:179). The purposes of writing and mathematics were thus at first strictly practical. Only with the passing of time did the former become a literary medium and the latter an instrument of research. However, both soon became specialized arts that could be mastered only through prolonged training. As a result, temple and court schools arose, and, with the establishment of these, specialized formal education was well under way. In due time these schools were of course destined to do much more than train professional scribes. They were to serve in addition as centers of research and the systematization of knowledge.

Mesopotamia from Hammurabi to the Fall of Nineveh

In an earlier context we traced the rise of Sumerian and Babylonian culture through the Age of Hammurabi (ca. 1947–1905 B.C.), and pointed out that this was to influence the development of civilization in southwestern Asia profoundly for the next twenty-five centuries. It remains to be noted now that Hammurabi's dynasty at Babylon scarcely survived his death. From about 1900 B.C. on, the Kassite invaders from the east by degrees made themselves masters of the country, and Babylon remained under their control for nearly six centuries. Little is known regarding its cultural development during this interval. Meanwhile, Assyria—which had become a well-organized kingdom in the upper Tigris valley during the middle of the second millennium B.C.— began to emerge as the dominant power in Mesopotamia (16: 239). It was to continue the sequence of Sumerian and Babylonian culture down to the fall of Nineveh in 612 B.C. Actually, Assyrian ascendence was to be achieved only by degrees. Tiglath-Pilesar I (ca. 1116–1093 B.C.) captured Babylon (16:240); in 689 B.C. Sennacherib (ca. 705–681 B.C.) destroyed it (16:243); and Essarhadden (ca. 681–668 B.C.) later undertook its restoration (16:243). The Assyrian Empire reached its height under Sargon II (ca. 722–705 B.C.) when it extended "from the Nile and Halys rivers in the west to the Persian Gulf and Lake Urmia in the east" (16:240–241). His successor, Sennacherib (ca. 705–681 B.C.) built the great capital at Nineveh. With the destruction of this in 612 B.C., the Chaldeans came into power, and Nebuchadnezzar II (ca. 604–562 B.C.) reconstituted Babylon into a city of unprecedented splendor. But, as Turner puts it, "The future belonged not to Babylon; rather it belonged to those Indo-European peoples who, quickly overthrowing the city's rule and finally destroying its structures, never forgot its glories. In the name of Babylon endured the organization and ideal of life to which the earliest urban cultures had given birth" (16:244).

The Sumerian System of Writing

As noted earlier, the Sumerians were a remarkably creative people. By 2700 B.C. they had evolved a system of writing consisting of several hundred signs representing words, syllables, and determinatives. The syllable signs enabled them to form new words, many of them denoting abstract concepts. The determinatives served as classifiers to designate categories of things. In writing, the Sumerians impressed their cuneiform or wedge-shaped characters upon moist clay tablets by means of a reed stylus. Since the tablets were subsequently sun-dried or baked they proved extremely durable (4: Chapter 2). The cuneiform script was later adapted to the Semitic languages of Babylon and Assyria. In the face of new vernacular languages, it became of course in time a dead language, to be studied and used much as Greek and Latin are in our culture.

There is abundant evidence to prove that the Sumerian writing system arose originally to meet practical needs. The same thing is true of their mathematics which early assumed respectable proportions. These practical needs had to do primarily with accounts, records, contracts, and correspondence incident to the administration of the great temple estates. Accounts apparently came first. The world's oldest account tablet, says Childe, was found in the first Temple at Erech. It bears impressions that are obviously numerals (5:146). Shortly before 3000 B.C., clay tablets bearing both characters and numerals are found at Erech in Sumer and at Jemdet Nasr in Akkad. "The characters are mostly shorthand pictures—a jar, a bull's head, two triangles, and so on. The script is therefore termed pictographic. You can guess what the signs mean by looking at them" (5:180–181). However, among these there is already a sprinkling of ideographs and phonograms. The Sumerian script is clearly in the making.

In the Shuruppak or Fara tablets, which belong to the period shortly after 3000 B.C., the Sumerian script is already highly conventionalized. The content of these tablets is limited to temple accounts and classified lists of items—fish, birds, animals—used as school texts. However, at about this same time there also begin to appear tablets with other contents—"at first mainly names and titles, then treatises, liturgical and historical texts, spells, and fragments of legal codes" (5:182–183). And appreciably before 2500 B.C. the Sumerian script came to be used to transcribe the language of the Semitic Akkadians.

Libraries and Literary Compilations

Although the Sumerian writing system arose as a practical device to record temple transactions, it was destined in time to become the vehicle of a remarkable literature. Taking the form of ritual hymns, legends, and epics, this literature has, apart from scattered fragments, come down to us primarily through Assyrian recordings of Babylonian versions. As Chiera observes, the probability is that much of this was long transmitted orally. However, most of it is known to have been committed to writing by about 1900 B.C.—at a time when the Sumerians had long since been under Babylonian rule. Hammurabi and the priestly scholars of this epoch seem to have sensed the greatness of Sumerian culture and to have made a desperate effort to preserve it for posterity (4:110–114).

The Assyrians, too, appear to have been bent upon preserving the culture of their predecessors. The great royal library of Ashurbanipal (ca. 669–626 B.C.) at Nineveh, consisting of some 30,000 tablets, bears eloquent testimony to this (7:277). This library had been systematically collected at the orders of the king who was himself an accomplished student of Sumerian (2:173). However, as Chiera stresses, the Assyrians were much more than collectors and copyists. "After they had copied texts written in the Sumerian language, the task the kings set themselves was to retranslate this whole mass of material into the vernacular and adapt it to the needs of the time. The old Sumerian stories were published as they were found, with an inter-linear translation in the Assyrian language. It must have required an immense amount of time and a great number of learned scholars to bring this work to completion" (4:174).

The Temple Schools of Mesopotamia

The cultural developments in Mesopotamia—from the emergence of the Sumerian script to the assemblage of Ashurbanipal's great library at Nineveh—were, as might be expected, to a great extent conditioned by an effective system of formal education. As Childe stresses, the system of writing, the numerical notation, and the standardized weights and measures that came into use very early depended upon conventional symbols and units—not only in one city but throughout the country. These had to be taught and learned, and by degrees extended. As a result, schools, with a priestly personnel in charge of them, became regular adjuncts to the temples (6:98–105). The priests not only trained scribes, clerks, and other functionaries, but they also extended and systematized knowledge. They were responsible for mathematical and scientific developments and for the elaboration of such pseudosciences as astrology and alchemy. To them we owe most of the technical and historical documents that have come down to us. And upon them devolved the development and maintenance of the libraries that were regularly attached to the temples. That such libraries assumed significant proportions, even before the middle of the third millennium B.C., is attested by the fact that those excavated at Tello and Nippur yielded 30,000 and 20,000 tablets respectively (10:44–46).

Temple schools apparently arose very early. The sign lists found on the Erech and Jemdet Nasr tablets could, as Childe points out, very well have been used as school texts. The Fara tablets, which belong to the beginning of the historical period, consist of temple accounts and sign lists that actually served as school texts (5:182). As Turner observes, the sign lists show that the schools had already gone beyond the mere teaching of writing and reading and were transmitting a gradually accumulating cultural tradition (16:147). And, presently, as noted above, the content of the tablets is extended to include other materials—liturgical, historical, and legal. All of which simply means that the content of the curriculum was keeping pace with a growing culture. And it was to do this indefinitely.

"From the earliest to the latest period," says Jastrow, "the priests continued to act as the teachers of the people. With the art of writing in the hands of the priests, the secrets of the gods could be unlocked by them only. The mysterious art naturally formed the basis of an education which the priests alone could impart. On the tablets all the extant knowledge was recorded, and to the tablets the wisdom and experience of the past was committed. Only through the handbooks was it possible to aquire the details of the various rituals and to carry out the requirements without danger of missteps. To provide for the uninterrupted continuance of religious tradition and its expression in the cult, the priests of the coming generation had to be trained by the present one. In all the larger temples and no doubt in the smaller ones as well, schools were established by the priests to hand down to their successors the wisdom of the ages as recorded in the compilations and collections which each large temple made in response to practical needs, though only in so far as these needs dictated. For the benefit of the pupils, lists of the signs used in the script were prepared with their values as syllables and as words. Grammatical paradigms both for the Sumerian and the Akkadian texts were drawn up, exercises in the use of the phrases and terms occurring in the hymns, incantations, omens, and in legal and historical texts were worked out in almost bewildering profusion, and texts edited with commentaries to explain difficult or obscure passages. Much of the Babylonian literature has thus come down to us in the form of school editions; and this applies also to mathematical tablets, chronological and geographical lists and medical prescriptions for which long lists of trees, plants, herbs and stones served as supplements, just as lists of all kinds of animals, of vessels of all kinds were prepared as aids for instruction in the omen literature. There followed instruction in the temple service in all its ramifications, and for this purpose the scribes of each temple had committed to writing all the necessary details and had preserved from one generation to the other the incantation rituals, the hymns and prayers, the omen collections and also as supplements, closely bound up with the cult and the current beliefs, the myths and fables and miscellaneous productions of the past.—The sciences that were evolved out of the cult, such as astronomy and mathematics in connection with astrology, medicine and botany as an outcome of the incantation rituals were likewise in the hands of the priests and remained so till a very late period. The temple schools thus continued to be the intellectual centers of the country, and no doubt these schools furnished the incentive for the cultivation of the fine arts as well. The priest as scribe and as judge leads to the priest as teacher. In this threefold capacity he dominated the entire civilization unfolded in the course of millenniums" (10:275–276).

Private Instruction

Chiera suspects that a good many students—especially those preparing for minor clerical positions—must have acquired the art of writing privately from scribes who were not connected with the temple schools. They apparently apprenticed themselves to the scribes and became known as their sons. To the extent that this was the case, the temple schools thus served primarily those who wished to prepare for the more exacting offices (4:165–166).

Chiera also presents an abundance of evidence illustrative of the manner in which the students learned to write. They began with simple exercises, progressed by copying literary works, and finally ended up by taking dictation (4:166–173).

Egypt from the Hyksos Through the Imperial Pharaohs

In an earlier context we traced the rise of Egyptian culture throughout the Middle Kingdom culminating in the brilliant achievements of the Twelfth Dynasty. The next two centuries marked a period of internal disorder and dissension. During this time the Hyksos invaded the country and by degrees gained control over it. Little is known about them, except that they introduced the horse and the war chariot. During the Seventeenth Dynasty organized rebellion against them got under way at Thebes, and about 1580 B.C. Ambrose I, the founder of the Eighteenth Dynasty, succeeded in driving them out completely (15:58).

With this, Egypt entered upon a spectacular era of empire-building and cultural elaboration. At its height, as Breasted points out, the Egyptian Empire "extended from the Euphrates in Asia to the Fourth Cataract of the Nile in Africa," and it "lasted from the early sixteenth to the middle of the twelfth century B.C.—somewhat over four hundred years" (2:96). Rising slowly at first, it achieved its greatest splendor under Amenhotep III (ca. 1411–1375 B.C.) (15:65). At this time, as Turner puts it, "Egypt was supreme in power, rich in all the products of the fields, shops, and mines, and splendid with the artistic products of a burst of creative genius, equaling, if not surpassing, the achievements of the great Pyramid Age. To her capital, Thebes, and the great cities, Abydos and Memphis, came traders of all nations, and to her court came messengers bearing gifts and asking favors—. The Pharaohs, like the sun, seemed to shed a beneficence over the entire world" (16:230).

Amenhotep IV (ca. 1375–1358 B.C.), generally known as Ikhnaton, undertook sweeping religious and social reforms. The priesthood of Ammon had by this time achieved tremendous prestige and power, and the professional army represented a formidable faction. Ikhnaton dispossessed the priesthood and neglected the army. The opposition engendered by this policy, together with incipient Asiatic dissertations, precluded the continuance of his reforms. Under his successor, Tutankhamen, the priesthood of Ammon was reinstated, and with its assistance, Haremhab (ca. 1350–1315 B.C.), a general, became the last pharaoh of the Eighteenth Dynasty (15:68).

Although the Empire was to endure to the middle of the twelfth century B.C., it had now passed the zenith of its greatness and its decline was definitely under way. Several able pharaohs of the Nineteenth and Twentieth Dynasties, notably Rameses II (1292–1225 B.C.) and Rameses III (ca. 1198–1167 B.C.), managed to stem the tide for a time. But, due to the fact that both internal and external conditions were growing steadily worse, their efforts had no lasting effects. Externally, the rise of new Asiatic peoples, and shifting alliances among existing ones, were slowly but surely undermining Egypt's power abroad, and thereby cutting off her sources of trade and wealth (7:215). Internally, the powerful priesthoods were tightening their hold upon the government and its economic resources (3:489–491). In the end, a high priest of Ammon actually usurped the throne (15:71). With this, as Durant observes, "the Empire became a stagnant theocracy in which architecture and superstition flourished, and every other element in the national life decayed" (7:214–215).

Egypt made notable achievements under the imperial Pharaohs. A powerful central government established order and harmony. An imperial nobility made up of court and administrative officials replaced the old feudal nobility. A planned economy, strictly regulated by the government, brought prosperity and security. A sizable middle class, made up of scribes, soldiers, lower government officials, artisans, and traders, gained a firm foothold. Within this class there was considerable mobility so that the ambitious were able to rise (1:95). Abroad, an admirable system of imperial administration was set up (1:92). At home great strides were made in agriculture, industry, commerce, and engineering (7:156–160). Architecture, sculpture, and the minor arts flourished. The most brilliant architectual achievements were of course the magnificent temples at Karnak and Luxor (7:185). Under the tutelage of the priests, science and learning advanced, and literature took on an increasingly spontaneous and natural turn (15:75).

Turning now to the rise of formal education in Egypt, we find that the motive forces back of this were essentially the same as in Mesopotamia. In each case the urban revolution produced an economic surplus that had to be administered. In Egypt, as Childe points out, the surplus was in the hands of an absolute monarch; in Mesopotamia it was in the hands of priestly corporations in city temples (5:157, 166). In either case techniques had to be devised for its effective administration. This called, among other things, for a system of writing, a numerical notation, and standardized weights and measures. The use of these techniques in turn demanded a class of trained scribes and clerks. This appeared early in both countries, and its profession became a highly respectable one (5:187–188). In Egypt, as in Mesopotamia, formal education arose initially to supply training for this profession. In due time it was of course extended to include higher mathematics, astronomy, medicine, surgery, and the ancient scripts. These subjects were developed by the priests and taught by them (5:190–191, 220).

The Egyptian System of Writing

Since the Egyptian system of writing had already reached a relatively advanced stage in the earliest known documents, we do not see it unfold before our eyes as we did the Sumerian. However, indirect evidence leaves no doubt but that it began with the customary pictographs. Very early many of these began to lose their pictorial values and came to represent phonograms—words and syllables—that could be combined to form new words. These enabled the Egyptians to express not only the concrete but also abstract concepts that could not be pictorially represented. Very early, too— even before the time of Menes—they hit upon a series of signs each of which represented only one letter. With twenty-four of these, they had at their command an alphabet that would have enabled them—had they seen fit to do so—to write their language phonetically as we do ours (2:59–60).

The oldest surviving Egyptian documents are, as Childe points out, "names and titles on sealings and vases, notes of accounts or inventories, and short records of events" (5:184). However, as he stresses, it is the use to which writing is actually put during the earliest dynasties, rather than such documentary evidence, that points to the motive force back of the invention of writing. Writing is clearly serving practical ends. "Scribes are explicitly mentioned among the royal officials. The observations on the height of the Nile—must have been written down. In later tomb pictures we see the scribes busily scribbling down the rent or tribute brought in by tenants and herdsmen. In the workshop scenes they are recording the materials removed from store to be worked up by the individual artisan."

"The scribes are officials, members of an organized and permanent public service. Their accounts and records must be intelligible to their colleagues, their superiors, and, in the last resort, to their supreme master, who is an earthy god. They must, as in Sumer, conform to a social convention; reading and writing must be learnt" (5:185).

The writing equipment of the Egyptians stood in marked contrast to that of the Mesopotamians. It consisted of paper manufactured from thin strips of the *papyrus* reed, ink made from soot and vegetable gums dissolved in water, and a pointed reed brush. By pasting the papyrus sheets together they contrived long rolls that could be stored in jars and filed in true library fashion (7:171, 174; 2:88–89). Of the three scripts, the stately Hieroglyphic was reserved primarily for monumental purposes; the Hieratic, roughly comparable to our own handwriting, was the chief medium of secular expression; and the Demotic, a post-Empire simplification of the Hieratic, was in use in commercial circles (16:190–191).

The Schools for Scribes

As noted above, formal education in Egypt arose to supply training for scribes. The latter embraced a large and varied class of civil servants, ranging, as Maspero points out, all the way from the humblest clerk to the priest and the literary noble. "Every one was a scribe who knew how to read, write, and cipher, was fairly proficient in wording the administrative formulas, and could easily apply the elementary rules to book-keeping" (11:288). Actually, the education of the priestly scribes went far beyond these minima, for upon them devolved the task of developing Egypt's learned tradition—

its mathematics, science, medicine, and surgery. And the priests were of course the masters of the sacred Hieroglyphic script.

Despite its varied character, the scribe class enjoyed on the whole a privileged position in Egyptian society. Membership in it was eagerly sought for and highly prized. Scribes were exempt from forced labor, and their means of livelihood was assured. And they had ready access to official positions. Scribes were so numerous that authorities often refer to them as an army. The reason for this seems to have been, as Erman observes, that the Egyptians had an obsession for records. "Nothing was done—without documents; lists and protocols were indispensable even in the simplest matters of business" (8:112). As a result, every official, from the highest to the lowest, had a coterie of clerks and scribes.

The education of the scribe was at best a prolonged and trying ordeal. Except in the case of the lowest ranks, he had not only to achieve proficiency in reading, writing, and arithmetic, but he had to become familiar with Hieroglyphics, and study the laws, administrative regulations, and government correspondence (12:269). And in some cases he may also have been required to study existing scientific generalizations and knowledge about the world (14:46). And there was of course no end of emphasis upon good manners and moral precepts. Even so, there can be no doubt but that the core of the curriculum was basically linguistic. After stressing the revolutionary influence of the Hieratic script upon Egyptian government and society, Breasted says: "It was the acquirement of this method of writing which enabled the lad to enter upon the coveted official career as a scribe or overseer of a magazine, or steward of an estate. Hence, the master put before the boy model-letters, proverbs, and literary compositions, which he laboriously copied into his roll, the copybook of this ancient school-boy. A large quantity of these copybooks from the Empire, some fifteen hundred years after

he fall of the Old Kingdom, has been found; and many a
:omposition which would otherwise have been lost, has thus
urvived, in the uncertain hand of a pupil in the scribal
chools" (3:99).

The character of the schools in which the scribe received
iis training has not been too consistently delineated—prob-
bly in part at least because different authorities have
tressed different historical periods. It seems fairly clear,
iowever, that during the Old Kingdom the court school,
vhere boys from varying social ranks were educated along
vith the sons of the nobles, played a conspicuous role. Upon
he completion of this, the aspiring scribe appears to have
)een assigned to some government official for practical train-
ng and gradual induction into the office of scribe. During
he imperial period schools appear to have been established
nd maintained in connection with different government de-
)artments. This means that a prospective scribe could now
eceive both his preliminary and his practical training in one
)lace under the tutelage of important officials (8:329). Mean-
vhile, court schools apparently continued to supply training
or the children of the nobility and for hostages from abroad.
And others may have been included. Thus, Petrie points out
hat during the Nineteenth Dynasty children born on the
ame day as the heir were customarily brought up with him
13:125).

Temple Colleges

In addition, the imperial period witnessed the establish-
nent of temple colleges at such centers as Memphis, Heliopo-
is, and Thebes (9:36). These were of course designed for the
)riestly class, and the training which they supplied was
ssentially professional in character. At these centers Egyp-
ian mathematics, science, medicine and surgery flourished
.long with no end of magic and superstition. And it was
ere that the sacred documents were studied and preserved.

The Practical Orientation of the Egyptians

From beginning to end, education was strictly a practical device for the Egyptians. They valued it for its utilitarian benefits. It elevated the scribe from the ruled to the ruling class, and it gave the priest power over the unseen. Their intellectual activities were motivated by the same considerations. "It never occurred to the Egyptian," says Breasted, "to enter upon the search for truth for its own sake" (3:100). They were, as Trever puts it, "not primarily thinkers and investigators," but rather "acute observers, interested in practical ends. Their mathematical, medical, astronomical, or chemical knowledge was the direct outgrowth of immediate needs such as land measurements; the erecting of great irrigation works, pyramids, statues, and temples; the dissection and mummification of bodies in connection with religion; the making of a calendar; the study of the stars in relation to human destiny; and manufacture of metals, pottery and glass (15:49).

In Egypt, as in Mesopotamia, formal education was not destined for the masses. In both societies, apparently more so in Egypt than in Mesopotamia, an able and ambitious individual had some opportunity to improve his lot through education. However, this affected a small proportion of the population. The children of the masses received their occupational training either through their families or through apprenticeship. In Egypt, as in Mesopotamia, trades were frequently confined to given families for generations, and free craftsmen were rather well organized (7:159).

BIBLIOGRAPHY

1. Barnes, Harry E., The History of Western Civilization, Volume I New York: Harcourt, Brace and Company, 1935.
2. Breasted, James H., The Conquest of Civilization. New York: The Literary Guild of America, 1938.
3. Breasted, James H., A History of Egypt. New York: Charles Scribner's Sons, 1911.

4. Chiera, Edward, They Wrote on Clay. Chicago: University of Chicago Press, 1938.
5. Childe, V. Gordon, Man Makes Himself. London: Watts and Company, 1936.
6. Childe, V. Gordon, What Happened in History. New York: Penguin Books, 1946.
7. Durant, Will, The Story of Civilization—Our Oriental Heritage. New York: Simon and Schuster, 1942.
8. Erman, Adolf, Life in Ancient Egypt. London and New York: The Macmillan Company, 1894.
9. Graves, Frank P., A History of Education—Before the Middle Ages. New York: The Macmillan Company, 1914.
10. Jastrow, Morris, The Civilization of Babylonia and Assyria. Philadelphia: J. B. Lippincott Company, 1915.
11. Maspero, G., The Dawn of Civilization—Egypt and Chaldaea. New York: D. Appleton and Company, 1894.
12. Moret, Alexandre, The Nile and Egyptian Civilization. New York: Alfred A. Knopf, 1927.
13. Petrie, W. M. F., Social Life in Ancient Egypt. London: Constable and Company, 1923.
14. Schneider, Hermann, The History of World Civilization. New York: Harcourt, Brace and Company, 1931.
15. Trever, Albert A., History of Civilization—The Ancient Near East and Greece. New York: Harcourt, Brace and Company, 1936.
16. Turner, Ralph, The Great Cultural Traditions, Volumes I and II. New York: McGraw-Hill Book Company, 1941.

CHAPTER III

CHAPTER III

Culture and Education in Ancient India

The Indus Valley Cultures

IN an earlier context we sketched the rise of urban culture in the Indus valley, and called attention to their mysteri ous disappearance after the middle of the third millennium B.C. Little is known at present regarding the relationship between the Indus valley people and the people of pre-Aryan India. However, the Indus valley culture bears resemblance to pre-Aryan cultures, and it is clearly non-Aryan. As Rawlin son observes, man is not a late arrival in India. Both Paleo lithic and Neolithic remains have been found in various re gions. The Dravidians, whom the Aryan-speaking invaders encountered, appear to have comprised several racial groups with a common language. They had developed a fairly ad vanced culture, with copper in use in the north and iron in the south. They were dark-skinned people (10:8–11).

The Aryan Invaders of India

The Aryan invaders, with whom the history of India begins, arrived in successive waves through the northwest passes before 1000 B.C. They were immigrants who brough their families and herds with them (10:20). Although they were generally fair-skinned and long-headed, they were no necessarily a racial unit. Their bonds were linguistic and cul tural. They spoke related Indo-European dialects, and wor

hipped similar gods. Their earliest literature was composed
n a special language which in time developed into the sacred
anscrit. In temperament, habits, and outlook these people
liffered strikingly from the type into which they later
volved. As Turner puts it, they "ate beef, drank beer,—went
o battle in chariots, and allowed their women a great deal
f freedom.—Their chief amusements were gambling, hard
rinking, and horse racing" (11:375). Child marriage was
nknown, and, although several social classes were in evi-
ence, there were no signs of castes.

The basic social unit was the family headed by the warrior-
riest father. A group of several hundred families in turn
onstituted a village. This appears to have taken the form of
primitive republic ruled by a patriarch (11:378). At the
ead of the tribe was the king whose powers were limited
y a popular assembly (10:24). Initially, at least, the Aryas
ere a semi-pastoral people who moved frequently (11:375).

The religion of the Aryas was fundamentally animistic.
here were gods of heaven, gods of the sky, gods of the
arth, and no end of spirits. Varuna, representing cosmic and
oral order, was the great god of heaven; Indra, manifested
thunder, lightning, and rain, ruled the sky gods; and Agni,
e mediator between gods and men, was the god of fire (11:
31). Very early the priestly class assumed a position of dig-
ity and importance, for it alone knew how to propitiate the
ds and spirits (3:11). "Vedic ideas of life after death," says
awlinson, "were as vague as those of the Homeric Greeks.
he soul departed to 'the fathers,' where it was received by
ama, the first man to die and now king of the dead, and
warded or punished according to its deeds" (10:32). There
as as yet no evidence of the doctrine of transmigration.

The Aryas Encounter the Dravidians

As the Aryan invaders pressed eastward in their migrations
ey encountered the Dravidians. The inevitable result was

a long drawn out conflict between the two peoples. The Aryas
not only wanted the Dravidian lands, but they despised their
color and religion and looked upon them as generally inferior
Although the Dravidians fared badly at first, they were so
numerous that the Aryas were unable in the long run to ex
terminate or enslave them. Neither were they able to conver
them wholly to their way of life (11:376). In consequence, the
two peoples and cultures gradually fused, the Dravidian
making no inconsiderable contribution to subsequent Hindu
ism (10:22).

Initially, however, the struggle served to unify the Aryan
tribes. They became more settled and improved their agri
cultural production. In due time villages began to coalesc
into cities. Urban cultures, appearing first during the eightl
century B.C., had become fairly numerous by early Buddhis
times (11:378). In the wake of cities came states and king
doms. And with these well under way, empires began t
appear.

The Vedic Hymns and Their Elaboration

Our knowledge of the Aryan invaders, as sketched above
is derived from their early literary productions—the Vedi
Hymns, composed between 1500 and 1000 B.C. There ar
four of these—the Rig-Veda, Sama-Veda, Yahura Veda, an
Atharva-Veda. The first consists chiefly of hymns in praise o
different gods, the second of chants selected from the Rig
Veda, the third of sacrificial prayers and prose commentarie
and the fourth of spells and magic formulas (3:6). "As literar
works," says Turner, "the Vedas show a fine feeling for natur
and a deep sense of the dignity of man" (11:388). They wer
composed by priests, and regarded as inspired.

When the Vedas reached their final form, the Aryas ha
penetrated eastward to the Ganges. At this stage Vedic elabo
rations began to appear—first the Brahmanas and Aryanaka
then the Upanishads and the Sutras. The Brahmanas wer

rose manuals dealing primarily with ritualistic instructions
or priests. The Aryanakas were speculative and meditative
uides for aged Brahmans who had retired to forest retreats.
he Upanishads are philosophical utterances pointing rather
efinitely to an imminent religious reorientation (3:7). The
utras were terse condensations of the Brahmanas designed
or popular use (11:389).

The period of the Brahmanas and the Upanishads falls
oughly between 800 and 600 B.C. By the end of this period
ryan life and culture had undergone significant changes.
ities and states had multiplied. With these came occupa-
onal and class differentiation. The priests rose to great
ower. And the castes, growing out of existing social classes,
ecame firmly established.

The Rise of the Caste System

Authorities are not wholly agreed regarding the factors
sponsible for the rise of the caste system—a system that has
o counterpart in any other culture (6:126; 10:26). However,
variety of forces—racial, religious, economic—appear to
ave been operative. The struggle between the Aryas and the
ravidians spurred proscriptions against inter-marriage (11:
4). The Brahman's exclusiveness and complete monopoli-
tion of religious functions suggested retaliative action to
her groups (10:25). The growth of cities in turn favored
e formation of special interest groups, especially along oc-
pational lines. In any event, by the close of the period
der consideration the four basic castes—the Brahmans or
iests, the Kshatriyas or warriors, the Vaisyas or cultivators,
d the Sudras or serfs—were firmly established (6:135).

Each caste was now an endogamous unit, the members of
hich married outside of their families but within the group.
ch had its own *dharma* or rules of life that defined its
ties and obligations, and a governing board to deal with
olations of them. This meant in essence that each caste had

its own distinctive social system—it was a self-governing bod
within the larger society (3:16).

Only the first three castes were of course within the pal
of Aryan society. They alone were eligible for the ceremon
of initiation which invested them with the sacred threa
and classed them among the twice-born. The Sudras wei
completely excluded. They could neither recite, nor listen i
the recital of, the sacred texts (6:137). Below them arose i
time an Out-caste system. Out of this grew the 40,000,0C
Untouchables of contemporary India (4:399).

In power and prestige, the Brahmans rose now by degre
far above their nearest competitors, the Kshatriyas. The pric
had long occupied an important place in Aryan society. Hov
ever, until the rise to extreme power in post-Vedic times, I
had been, as Turner puts it, primarily "a singer of songs
praise of gods, an utterer of prayers, and a maker of sacrific
according to strict formulas" (11:385). By the time the Ary
had penetrated eastward to the Ganges, ritualism had becon
so complex and elaborate that nothing could be done witho
priestly direction. However, the Kshatriyas or warriors we
still the dominant group. Only after the destruction of mai
of them in connection with subsequent invasions and inte
tribal wars did the Brahmans succeed in seizing suprem
power. But once they had seized it they were to retain
longer and exercise it more tyrannically than any other prie:
hood in the annals of history (4:487).

Religious Unrest

The religious reorientation that was now getting under w
was to lay the foundation for subsequent Hinduism. It mai
fested itself in a variety of ways. Pessimism and disillusic
ment were rampant. Life seemed to be an evil, and there w
a growing desire for release from it. The old polytheistic b
liefs no longer satisfied the more intelligent. They were gro

ing for an all-embracing principle of being (6:100). In the Upanishads this took the form of a World Soul—Atman—an impersonal essence that is present in all things (10:41). As a natural sequel, came the doctrine of transmigration and the related concept of Karma or action. According to the former, the soul is reborn many times in various forms; according to the latter, progress toward release is achieved through actions in previous existences (10:41). With actions, good or bad, determining rebirth, the idea naturally suggested itself that release might be gained through complete abstention from all activity and desire. This, as Farquhar observes, made the ascetic the only truly religious person (5:40).

In the wake of ideational reorientation came significant changes in practice. Ritualism became more complex and elaborate. The father, as head of the family, was forbidden to eat with his wife. Boys of the twice-born castes were regularly sent to Brahman teachers (3:21–22). Child-marriage and the use of idols in worship received full-fledged recognition. Only childless widows remained free to remarry. And there was a drift toward abstention from flesh-eating.

The Beginning of Authentic History

Down to 600 B.C. the development of the Indian cultural tradition has to be largely inferred from literary works. Thereafter, although it is punctuated by long intervals for which there are few inscriptions and documents, authentic history begins (3:30). Among the major events demanding our attention from this point on are the rise of two religions and the establishment of several great empires. The two religions were of course Jainism and Buddhism, founded by Vardhamana Mahavira (ca. 540–468 B.C.) and Gautama Buddha (ca. 563–483 B.C.), respectively (3:33). Their rise was, as Durant points out, almost inevitable at this stage of Indian cultural development. The materialistic school of philosophers, known as Charvakas, had so effectively undermined the old beliefs that a new outlook was urgently needed (4: 419).

Up to a certain point these two religions had much in common. Both were founded by members of the Kshatriya caste; both revolted against the tyranny of the Brahmans; both challenged the sanctity of the Vedas; both ignored caste distinctions; both were atheistic; both were pessimistic in the sense that they regarded life as an evil; both sought release from life through right living; both featured monastic orders; and both initially utilized the vernaculars in place of the Sanscrit (10:43). From this point on they diverged. The asceticism of Jainism was extreme; that of Buddhism moderate. In place of self-torture, Buddism stressed meditation. Jainism enjoyed complete *ahimsa*— abstention from injury to all living things (4:421); Buddhism merely prohibited needless killing and flesh-eating. Finally, the social element was appreciably stronger in Buddhist than in Jain ethics (11:397, 403–404).

In part at least because of its extreme asceticism, Jainism failed to appeal to the masses and became instead the religion of a select group. By way of contrast, Buddhism, although it never succeeded in supplanting Brahmanism completely, spread rapidly, and was destined in time to become a world religion. It reached the peak of its development between the reigns of Asoka (ca. 274–184 B.C.) and Harsha (ca. A.D. 606–648). After the twelfth century A.D., it practically ceased to exist in India (3:99).

The Maurya Empire

The Maurya Empire (ca. 321–184 B.C.) was the first great Indian empire to be established. It was to last for one hundred and thirty-seven years, extend over most of India, and produce one of its foremost rulers—Asoka. Its founder, Chandragupta Maurya, after expelling the last vestiges of the

Greeks from the Indus valley, built a splendid capital at Pataliputra, and set up a powerful government. The greatest extension of the Empire and the most significant internal developments occurred during the reign of his grandson, Asoka (ca. 274–236 B.C.). At first primarily a conqueror and an organizer, Asoka by degrees became an ardent reformer. Through the influence of a great teacher he was converted to Buddhism, and later became a monk (10:76). Thereafter, he devoted himself unsparingly to the application and dissemination of Buddhist principles. He appointed high officials to teach piety to his subjects, to alleviate abuses, and to set up charitable organizations (3:49). The royal kitchens became vegetarian, and kindness to living things was strictly enjoined (10:77). Early in the course of his reign he began to have his edicts inscribed upon granite rocks and massive pillars in the language of the people. In spite of his unqualified devotion to Buddhism, he insisted upon complete religious toleration. Under his influence Buddhism spread throughout India, and in addition missionaries were dispatched to Ceylon and Burma, and to Syria, Egypt, and Greece. And Asoka was lavish in his endowment of monasteries. Shortly after his death the Empire disintegrated and the Maurya dynasty came to an end.

The Kushan Empire

Almost six centuries intervene between the death of Asoka (232 B.C.) and the establishment of the Gupta Empire (A.D. 320). The events which occurred during this long interval are, as Durant points out, for the most part so meagerly documented that they have to be largely inferred (4:450). For our purposes we may, with one exception—the rise of the Kushan Empire (ca. A.D. 50–226)—by-pass them. The Kushans, a central Asiatic people, invaded Gandhara during the middle of the first century A.D., and by degrees built up an extensive

58   ANCIENT EDUCATION

empire in northern and central India. Their greatest ruler—
and the only one about whom there is definite information—
was Kanishka (ca. A.D. 120–162). Like Asoka, he was converted to Buddhism, and became an ardent protagonist of it.
In the hope of reconciling the many conflicting sects and
scriptural interpretations that had by this time arisen, he
called a general council of Buddhist monks (10:96). This, as
Durant puts it, "lowered Buddha's philosophy to the emotional needs of the common soul, and raised him to divinity"
(4:451). Out of its deliberations emerged by degrees the
northern or Mahayana branch of Buddhism that was subsequently to spread to China and to Japan (10:96–97). Beyond
this, Kanishka was an enthusiastic patron of the arts and sciences, and his era appears to have been one of unusual prosperity and splendor (10:98–99).

The Gupta Empire

Little is known about the century intervening between the
disintegration of the Kushan Empire and the rise of the
Gupta Empire (ca. A.D. 320–484). Founded by Chandragupta
I (ca. A.D. 320–330), the Gupta Empire reached the zenith
of its greatness during the reign of Chandragupta II (ca. A.D
380–415). It collapsed toward the close of the fifth century
A.D. under the onslaught of the White Hun invaders.

The Chandraguptas were not only great conquerors, but
also able rulers and liberal patrons of the arts, learning, and
religion. They erected splendid buildings, and surrounded
themselves with brilliant philosophers, scholars, and artists
In contrast with the Maurya, their religious sympathies were
definitely, though not fanatically, Brahman. Fa-hsien, the
Chinese pilgrim who was in India during the first ten years
of the fifth century A.D., speaks in glowing terms of pros
perity and contentment, of hospitals and charitable institu
tions, of great monasteries, of large cities, and of splendid
imperial palaces. Indeed, so much was he impressed with the

elegance of the age that he completely failed to sense the Brahman reaction that was getting under way (4:451–452).

Harsha Vardhana

The collapse of the Gupta Empire was followed by a chaotic century. Then, another of India's great empire builders arose. At the beginning of the seventh century A.D. Harsha Vardhana (A.D. 606–647), a descendant of the Guptas, became ruler of Thanesar. Within a few years he had built up an extensive empire in northern India (3:74–75). And there ensued another brilliant period in India's cultural history. Harsha was an able and beneficent ruler. Although Brahman reaction had become strong by this time, he leaned toward Mahayana Buddhism. He built shrines throughout his dominions, and was generous in his endowment of monasteries. At intervals he called great public assemblies to encourage discussion and excange of ideas. And he was a great poet and dramatist in his own name (4:453).

Once more we have the testimony of a Chinese pilgrim—Hsuan-tsang—who spent fifteen years in India (A.D. 630–645), eight of them in Harsha's Empire. He was deeply impressed with the prosperity and beneficence which he found everywhere, with the spirited public assemblies, and with the esteem accorded learning at such monastic centers as Nalanda. The Brahman reaction had now become conspicuous, and the caste system was again in full force. Significantly enough, the Vedas had not yet been committed to writing (10:113–121).

Under the Guptas and Harsha classical Indian culture reached its climax. With the death of Harsha, chaos once more ensued, and it was, as Durant puts it, to continue "for almost a thousand years. India, like Europe, now suffered her Middle Ages, was over-run by barbarians, was conquered, divided, and despoiled. Not until the great Akbar would she know peace and unity again" (4:454).

Hinduism

It remains to be noted that Hinduism, as it is known today, began to emerge during the reigns of the Guptas and Harsha (10:123). Buddhism, although it enjoyed the patronage of powerful rulers, had never been the religion of the masses. With the twelfth century A.D. it disappeared from northern India (3:99). Long before this it had begun to assume an increasing semblance to Hinduism. The Brahmans who had been temporarily under eclipse were now actively reasserting themselves. Eager to regain their control over the Indian mind, they were willing to meet challenges with compromise. As a result, new deities—among them Brahma, Vishnu, and Siva— replaced the old; and the Puranas—mythological accounts of the world and the gods—together with the great epics, the Mahabharata and the Ramayana, became the sacred literature of popular Hinduism (11:767). Beyond this, anthropomorphism became conspicuous, the gods being represented by idols dwelling in temples, and the cow becoming a sacred animal (10:128).

"Hinduism," says Rawlinson, "is hard to define. It is not a creed, like Christianity or Islam, but a way of life—a collection of rites, traditions and mythologies, sanctioned by the sacred books and propagated by Brahmanical teaching All Hindus, however, believe in caste and pantheism; they regard all their countless deities as merely manifestations of the all-pervading divine energy. With these they associate the doctrines of rebirth and Karma.—The keystone of the system is the Brahmin—" (10:129).

Religious and Oral Bases of Education in Vedic India

In contrast with Mesopotamia and Egypt, the rise of formal education in India was, on the surface at least, unique in two respects. It occurred without benefit of a system of writings and the motivation back of it was exclusively religious. The Vedas, about which Brahman education centered, were trans mitted orally, and not committed to writing until the eighth or ninth century A.D. (1:147). And while the content of Brahman education came very early to include much more than the memorization of one or more Vedas, its purpose was strictly religious, as is abundantly attested by the six Angas— phonetics, meter, grammar, etymology, astronomy, and ceremony—without which an adequate understanding of the Vedas and their proper use in ritual would have been out of the question (1:111). Finally, Vedic India restricted teaching to the priestly class—only Brahmans could give instruction.

What has been said above does not imply that cultural evolution in India followed a course that was fundamentally different from that which it followed in Mesopotamia and Egypt. It means rather that we observe it at a different stage and under somewhat different circumstances. In Mesopotamia the system of writing unfolded before our eyes and we were able to follow subsequent developments and elaborations terminating in an extensive literature and an elaborate system of temple schools. The priestly class concentrated upon mundane matters and was not obsessed with other-worldly affairs. The Egyptian system of writing was already highly developed when we encountered it, but it was clear that it had followed essentially the same course as in Mesopotamia. Subsequent literary and educational developments occurred within our purview. The Egyptians were religious and deeply concerned with after life, but not to an obsessional degree. The priesthood did not rise to power until late.

The situation that confronts us in India stands in strong contrast. Apart from the Indus valley cities where cultural evolution had followed essentially the same course as in Mesopotamia and Egypt, we have very little definite information regarding early cultural developments. When we first catch sight of the Aryan invaders, they are already in possession of the horse and the plow and they have a cultural tradition that is being handed down orally. Beginning with the eighth century B.C., some of them have accumulated an economic surplus and are building cities. The administration of this surplus must have demanded—as it did in Mesopotamia, Egypt, and the Indus valley—some sort of writing, a numeral notation, and standardized weights and measures. But we have no direct evidence of them. The earliest existing examples of Indian writing are Asoka's inscriptions executed during the third century B.C. Significantly enough, however, these are so skillfully executed that writing is assumed to have been in use long before this time (10:81). Yet, there are no extant manuscripts antedating the fourth century A.D. However, by this time books were in widespread use throughout India (10:130). They were written on birch bark and palm leaves with an iron or reed stylus, the pages being assembled on cords (4:556).

Indirect evidence pointing to the early use of writing for practical purposes is supplied by the fact that traders appear to have brought the Brahmi script—the parent of all existing Indian alphabets—from western Asia to India as early as the eighth century B.C. This, it will be recalled, coincides with the time when Indian cities were rapidly getting under way. The Brahmi script was Semitic in character, consisting initially of consonants only. In the course of the next few centuries the Indians elaborated it in a most ingenious manner into a system that records speech forms with complete phonetic accuracy (8:532–533; 2:289).

The proscription against writing originated of course with the Brahmans, and it concerned primarily the Vedas. These were handed down from one generation to another in Brahman families and zealously guarded. The Brahmans composed them, and they alone knew how to recite and interpret them. Had they been committed to writing they might have reached the profane non-Aryans. For a Sudra to have gotten the remotest inkling of the content of the Vedas would have been a supreme calamity, and it would have constituted a crime punishable by unspeakable torture (4:485–488).

While the proscription against committing the Vedas to writing may have had a retarding influence upon writing in general, there are indications that it came increasingly into use during the period between Asoka (274–236 B.C.) and the Guptas (A.D. 320–484) (5:87). And it may have been fairly prevalent earlier. However, Panini, who developed the science of grammar a century before Asoka's time, failed to use or mention it (11:391). Thomas suspects that the Sutras may have been the first of the Vedic elaborations to have been put into writing (6:62). The Buddhist canon was not written down until the first century B.C. The great epics— the Mahabharata and the Ramayana—did not appear in writing until Gupta times. And these, it should be borne in mind, were accessible to women and men of all castes (5:89).

Brahman Education

During the earliest stages, Brahman education appears to have been administered by the father—each experienced priest teaching his own sons—and its purpose was obviously to train priests (7:13). Later, when the various family traditions had been incorporated in the Vedas, schools or associations of priests corresponding to the several Vedas, arose. The ceremonial functions of these became differentiated and somewhat specialized (7:37). From this point on the Brahman student received his training from a priest of the school in which he wished to specialize (7:13–17). It should be borne in mind, however, that he did not enter a school. There were no schools in the technical sense of the term. There were merely priests who received and trained students by special arrangement (1:245–246). Instruction was on an individual basis (7:41).

The core of the student's curriculum was the Veda of his particular school. He was of course free to master all four of them. However, since it presumably took twelve years to master one, this must have been a rare occurrence. And Altekar suspects that the emphasis upon Vedic study may have sharply decreased during the period of the Upanishads and the Brahmanas in the interest of such subjects as grammar, philosophy, and law (1:130–131). However that may be, students were traditionally required to memorize one of the Vedas. Along with this, they received instruction in the meaning of the hymns, the details and intricacies of the ritual, and the duties of the priests. At first administered informally, exegetical instruction of this type finally culminated in the Brahmanas of the different schools (7:17–18). Beyond this, as implied earlier, the six Vedangas—phonetics, meter, grammar, etymology, astronomy, and ceremony—developed by degrees into formidable studies, so much so that they subsequently became the point of departure for specialization (7:44–45).

The regulations governing Brahman education—and practically every other phase of Indian social life—were incorporated in the *dharma-sastras*. The greatest of these was the Code of Manu which reached its final form about A.D. 200 (4:483–488). Tremendous stress was placed upon the relationship between the student and the teacher. And the student was of course required to lead a rigorously disciplined life. Admission to student status began with *Upanayana*—the ceremony of initiation into the twice-born castes—at about age eight (7:28). After this the student became virtually a member of the priest-teacher's household.

Sometime before 500 B.C. the education of the Kshatriya and Vaisya castes likewise passed under Brahman control. With this, the boys of these castes were expected, after the ceremony of initiation, to enter upon Vedic studies (7:26–27). However, since these had less occasion to use Vedic lore, and moreover needed training in other fields, the probabilities are, as Altekar observes, that Vedic memorization may have been reduced to a bare minimum. And in the case of the

Vaisya, who were becoming increasingly entangled with the Sudras, it may have disappeared altogether (1:164–166). Even so, the Brahmans had greatly strengthened their hold upon Indian life.

Buddhist Education

Buddhist education differed from Brahman education in certain important respects; in others it resembled it rather closely. The chief differences lay in the fact that it ignored caste distinctions and the Vedas, and was monastic in character. Beyond this, the two had much in common. The age intervals were closely comparable. There was the same close relationship between the student and the teacher or preceptor. Oral instruction and memorization were conspicuous in both.

With the Vedas out of the way, except in higher institutions, the core of the general curriculum naturally shifted to Buddhist literature—the Tripitaka and various related works. In the study of this, tremendous emphasis appears to have been placed upon grammar—both Pali and Sanscrit—followed by logic, metaphysics, and philosophy (1:289). Upon the completion of such a program, the monk was prepared to teach others, but he was enjoined to remain a life-long student himself (1:141). This explains in part at least the extensive provisions for advanced study in numerous Buddhist monasteries.

Brahman Centers for Higher Education

As noted above, during the period of the Brahmanas and the Upanishads interest in Vedic study declined and there was a growing tendency to specialize in such fields as grammar, law, logic, philology, and comparative philosophy (1:131). This in turn appears to have served as a stimulus to the development of centers for higher education. The Brahmans did not, as Altekar stresses, establish formal institutions to this end, but they encouraged learned men to congregate in centers for the purpose of giving instruction (1:245–247). A considerable number of them actually sprang up by degrees. The earliest and most illustrious one arose at Taxila, the capital of Gandhara. As early as the seventeenth century B.C., it was attracting famous scholars from all over India, and it appears to have continued to function to the end of the Kushan Empire (ca. A.D. 226). It was there that Panini compiled his great grammar. The offering apparently extended over a wide range, including the Vedas and some eighteen arts and professions (1:248–254).

Buddhist Centers for Higher Education

Corporate institutions came into being with the Buddhist monastic system (1:246). The fact that Buddhist monks were enjoined to be life-long students must in part at least have been responsible for the development of Buddhist higher education. In any event, as the monasteries grew larger and more numerous, during and after Asoka's time, many of them developed centers for higher education—at first for inmates and then for outsiders as well (1:246). The most famous of these was Nalanda in eastern India. It rose to prominence rather abruptly about the middle of the fifth century A.D. under the sponsorship of the Guptas. Hsuan-tsang, the Chinese pilgrim who spent five years there shortly before the middle of the seventh century A.D., speaks of superb monastic buildings running into several stories, of thousands of monks, and of famous scholars (1:262–266). The offering included among other things medicine, mechanics, grammar, logic and metaphysics (10:117). Instruction in religion, philosophy, and literature appears to have been broad and cosmopolitan, stressing contrary as well as accepted views. And the monastery featured, as might be expected, a great library (1:266–268).

Primary Education

Information regarding primary education in ancient India is so sketchy that we shall make no attempt to analyze it. To the extent that such education existed it appears to have served two separate and distinct purposes—to prepare boys for Vedic studies (1:204–206), and to meet a popular demand for training in reading, writing, and arithmetic (7:144). These two types of training obviously could not have been administered by the same teachers or schools. In general, Altekar assumes that by the end of the eighth century A.D. about 40 per cent of the boys of school age were receiving primary education (1:213). This seems at best excessive when we bear in mind that India's population is to this day 90 per cent illiterate.

The Education of Women

As Altekar observes, the development of the status of women has followed a unique course in India. In most societies the status of women has improved by degrees; in India it deteriorated progressively until they came to be regarded as substantially on a par with the Sudras (1:220–230). In Vedic times women qualified for Upanayana. They pursued Vedic studies under relatives and participated in sacrifices. During the period of the Upanishads such privileges became restricted to women of the upper classes. And subsequently, Upanayana for women became a meaningless formality, and Vedic studies virtually ceased (1:232). The Buddhists, although they established nunneries, and may have encouraged learning among women in aristocratic circles, appear on the whole to have shared the Brahmans' attitude toward woman (7:111–113). Under such circumstances, literate learning for the rank and file of India's women dwindled to negligible proportions.

Occupational Education

Apart from the professional training carried on at university centers—as in the case of Taxila and Nalanda—in such fields as medicine, commerce, agriculture, and the military arts (1:2:54), occupational education in ancient India was supplied almost exclusively on family and apprenticeship bases. The large freedom in occupational choice that prevailed in Vedic times disappeared as the castes became fixed and highly differentiated (1:168–170). With this, occupations became increasingly restricted to families and castes. And it was within these, that they came to be transmitted from one generation to another. In time the family and caste systems were supplemented by guilds. The functions of these were largely regulatory (1:193–195).

BIBLIOGRAPHY

1. Altekar, A. S., Education in Ancient India. Benares: The Indian Book Shop, 1934.
2. Bloomfield, Leonard, Language. New York: Henry Holt and Company, 1933.
3. Dunbar, Sir George, A History of India, Volume I. London: Nicholson and Watson, 1943.
4. Durant, Will, The Story of Civilization—Our Oriental Heritage. New York: Simon and Schuster, 1942.
5. Farquhar, J. N., A Primer of Hinduism. London: Oxford University Press, 1912.
6. Garratt, G. T. (editor), The Legacy of India. London: Oxford University Press, 1937.
7. Keay, F. E., Ancient Indian Education. London: Oxford University Press, 1918.
8. Kroeber, A. L., Anthropology, New Edition. New York: Harcourt, Brace and Company, 1948.
9. Mulhern, James, A History of Education. New York: The Ronand Press Company, 1946.
10. Rawlinson, H. G., India—A Short Cultural History. London: The Cresset Press, 1948.
11. Turner, Ralph, The Great Cultural Traditions, Volumes I and II. New York: McGraw-Hill Book Company, 1941.
12. Woody, Thomas, Life and Education in Early Societies. New York: The Macmillan Company, 1949.

CHAPTER IV

Culture and Education in Ancient China

The Prehistory of China

THE prehistory of China is still relatively obscure. However, Neolithic implements are widely distributed, and archeological evidence points to several fairly advanced Neolithic cultures in the Yellow River, Wei and Feng valleys shortly after the opening of the third millennium B.C. (13:34). Somewhat later, a still more advanced culture, the Yang Shao, appears to have penetrated from the west and mingled with some of these. At the beginning of the second millennium B.C., some peasant-village cultures were evolving into urban centers (18:407–409).

The Beginning of Authentic History

Traditional Chinese history begins with three dynasties—the Hsia (ca. 2000–1500 B.C.), the Shang (ca. 1500–1100 B.C.), and the Chou (ca. 1100–221 B.C.). Since there is as yet no scientific evidence in support of the first of these, authentic history begins with the Shang Dynasty, the capital of which has been unearthed at Anyang, along with numerous corroborating inscriptions—most of them on oracle bones. Shang culture was already far advanced and must have had a long history back of it (6:104). Its system of writing was highly sophisticated and its decorative art exquisite (3:35). It was a bronze-using culture, resting upon an economic base of agriculture and skilled crafts. Although there are indications

69

of expert diviners, there appears to have been little if any differentiation between the ruling military class and a priestly group (18:410–412).

The Chou Foundations of Chinese Civilization

During the succeeding Chou Dynasty the foundations of Chinese civilization were rather securely laid. The long interval over which this dynasty extends is frequently divided into three sub-periods—the early, the middle, and the late (7:18). During the first of these the Chou kings, although the realm was divided into principalities, were the real rulers of the country. During the second, which began with the removal of the capital from the Wei valley to Loyang, control drifted into the hands of the feudal states, much as in Medieval Europe, leaving the Chou kings with little more than priestly powers (13:46). The third, sometimes characterized as the period of the contending states, was marked by the rise of rival states which waged almost incessant war to the time of the emergence of the Ch'in Dynasty (13:50).

Despite the social and political turmoil that characterized much of it, the Chou period was a remarkably creative one. "The Chinese," says Goodrich, "consider this their classical age—when some of their most memorable poetry and prose were composed; when the laws were written down for everyone to see; when market places increased and a money economy appeared; when advances in craftsmanship and methods of production, notably fertilizers, irrigation, and the traction plow, were made; when iron began to displace bronze in common tools and weapons; when science and thinking took great leaps forward, and increasing numbers of new ideas began to seep through the land barriers to the west and southwest to stimulate their own native genius. The very fact that China was in turmoil may have aided these developments. There was no set pattern, no orthodox church, no dominant policy" (7:23).

Confucius and His Immediate Followers

Of primary interest to us are the philosophical developments that took place during the later Chou centuries. These were to have a profound influence upon China's future moral and political orientation. The most influential system of philosophy originating at this time was of course that of Confucius and his immediate followers—Mencius and Hsun Tzu. Confucius (ca. 551–479 B.C.) was not a profound or systematic philosopher. He avoided metaphysical and theological issues, and concerned himself instead with moral and political problems (5:666–667). Although he drew heavily upon the past, and considered himself a transmitter rather than an originator, his analysis of the social order was clear and searching. His moral standards were so exacting that, as Shryock observes, a sincere Confucian would have been a good citizen in any society (15:247). Of men he demanded intelligence, sincerity, good will, and discipline—in respect to the self, the family, and the state. As the chief instruments of government he stressed good examples, good appointments, and good manners—proper relationships between functionaries. A disciplined and ordered society was to be achieved through education rather than force or law. The traditional social order that he idealized was of course the feudal system of the Shang and early Chou.

The most influential followers of Confucius were Mencius (ca. 373–288 B.C.), and the slightly younger Hsun Tzu. While Mencius' views were in close agreement with those of Confucius, he appears to have placed even greater stress upon man's natural goodness and his amenability to education and good examples. By the same token, he appears to have made greater demands upon the state as an instrument of social welfare. His views are recorded in the Meng Tzu Shin or Book of Mencius. Hsun Tzu looked upon human nature as fundamentally bad, but amenable to, and indefinitely improvable through, education.

The Confucian Canon

As noted above, Confucius drew upon the past for his didactic and illustrative materials. Of the five works attributed to him, four—*Li-Chi* (Book of Rites), *I-Ching* (Book of Changes), *Shih-Ching* (Book of Poetry), and *Shu-Ching* (Book of History)—were edited or compiled by him, and one—*Ch'un Ch'iu* (Spring and Autumn Annals)—was written by himself. His own teachings are most authentically recorded in the Lun Yu (Discourses and Dialogues). The volume was compiled by his followers sometime after his death. These six volumes plus three additional works—the *Ta Hsueh* (Great Learning), the *Chung Yung* (Doctrine of the Mean), and the *Meng Tau Shu* (Book of Mencius)—constitute the original Nine Classics (5:664–666). In the course of the Han dynasty the list was extended to thirteen through the addition of *Erh Ya* (a dictionary), the *Hsiao Ching* (Classic of Filial Piety), the *I Li* (a collection of rites), and the *Chou-li* (Rites of the Chou). As the Canon stood now, some of the original titles must have been, as Turner suggests, "Han renderings of earlier works" (18:833).

The Taoists, Mo Ti, Yang Shu, and the Legalists

Among other notable contributors to the philosophical developments of the late Chou period were the Taoists, Mo Ti, Yang Shu, and the Legalists. Apart from Buddhism, which was an import from India, Taoism came in time to be the chief competitor of Confucianism. Lao Tzu, the traditional founder of Taoism, is supposed to have been an older contemporary of Confucius. However, the *Tao Te Ching* attributed to him appears to belong to the third century B.C. Chuang Tzu, the most influential Taoist writer, did his work during the latter half of the fourth century B.C. (13:73).

The frame of reference of Taoism was as mystical as that of Confucianism was realistic. And in place of action it called for inaction. Tao, the Way, seems to have been vaguely synonymous with nature or the natural course of things. Social institutions were bad because they represented a departure from it. Harmony with it could be achieved only through complete acquiescence—by doing nothing about anything. This point of view, as Durant observes, falls in the same general category as that later propounded by Jean-Jacques Rousseau (5:657). The attitudes engendered by it were in the very nature of the case thoroughly hostile to the positive social action proposals of the Confucianists. And the very semblance of education came to be looked upon as intrinsically evil. As might be expected, Taoism was subsequently to prove friendly to Buddhism.

Mo Ti, the founder of Mohism, did his work during the middle of the fifth century B.C. He was an altruist and prophet of universal good will, exhorting all men to love one another. He assumed the natural goodness of man, and believed him capable of effecting his own improvement. He condemned agressive warfare, and frowned upon prevailing class distinctions and restricted family loyalties. In some respects his views bore a close resemblance to those of the early Christians (13:75–76).

The pessimistic and cynical doctrines propounded by Yang Shu a century later stand in strong contrast to those of Mo Ti. For Yang Shu, life was basically evil and man a mere puppet of fate. All attempts at social amelioration were futile (13:76). Under such circumstances there was but one thing man could do—accept his lot and extract from life whatever vantages it might casually offer (5:679–682).

Another group of philosophers, loosely known as the Legalists, functioned during the fourth century B.C. The chief point of agreement among them appears to have been that man, although improvable through education, is not sufficiently good by nature to respond to good example alone. Accordingly, they demanded, in addition, the employment of force guided by laws impartially set up and fairly administered. On most other issues they differed widely (13:77–80).

The Empire

The collapse of the Chou Dynasty in 221 B. C. marked the transition to the Empire. Under varying vicissitudes, this was to persist down to A.D. 1912 (16:72). Our concern with it is restricted to the period ending with the T'ang Dynasty in A.D. 907. This period falls into five main subdivisions—the Ch'in Dynasty (221–206 B.C.), the Han Dynasty (206 B.C.– A.D. 221), the so-called age of the Six Dynasties (A.D. 221– 589), the Sui Dynasty (A.D. 589–618), and the T'ang Dynasty (A.D. 618–907).

The Ch'in Dynasty

Despite its short duration, the Ch'in Dynasty made a lasting impression upon China. The Emperor, Shih Huang Ti, and his chief minister, Li Ssu, were men of exceptional ability. Since their orientation was basically Legalistic, they made large use of power. The last vestiges of feudalism were promptly stamped out, peasant proprietorship of land was instituted, and an enduring administrative organization was set up (13:89). In addition, Shih Huang Ti undertook large-scale public improvements, standardized weights and measures, and reduced the varied systems of writing to one (7:31–32). When the Confucian scholars became too outspoken in their criticism of Shih Huang Ti's policies, Li Ssu advised him to have most of their books burned, and the order was promptly issued (5:696–697). Upon the Emperor's death in 210 B.C., revolts broke out and anarchy prevailed until the Han Dynasty came into power.

The Han Dynasty

The long Han Dynasty, broken by a brief Interregnum (A.D. 9–23) during which Wang Mang ruled, falls into two divisions—the Early or Western Han Dynasty (202 B.C.–A.D. 9) with its capital at Ch'angan, and the Later or Eastern Han with its capital at Loyang (A.D. 23–221). The Han, as Latourette observes, were to give permanence to the work which the Ch'in had begun, and the centuries during which this Dynasty ruled proved to be among the most illustrious in Chinese history (13:100). Together the Ch'in and the Han developed a state the strength of which was rivaled only by Rome. In so doing, they forestalled in China the type of sectional nationalism to which Europe later succumbed. The agencies primarily responsible for this achievement were the administrative machinery supplied by the Ch'in and the political philosophy developed by the Han (13:137).

Kao Tsu (Liu Pang), the founder of the Han Dynasty, proved to be an able ruler. By the time of his death in 195 B.C. the Dynasty was firmly established. Although making some concessions, by way of decentralization, he retained the chief features of the Ch'in administrative organization. He made no attempt to restore Ch'in Legalism, but adopted instead a policy which prepared the way for the gradual reinstatement of the Confucian scholars. Shortly after his death the Ch'in restrictions upon freedom of speech and the use of unauthorized books were abolished (13:103).

The greatest Emperor of the Earlier Han Dynasty was Wu Ti (140–87 B.C.). During his reign the boundaries of China were extended in all directions, trade and commerce flourished, and extensive public works got under way. Efforts were made to secure abler men for government positions. A higher school for the training of public officials was founded, and the system of civil service examinations was set up. Although diverse philosophical views were entertained at Wu Ti's court, Legalism was definitely on the way out, and a modified

Confucianism was gaining increasing favor (13:109–110).

Wang Mang, who seized the throne at the end of the Early Han Dynasty, and ruled during the Interregnum, appears to have been an able statesman bent upon economic and social reforms that were too drastic for his time (5:700–701).

Kuang Wu Ti, the first Emperor of the Later Han Dynasty, by degrees restored internal order and reasserted his authority over border states that had revolted. By the end of his reign the Empire had regained its integrity. Since there was nothing unusual about the Emperors who succeeded him, we shall by-pass them and note instead certain cultural developments. Although it was not to gain a firm foothold until after the third century A.D., Buddhism appears to have entered China near the beginning of the Later Han Dynasty (13:129). Confucianism, in modified form, had been gaining favor during the Earlier Han Dynasty. In the course of the Later Han Dynasty it became firmly established. It had by this time become a composite product drawing in one way or another upon most of the leading Chou philosophies. As such it became the chief means of promoting the cultural unity of the Empire (13:132). And there were religious developments. Ancestor worship and the worship of Heaven had long been in use. To these the Later Han added the worship of great men of the past (13:134).

The great intellectual activity of the Han period was kept within restricted bounds by an increasingly dominant Confucianism. Scholars were bent primarily upon conservation. Among other things, the writing of authentic history got under way at this time (7:50–51). However, the great literary achievement of the Han period was the collection and final editing of the books of the Chou period. As noted earlier, by the end of the Han period thirteen of these works had been set up as canonical. The invention of paper, near the begin-

ning of the second century A.D., naturally facilitated the
literary activities of the Han (13:135).

The Six Dynasties

During the period intervening between the collapse of the
Later Han Dynasty (A.D. 221) and the rise of the Sui Dynasty
(A.D. 889)—sometimes referred to as the Age of the Six Dynasties—the Chinese Empire temporarily disintegrated into
smaller political units which were almost constantly at war
with each other. In spite of the turmoil and the uncertainty
that characterized the age, Chinese culture not only maintained its integrity but actually experienced growth in certain
directions. One of the signal events of the times, for example,
was the rapid spread of Buddhism (14:86–87).

The Sui Dynasty

Under the ensuing Sui Dynasty the Empire was quickly
and effectively reunited, and during this and the succeeding
T'ang Dynasty, it was to experience three of its most brilliant
centuries (16:81). The two Sui Emperors—Yang Chien (Kao
Tsu) and his son, Yang Kuang (Yang Ti),—although in some
respects erratic, were able generals, skilled organizers, and
great promoters. They subdued rebellious factions, constructed great canals, and built magnificent palaces. Yang
Kuang set up schools and strengthened the examination system (13:181).

The T'ang Dynasty

Li Yuan (Kao Tzu), the first Emperor of the Y'ang Dynasty,
after a short reign, abdicated in favor of his son, Li Shih-min
(T'ang T'ai Tsung). The latter was to be one of the ablest of
the twenty-one T'ang Emperors (16:83). During his reign
(A.D. 627–649) the Empire was thoroughly unified, and the
boundaries extended. The central administrative organization was strengthened and the legal code revised. State

schools were encouraged and the examination system was elaborated and put into wider use. The age was prosperous and culture flourished (16:83–84).

The T'ang Dynasty reached the height of its glory during the reign of Hsuan Tsung (Ming Huang) (A.D. 712–756). The boundaries were further extended, especially in the west. Industry and commerce flourished. Wealth and luxurious living were commonplace. Ch'angan, the capital, was beautiful and cosmopolitan. At the court were great poets, painters, and sculptors. The Hanlin, an academy that brought together the most distinguished scholars of the day, was founded at this time. There was large-scale establishment of schools. And printing appeared for the first time (16:85).

However, even before the end of Hsuan Tsung's reign decline began to set in. The T'ang regime was to persist for another century and a half, but, apart from occasional temporary spurts, its great days were over (13:189–192).

That the China of the T'ang Dynasty should exert a profound influence upon such neighboring cultures as the Korean and the Japanese is to be expected. However, it was itself the constant target of foreign influences, notably so in religion. Zoroastrianism appeared during the sixth century A.D., and subsequently Nestorian Christianity and Islam gained footholds. Buddhism continued its conquest until the middle of the ninth century A.D., when secularization checked it —by that time it had of course become an integral part of Chinese culture (7:122–132). Meanwhile, in respect to domestic cults, Taoism enjoyed some popularity, but in no sense in a degree comparable to Confucianism, the power and influence of which were greatly augmented under the T'ang (13: 204–205).

The Chinese System of Writing

The Chinese system of writing was already well developed when we first encountered it on the Shang oracle bones in the fourteenth century B.C. Although its pictographic origin is obvious, it had passed far beyond this stage, embodying, as Creel points out, in varying degrees every important principle governing the modern system (4:159–160). Some characters were clearly pictures of objects, many were ideographic, and a few served phonetic purposes. And there are indications, further, that the Shang had hit upon the use of the brush and ink in the formation of characters (4:172–173). Although the inscriptions on the oracle bones are mainly records of consultations with the gods, writing appears also to have been used in keeping chronicles (14:57–58).

While the ability to write may have been restricted to the few in Shang times, it appears to have become widely diffused among the aristocracy during the succeeding Chou period. At this time records were frequently inscribed upon bronze ceremonial vessels. However, as Turner observes, writing served a wide variety of purposes. "Written documents certifying ownership were given with gifts, even if the gifts were without value. Orders were written down, edicts recorded, and notes taken. Special priestly scribes were kept at the royal court and, later, at the feudal courts in order to prepare state documents. Even deities kept accounts, and letters were addressed to the gods" (18:419). And, while there may not have been a regular postal service, the exchange of letters by messengers appears to have been commonplace (4:255–256). Nor was writing restricted to purely practical purposes. "Treatises on ceremonial, on poetry, on discourse, on music, and especially on history," says Creel, "were prized and were studied—by youthful aristocrats" (4: 258–259).

As noted earlier, the Chinese writing system was standardized under Shih Huang Ti (221–206 B.C.). In this form it was, with only minor changes, to persist to the present (13:135). It is not, as Creel stresses, a primitive system, but rather a highly sophisticated one (4:158–159). It makes large use of the phonetic principle by combining its numerous homonyms (words of like sounds but different meanings) with its two hundred and fourteen radicals. Thus, the homonym *fang* connotes 'district' when combined with the symbol for 'earth,' and 'spin' when combined with the symbol for 'silk' (2:286). While this system of writing, comprising as it does nearly fifty thousand characters, is thoroughly adequate for the representation of ideas, it is too difficult to master to be educationally economical (13:773).

Inscriptions and Books

The earliest Chinese inscriptions are incised upon animal bones, tortoise shells, bronze vessels, and weapons. However, writing with brush and ink on more perishable materials, such as wood, bamboo, and silk, may also have been in use (8:52). In any event, these materials become conspicuous later on. The earliest books were made of narrow strips of bamboo or wood fastened together with leather thongs (1:336). During Early Han times silk fabrics began to displace wood and bamboo, and with the Later Han paper came into use (13: 135). Block printing was discovered under the Sui Dynasty, and was in widespread use by the tenth century A.D. (7:137).

In contrast with the Indians, the Chinese had no prejudice against committing their canonical works to writing. Confucius' own work set the model in this respect. And as already noted, during Han times the ancient works were zealously collected and edited. On the other hand, for reasons which are not too clear, the Chinese were slow in committing their popular literature to writing. This did not generally occur until sometime during the ninth century A.D. (19:389). This may have given rise to the custom of memorizing. In any event, memorizing came in time to play almost as conspicuous a role in Chinese, as in Indian education. Indeed, as Hsu points out, by the middle of the last imperial dynasty a scholar who had not memorized several hundred classics commanded very little respect (10:787).

The Humanistic and Secular Orientation of Chinese Culture

The character of formal education in China, as it emerged by degrees, was determined by the orientation of Chinese culture. The latter, as implied earlier, stood in striking contrast to that of India. The orientation of Indian culture was metaphysical, religious, and mystical. Its concern was with the gods, the religious life, and the future. The orientation of Chinese culture, on the other hand, was humanistic, secular, and rational. Its concern was with man—his nature, improvement, government. The approach was intellectual and practical—its main ends were to be achieved through knowledge and good example (11:221–222).

In spite of these initially remarkably sound foundations, the Chinese succumbed in the end to a fatal error. They accepted tradition as knowledge, and neglected direct observation and experimentation. The classics became the authoritative guide for education and social improvement. The scholar —the most influential person in ancient China—came to be one well-versed in tradition and skilled in literary expression. As a result, science and technology failed to develop on an adequate scale, and China not only lagged industrially, but became increasingly provincial in outlook.

Traditional Claims Regarding Early Chinese Education

Due to its involvement with myth and legend, any attempt to appraise the extent of formal education in ancient China is at best hazardous. Traditional sources make extraordinary claims. Kuo has summarized these in some detail (12). Among other things, they maintain that there already existed in pre-Shang and Shang times a fairly elaborate system of formal education, in charge of state officials, comprising not only colleges for the sons of the nobles, but also schools for the children of the common people (12:7–14).

The claims advanced for the Chou period are, as might be expected, even more elaborate. If these were authentic, Chou times would have witnessed the best educational system China ever had. As characterized by Kuo, the system comprised two types of schools—a variety of colleges in the capitals of the kings and the feudal barons, and schools scattered throughout the feudal domains in hamlets, villages, and districts. The system was highly organized and ably administered by a coterie of state officials (12:15–17).

The curriculum as a whole embodied: "the six virtues, the six praiseworthy actions, and the six arts." The six virtues were "wisdom, benevolence, goodness, righteousness, loyalty, and harmony." The six praiseworthy actions were "honoring one's parents, being friendly to one's brothers, being neighborly, maintaining cordial relationships with relatives through marriage, being trustful, and being sympathetic." The six arts consisted "of rituals, music, archery, charioteering, writing, and mathematics." A liberal education included "five kinds of ritual, five kinds of music, five ways of archery, five ways of directing a chariot, six kinds of writing, and nine operations of mathematics" (12:18). The methods of teaching and learning were strikingly modern—far in advance of those which came into use subsequently (12:21–22).

Unfortunately, scientific historians have every reason to be extremely skeptical about the authenticity of Chinese traditional accounts (6:13–18; 13:36–44). A variety of considerations forces them to regard these accounts as largely idealizations of the past by later writers. Nevertheless, recent archeological discoveries have shown that some of them rest in varying degrees upon factual bases. Future discoveries may authenticate more of them. Meanwhile, we must be cautious in our generalizations about education during the classical age. Since top-ranking nobles appear to have been literate in Shang times, and literacy was widespread among the aristocracy under the Chou (18:419), there must have been schools, and it seems reasonable that these should have been located in the capitals of the kings and the feudal barons. Beyond this, there is general agreement that in later Chou times scholars began to give private instruction in population centers to boys who wished to prepare for government service (7:25). This in time gave rise to one of China's most characteristic governmental features—the class of professional statesmen. And private instruction to this end was to play a conspicuous role throughout most of China's subsequent history.

Imperial Education and the Civil Service Examinations

The first steps toward setting up the civil service system were taken during the Earlier Han period by Emperor Wu Ti (13:109). However, for several centuries thereafter the examinations appear to have been given only sporadically. Under Yang Kuang, second Emperor of the Sui Dynasty, the system was extended and put into wider use (13:179). Li Shih-min, second Emperor of the T'ang Dynasty, placed the examinations on a strictly competitive basis and provided for their periodic administration both locally and in the capital. Under the Sung Dynasty (A.D. 960–1127), the examinations in the capital were placed on a tricennial basis. And by the beginning of the Ming Dynasty (A.D. 1368–1644) they had reached essentially the form they were to have until their abolition in 1905 (17:441–442). "The system," says Teng Ssu-yu, "was so adjusted that the student who passed a district examination was known as a *hsiu-ts'ai,* or budding genius; one who passed at a provincial capital became a *chu-jen* (ju-ren), or promoted man; and one who was successful at the national capital became a *chin-shih* (dzin-shzh), or achieved scholar" (17:441).

"In preparation for the imperial examinations," says Han Yu-shan, "students memorized the *San-tzu Ching* (Three-Character Classic), the *Pai Chia Hsing* (One Hundred Surnames—actually there are more than four hundred), the *Ch'ien-tzu Wen* (Thousand Character Essay), the Four Books: the *Lun Yu* (Analects, or Dialogues, of Confucius), the *Ta Hsueh* (Great Learning), the *Chung Yung* (Doctrine of the Mean), the *Meng Tzu* (Works of Mencius); the Five Classics: the *Shu Ching* (Book of Documents, or Book of History), the *Shih Ching* (Book of Poetry or Book of Songs) the *I* (or *Yi*) *Ching* (Book of Changes), the *Li Chi* (Book of Rites), the *Ch'un Ch'iu* (Spring and Autumn Annals). Every day the students practiced calligraphy and the composition of essays and poems. This amount of work may seem impossible, but it was standard" (9:10).

We shall make no attempt to characterize the examinations as such. That they were severe is attested by the fact that of the two million candidates examined each year not more than two to three per cent were advanced to the first degree (9:14). Paralleling the literary examinations was a somewhat comparable system of military examinations.

Facilities for the Training of Candidates

The maintenance of such an elaborate examination system would of course have been quite out of the question apart from facilities for the training of candidates. And significantly enough, historical accounts of the improvement of the examinations are almost invariably accompanied by references to the extension of school facilities. Thus, Wu Ti is reported to have established a higher school in the capital and to have encouraged schools in the provinces and districts (13:109). Yang Kuang, likewise, is credited with the encouragement of schools and the enlargement of the imperial library. Li Shih-min is said to have maintained and reinforced state schools (13:192). The Sung are reported to have set up a system of schools extending from the capital to all the administrative subdivisions of the Empire (7:151). And the Ming are credited with a plan that called for a school in every village and a higher institution in the capital (13:790).

Traditional accounts, as summarized by Kuo, make much more elaborate claims, especially for the T'ang and Ming Dynasties. Under the T'ang, for example, they credit the imperial capital with six colleges under the control of a national university, and the Empire at large with a public school in each prefecture, district, and village (12:41). The Ming school system at its best is said to have included a college for the education of young nobles and a national university in the capital, and a public school in each prefecture, department, district, and village (12:54-55).

However, despite sporadic reports and claims, China appears at no time to have had—apart from the state colleges maintained in the capital—a real system of public schools. "The state," says Hsu, "provided no public education of any sort, except on the highest level for scholars who had already advanced themselves through the imperial examinations. Education was a private affair. A wealthy family in a village might decide to hire a tutor for the benefit of its sons but allow sons of relatives and neighbors to attend the lessons also. Sometimes several families in the community would form a tutor-school jointly, sharing the salary and keep of the teacher. Or an elderly scholar might decide to form a tutor-school of his own, charging the parents of his students a sum for tuition each year. In all cases the ability to pay determined the amount of tuition.—School and state met only in the imperial examinations" (10:786–787).

Although school and state met only in the imperial examinations, the private schools of China, both primary and advanced, and the higher schools maintained by the state, were dominated by a common ideal—Confucian literate learning. The curriculum began with the classics and ended with the classics; and it was—except possibly on the highest levels —essentially the same for all as long as they stayed in school

(13:792). Since only a small percentage of those who entered schools reached the examinations, and only a negligible proportion of these managed to pass them, the system supplied China with a respectable body of literate citizens, as well as with a select body of highly trained servants of the state. In theory the system was democratic since anyone could avail himself of it; in practice, due to the severe sacrifices entailed, it was heavily weighted in favor of the prosperous. It made of course no provisions for girls. And yet, ancient China was not wholly without literate women.

While the instructional techniques employed in these schools stressed memorization and discouraged originality, the Confucian ethical code that pervaded the curriculum from beginning to end supplied a moral discipline that has rarely been equalled in the schools of other countries. It may well, as Latourette suggests, have been in no small part responsible for the remarkable coherence and stability of Chinese culture (13:792–793).

Occupational Education

As in other early societies, practical education in ancient China was in the hands of guilds and was administered on an apprenticeship basis. This was true not only of the arts and crafts, but of commerce and industry, and the professions as well (18:808). Indeed, there appears to have been no urban occupation of any consequence without a corresponding guild. Not only did the guilds control occupational education, but they were almost completely self-governing in every other respect. They made their own laws, fixed prices and wages, and provided for the arbitration and settlement of disputes (5:777).

BIBLIOGRAPHY

1. Ayscough, Florence, "Calligraphy, Poetry and Painting." Chapter XXI in China edited by H. F. MacNair. Berkeley and Los Angeles: University of California Press, 1946.

2. Bloomfield, Leonard, Language. New York: Henry Holt and Company, 1933.

3. Creel, Herrlee G., Studies in Early Chinese Culture. Baltimore: Waverly Press, 1937.

4. Creel, Herrlee G., The Birth of China. New York: Reynal and Hitchcock, 1937.

5. Durant, Will, The Story of Civilization—Our Oriental Heritage. New York: Simon and Schuster, 1942.

6. Fitzgerald, C. P., China—A Short Cultural History. New York: D. Appleton–Century Company, 1938.

7. Goodrich, L. Carrington, A Short History of the Chinese People. New York: Harper and Brothers, 1943.

8. Goodrich, L. Carrington, "Antiquity: To the Fall of Shang." Chapter IV in China edited by H. F. MacNair. Berkeley and Los Angeles: University of California Press, 1946.

9. Han Yu-shan, "Molding Forces." Chapter I in China edited by H. F. MacNair. Berkeley and Los Angeles: University of California Press, 1946.

10. Hsu, Francis L. K., "China." Pages 731–813 in Most of the World, edited by Ralph Linton. New York: Columbia University Press, 1949.

11. Hu Shih, "Chinese Thought." Chapter XIII in China edited by H. F. MacNair. Berkeley and Los Angeles: University of California Press, 1946.

12. Kuo, Ping Wen, The Chinese System of Public Education. New York: Teachers College, Columbia University, 1915.

13. Latourette, Kenneth S., The Chinese—Their History and Culture. New York: The Macmillan Company, 1946.

14. Lattimore, Owen and Eleanor, China—A Short History. New York: W. F. Norton and Company, 1947.

15. Shryock, John K., "Confucianism," Chapter XV in China edited by H. F. MacNair. Berkeley and Los Angeles: University of California Press, 1946.

16. Teng Ssu, "From the Fall of Chou to the Fall of T'ang." Chapter VI in China edited by H. F. MacNair. Berkeley and Los Angeles: University of California Press, 1946.

17. Teng Ssu, "China's Examination System and the West." Chapter XXX in China edited by H. F. MacNair. Berkeley and Los Angeles: University of California Press, 1946.

18. Turner, Ralph, The Great Cultural Traditions, Volumes I and II. New York: McGraw-Hill Book Company, 1941.

19. Wang Chi-chen, "Traditional Literature: Nature and Limitations." Chapter XXV in China edited by H. F. MacNair. Berkeley and Los Angeles: University of California Press, 1946.

20. Woody, Thomas, Life and Education in Early Societies. New York: The Macmillan Company, 1949.

CHAPTER V

The Rise of Greek Culture

Aegean Antecedents

IN an earlier context we gave a brief account of the rise of
Minoan culture in Crete, and pointed out that three general developmental periods stand out, namely: the Early
Minoan, 3000 to 2200 B.C.; the Middle Minoan, 2200 to 1600
B.C.; and the Late Minoan, 1600 to 1100 B.C. It remains to
be noted now that at its height Minoan culture extended far
beyond Crete. Indeed, during the last centuries of its existence it spread throughout the entire Aegean basin (28:125,
133). It was at this time that the Achaean Greeks, whose
Mycenaean rendition of it was subsequently to replace it,
came under its sway. And indirectly, by virtue of far-reaching
commercial activities, Cretan influences reached of course
far beyond the Aegean basin—to Cyprus, to the coasts of
Syria and Asia Minor, and to the western Mediterranean. And
there were intimate contacts with Egypt (28:133–134).

Significantly enough, up to the time of the Minos dynasty
at least, Minoan cultures spread exclusively by peaceful pene-
tration. Although prepared to defend themselves, as evidenced by the extent of their fleet and by the abundance of
armor and weapons uncovered at Cnossos, the Cretans were
a peaceful people. Their cities were unwalled and their palaces unfortified (28:124). They excelled in commerce, in the
arts and crafts, and in graceful living. While their maritime
activities assumed tremendous proportions, especially in
Late Minoan times, the Cretans were anything but mere
traders. They were above everything else great craftsmen

88

THE RISE OF GREEK CULTURE

and fine artists. Their pottery and vases were elegantly designed and exquisitely decorated. Their fresco painting was superb. Much of the same thing was true of their modeling and carving, and of their spinning and weaving. And they were of course the first great architects in the northern Mediterranean. Beyond this, Cretan art was intrinsically functional rather than superficially decorative. It permeated every aspect of life and affected all classes of society. Not only were the palaces magnificent assemblages of the arts (10:18), but "beauty was expressed in the commonest things and in the lowliest homes" (28:136). Finally, Cretan art was dominated by spontaneity and naturalism. There was nothing artificial, stereotyped, or grandiose about it. It reflected the natural and graceful mode of life of a remarkably balanced and keenly sensitive people (29:221).

As noted earlier, the Cretan outlook on life was intrinsically secular. Although religious beliefs and practices permeate life, there are no indications of religious obsessions or priestly domination. Since their script has not been deciphered, and much of their literature may have been recorded on perishable materials (13:374), the character of Cretan social and political institutions and the extent of their learned tradition have to be largely inferred from archaeological evidence. Until Late Minoan times, when they were united under the Minos dynasty, the Cretan city-states appear to have been independent units ruled by kings. The palace at Cnossos, whence the Minos dynasty ruled, points to Minos as a monarch with absolute power. However, certain considerations, among them the prevalence of literacy and the democratization of art, suggest that the masses may have fared much better in Crete than in the Oriental monarchies. Finally, Crete accorded woman a position of freedom and dignity that was approximated in no Oriental culture except the Egyptian (28:138).

Aside from the fact that literacy appears to have been

widespread among them, we know very little about the learned tradition of the Cretans. Nothing is known regarding their literary and philosophical achievements. Beyond this, about all that can be said is that they were using a simple decimal system of numeration, the Egyptian version of the Babylonian weights and measures, a rudimentary currency, and a lunar calendar (4:16; 29:218).

The Cretan script emerged in Early Minoan times in the customary pictographic and ideographic form. During the Middle Minoan period it evolved through two hieroglyphic systems into a linear script employing less than one hundred characters designating mainly words, syllables, and letters (13:371). In this the signs were greatly simplified as in the Egyptian hieratic. In time this script spread not only over Crete but throughout the Aegean world. In Late Minoan times a special script reserved for the palace at Cnossos appears to have been developed (13:377–388). Early Minoan documents consist largely of pictographic and ideographic inscriptions on beads and seals. With the emergence of the linear script in Middle Minoan times the clay tablet came into extensive use. And Glotz suspects that the most important writings—religious, literary, legal—may have been inscribed on more perishable materials. If so, these have of course failed to come down to us (13:374).

What became of the Cretan script after it had spread throughout the Aegean world is not clear. The Greeks are known to have received the alphabet from the Phoenicians. The latter had presumably obtained it from the Egyptians through Semitic intermediaries. Actually, a considerable proportion—about one-third—of the Phoenician characters bear a close resemblance to the Cretan hieroglyphic and linear characters. This has led some authorities to suspect that both Cretan and Egyptian elements may have been incorporated into the alphabet which the Phoenicians borrowed from the Semites (13:371–373; 28:82–83, 134–135).

Writing in Crete, as in other ancient cultures, appears to have served a variety of practical purposes—administrative, legal, religious, and commercial. Thousands of clay tablets were found in the place at Cnossos—many of them apparently inventories of the contents of storerooms, and others obviously letters and dispatches (32:205). "Religious life," says Glotz, "involved much writing. Many ex-voto offerings bear dedications. The libation-tables, the ritual vessels, and in particular the spoons of clay or stone are often covered with characters.—In Crete, as in Phoenicia, trade seems to have made full use of the advantages offered by writing. Everywhere there are tablets similar to those of the royal archives; everywhere they were inscribed with signs representing goods of all kinds and with those of the ship, the ingot, and the scales—"(13:379).

After flourishing for more than a thousand years the brilliant bronze-age culture of the Cretans met with sudden disaster. About 1400 B.C. Cnossos and most of the other Cretan cities were sacked and burned—presumably by the Achaeans (28:126). With this the center of Aegean civilization shifted to southern Greece where the Mycenaean rendition of Minoan culture was to prevail for the next two centuries.

Who were the brilliant Cretans, and what is our indebtedness to them? They were a long-headed Caucasian people of the Mediterranean race (19:722). Their language appears to have been neither Indo-European nor Semitic (33:201). Although they borrowed extensively from Oriental sources, their culture was European in spirit rather than Oriental. In spreading this culture throughout the Aegean basin, they laid the foundation for Greek culture. It is difficult to conjecture what shape the latter would have taken and how far it would have gone without its Minoan base and orientation. One fact stands out clearly. Greek culture achieved its earliest and most spectacular brilliance among the Aeolian and Ionian settlers on the coast of Asia Minor where the Minoan-Mycenaean-Greek sequence was continuous, and it remained most backward in Epirus and Thessaly where Minoan influences had never been strong and where the Achaeans were driven out (28:128–129, 147–148).

The Achaeans and the Mycenaean Age

As already noted, with the fall of the Cretan empire the center of Aegean culture shifted to the Greek mainland—especially to Mycenae, Tiryns, and Orchomenos—where the Achaean Greeks were to elaborate the Mycenaean phase of Aegean civilization. The Achaeans, generally recognized as the first Indo-European rulers of Greece (29:452), had long been the dominant element in the population of southern and central Greece (28:125). They had penetrated Greece by degrees and had become—apart from their language which they retained—rather thoroughly Cretanized. About 1400 B.C. they revolted against Minoan domination and, as already noted, sacked and burned the Cretan cities. In contrast with the peaceful Cretans the Achaeans were a warlike people. Their cities—the first European urban centers—were impregnable fortresses whence they conducted raids by both land and sea (29:452). One of the most spectacular of these marauding expeditions resulted in the destruction of Troy about 1800 B.C.

On the material side the Mycenaean age was rich and prosperous. Industry and trade flourished. Skilled craftsmanship abounded. The palaces at Mycenae and Tiryns were elegant and unprecedentedly pretentious. And with it all, Mycenaean culture spread throughout the Mediterranean area. However, on the non-material side—in respect to the more subtle artistic and intellectual aspects of culture—the Mycenaean age failed to approximate Minoan achievements. Even the use of writing may have shrunk to negligible proportions (28:126–127).

The Dorian Conquest

Toward the end of the thirteenth century B.C. Mycenaean power began to wane, and in the course of the next two centuries it was to be completely destroyed by a new wave of Greek-speaking invaders—the Dorians. The latter poured in successive hordes out of Illyria and by degrees over-ran central and southern Greece, the Cyclades, Crete, Rhodes, and southern Asia Minor. They sacked and burned Mycenae and Tiryns and demolished Mycenaean strongholds wherever they went. The Achaeans, except in Attica and Arcadia where the Dorians failed to establish themselves, generally fled, some of them as far as the coast of Asia Minor.

The Dorians were not only more warlike than the Achaeans but they were culturally less advanced. In fact, they were still in the hunting and herding stage. However, they had one great advantage—they possessed iron in abundance. In every other respect they were inferior to the Achaeans, and, therefore, quite incapable of appreciating their culture. As a result, Mycenaean culture went into eclipse, and a chaotic period, sometimes characterized as the Greek Middle Ages, descended upon Greece. This was to impede cultural developments for centuries—down to about 800 B.C. The period was, however, by no means wholly or largely one of stagnation. Fundamental readjustments were underway—the blending of peoples, old and new; geographic redistributions; and the gradual assimilation of diverse Mycenaean cultural elements. "By the opening of the eighth century B.C.," says Turner, "when something like order returned to the Aegean lands, the Greek people—in three divisions, the Dorians, the Aeolians—and their chief cities—Sparta, Corinth, Argos, Megara, Athens, Thebes, Ephesus, and Miletus—had appeared" (29: 453). The same thing was true of the classical Greek physical type, and of the base of the cultural tradition that was subsequently to be elaborated into classical Greek culture. "This type and its tradition," as Turner adds, "are met first in the Homeric poems, the *Iliad* and the *Odyssey*, which had their setting in this age" (29:453).

The central theme of these poems is, it will be recalled, the Trojan War, the *Iliad* dealing with the war itself, and the *Odyssey* with the homeward voyage of Odysseus, one of the warrior princes. Up to 1870 when Schliemann's excavations revealed the actual city of Troy—and subsequently Mycenae and Tiryns as well—the events and characterizations in the Homeric epics were regarded as almost purely legendary. Since that time the close correspondence between archaeological revelations and much of the content of the poems has convinced authorities that they present within limits a fairly authentic picture of the material aspects of the Mycenaean age. Whether the non-material cultural conditions—religious, moral, political, and economic—portrayed in the poems are also those of the Mycenaean age, or whether they reflect those of the poet's own time—the ninth century B.C.—is an issue on which opinions are sharply divided. Some insist that the Homeric picture is Mycenaean in its entirety; others maintain that it is Mycenaean only in its material aspects—that the beliefs, ideals, and the economic political conditions portrayed are those of the poet's own age. For reasons which we shall not attempt to elaborate here the position of the latter seems more tenable than that of the former (28: 153; 25:276; 31:137).

The economic conditions reflected in the Homeric poems were simple and primitive, with herding and farming and war and plunder as the chief means of subsistence. Wealth was reckoned mainly in flocks and herds, and exchange was by barter. Industry was confined largely to the home. Trade was in the hands of the Phoenicians (28:153; 32:207–208). Although aristocratic in pattern, social life, too, was simple. No occupation was considered degrading, and noble men and women engaged in the most menial tasks (13:14). Skilled artisans were rare, and the professions were limited to priests, soothsayers, and physicians (32:208). Slavery had not become conspicuous. Initially, the political unit appears to have been the unwalled village, but appreciably before the beginning of historic times the characteristic city-state had become prevalent (23:30; 32:212–213). At the head of this was a king whose powers were limited by a council of notables and a popular assembly (28:153; 32:213–214).

The ethical and moral standards of the Homeric Greeks rested on a tribal basis. In general they called for hostility toward the out-group and loyalty to the in-group. Accordingly, we find on the one hand deceit and treachery and on the other a high regard for family and friendship ties. The sanctity of oaths and the obligations of hospitality were highly regarded, and woman was accorded a superior position (28:154–155; 32:208). As yet, goodness implied physical excellence rather than excellence in character.

The religious outlook of the Homeric Greeks was basically Hellenic rather than Mycenaean. Homer's pantheon on Mt. Olympus—including, as it did, Zeus, Apollo, Athena, Hera, Aphrodite, Artemis, Hephestus, and Hermes—is substantially the same as that of the classical Greeks (28:154). As Webster puts it, "stronger, wiser, more beautiful than mortals, ever living and ever young, are these Olympians, but nevertheless they are completely humanized. They have human form, need sleep and food, can feel intense physical pain, marry and procreate, and interfere constantly in mundane affairs on behalf of their favorites. Homer does not scruple to reveal their vanity, selfishness, lusts, and quarrels.—The Olympians, indeed, were no better than their worshipers" (32:209). As we shall note farther along, this rather flippant portrayal of the gods and goddesses was to exert a far-reaching influence upon subsequent Greek attitudes and outlook.

The Formative Age

The eighth, seventh, and sixth centuries B.C. are generally known as the formative age in the development of Greek civilization. During this period the Greeks elaborated the city-state, planted colonies throughout the Mediterranean world, and passed through an economic revolution. Politically, they progressed from monarchy through aristocracy and tyranny to the beginnings of democracy.

The city-state, the characteristic unit of Greek political organization, was not a Greek invention. It had arisen in the Orient, and had prevailed in the Aegean age. However, the Greeks did elaborate it into something that was unique—so much so, indeed, that they were never able to pass beyond it in either theory or practice.

For a time after the Dorian conquest—when they were subsisting upon a primitive economy of hunting, herding, and agriculture—the Greeks appear to have lived in scattered unwalled villages. Later, groups of such villages, either voluntarily or under compulsion, merged and assembled about a fortified height to form the *polis* or city. On top of the elevation were palaces and temples, at its base the market place, and beyond it stretched the lands owned by the people. Such a settlement, says Webster, "being independent, self-governing, and with power to declare war, conclude treaties, and make alliances,—is properly described as a city-state" (32:213). It had begun to appear at the close of the Homeric age, and was subsequently to spread throughout most of Greece. Apart from Sparta, Athens, and Syracuse, it was generally small in respect to both area and population (28:174).

Colonization began about the middle of the eighth century B.C. and continued to the end of the sixth century. "At the close of the era of expansion," says Barnes, "the Greek colonies dotted the ancient world from the Pyrenees in the west to the Caucasus in the east. Hellenic settlements lined the

Black Sea region; they were to be found along the Thracian coast, in Cyprus, in Italy and Sicily, along the coast of southern Gaul and eastern Spain, at the Nile delta (Naucratis), and in Libya in northern Africa" (1:204). Beginning initially in haphazard private ventures, colonization became in time a deliberate and well organized function of the city-states. The relationship between the founding city and the colony was close and sentimental. The parent city normally supplied the traditional hero for the colony (28:162). The colonists in turn brought with them a handful of earth to be strewn upon the foreign soil and the fire from the public hearth to start the civic fire in the new settlement (4:81; 10:128). Once it was founded the colony became an independent city-state, with no formal obligations to the parent city (23:32).

Initially at least the land problem appears to have supplied the chief incentive for colonization. Land was scarce, and for a variety of reasons—among them the encroachments of large-scale noble land owners— it was never equitably distributed. As the economic revolution progressed, commercial motives —the need for raw materials and facilities for the exchange of commodities—became operative. And then there was of course always the adventurous proclivity of the Greeks (28: 161).

Colonization had far-reaching effects upon the development of Greek civilization. The most profound of these was of course the economic revolution which by degrees transformed a primitive agricultural economy into an urban economy based on trade, industry, and money (28:166). Among the more subtle psychological outcomes were the broadened cultural horizon resulting from contacts with varied peoples and lands, and, by way of contrast, the deepened sense of Hellenic unity and superiority as reflected in the drastic distinction between the Greek and the barbarian (29: 458; 28:172).

The new urban economy naturally gave rise by degrees

to the production of commodities for export—among them pottery, textiles, and metal work. This, as Trever puts it, "contributed greatly to the expansion of trade and industry, to speculation, the growth of credit, loans, and interest, and the drive to gain a fortune by fair means or foul" (28:167–168). With new opportunities for gaining wealth, there grew up alongside of the old nobility a new aristocracy resting on general wealth. As time went on, this made increasingly insistent demands for social and political recognition. This naturally brought it into growing conflict with the old landed nobility (24:51).

Meanwhile, the lot of the peasant landholder grew steadily worse. Under the new economy the cultivation of the olive, the fig, and the vine, and stock raising were more profitable than the production of cereals. However, due to the fact that they demanded more time and labor, the small farmer could not compete successfully with the large landholder who had capital and slaves at his command. As a result, he either eked out a miserable existence or borrowed capital. If he did the latter, he was almost certain to lose his land and sink into serfdom or slavery. Under these circumstances, the estates of the landholding nobles grew larger and larger, and the small landholders all but disappeared (29:457).

And there appeared to be no promise of improvement. The landed nobles grew steadily more mercenary in their attitudes, not only toward the poor, but also toward the new commercial and industrial elements. With all this, social strife and discontent became the order of the day. It was, as Trever observes, a case of "nobles against merchants, poor against rich, nobles against peasants," and with this, "the stage was set for social and political revolution" (28:169).

In their political development the Greeks, as noted above, passed, in the course of the formative period, from monarchy through aristocracy to the beginnings of democracy. Monarchy prevailed down to about 750 B.C. Thereafter, the nobles began to take over the powers of the king. Within a century, the latter had either disappeared or his office had become largely titular (20:47). Between 650 and 500 B.C. tyrannies arose in most Greek city-states. These were not infrequently headed by nobles bent upon the amelioration of the economic and political conditions that gave rise to class strife and social discontent. Since the tyrannies normally disappeared in a generation or two, and usually brought about much needed reforms, they represented on the whole steps toward democracy.

Sparta

To the middle of the seventh century B.C., the development of Sparta does not appear to have differed fundamentally from that of other Greek city-states (4:113–114; 29:465). The original settlement represented a combination of five unwalled villages founded by Dorian invaders in the Eurotas valley. Although its growth was slow at first, by the close of the eighth century B.C. it had unified all of Laconia and conquered Messenia. With the opening of the seventh century B.C., Sparta was wealthy and culturally well advanced —especially so in poetry and the arts (28:179). Her nobles were as free and lived as luxuriously as the nobles of other city-states (4:123).

The Messenian rebellion, about the middle of the seventh century B.C., led to a radical reorientation in Sparta's cultural outlook. The Messenians and their allies were subdued with the utmost difficulty, and, when victory was finally achieved, the hostile subject population outnumbered the citizenry approximately twenty to one (1:197). As a means to survival under such conditions, Sparta now transformed herself— through reforms traditionally attributed to Lycurgus, but more probably brought about gradually—into a military machine. Everything that was typically Greek in spirit was deliberately sacrificed to this end (28:180).

The Spartan population now consisted of three classes—the Spartiates or citizens whose concern was exclusively with public affairs, the perioeci who lived in surrounding towns and were mainly engaged in industry and trade, and the helots or serfs who were tied to the soil and tilled the Spartiates' estates. The lot of the perioeci does not appear to have been particularly hard. They were not subjected to Spartan discipline and they enjoyed considerable freedom. The lot of the helots probably could not have been much worse than it was.

The iron discipline to which the Spartiates were subjected is too well known to require much comment. The worst feature about it was unquestionably the cultural impoverishment which it inevitably entailed. Authorities are not at all certain that the Spartiate as much as learned to read and write in competent fashion (34:241–242). Actually, as Thorndike suggests, the life of the Spartiates may not have been as dour as has traditionally been implied (27:108). And yet, discipline there was, discipline to one end only—the ruthless warrior. At seven the young Spartiate was removed to military barracks and subjected to intensive gymnastic training; at twenty he entered upon adult military training; at thirty he began to shoulder the duties of full-fledged citizenship; and not until sixty was he free to retire from active public service. Marriage and childrearing were obligatory, home life all but non-existent (32:215). There were neither opportunities nor incentives for the accumulation of wealth and the enjoyment of luxuries. The discipline of the Spartiate woman was about as rigorous as that of the man.

The government set up by the Spartan constitution embodied a combination of monarchial, democratic, and aristocratic features. At its head were two kings who had very little power except as alternate commanders of the army and as high priests. Theoretically, the real power of government was vested in the *apella*—the popular assembly comprising all adult male Spartiates in good standing. It elected the five *ephors* who represented the people, and also the *geronsia* or council of elders composed of twenty-eight nobles sixty years of age or over and the two kings. The ephors constituted the chief executive and judicial body. The council, among other things, prepared the legislation to be submitted to the assembly and ratified its acts. In practice, therefore, the popular assembly was in varying degrees subservient to the aristocratic council (24:54).

Athens

Attica appears to have been very little disturbed by the Dorian invasion. As a result, its population retained its indigenous Achaean-Mediterranean character (10:108). For a long time the territory was divided between a number of warring villages. By degrees—between 1000 and 700 B.C.—these were unified under the leadership of Athens (20:50).

Social organization in early Athens revolved mainly about kinship—families, clans, tribes. Ownership of land rested on a family and tribal basis. The government was monarchial, the powers of the king being, however, somewhat limited by a council of nobles and a popular assembly. In the course of the ninth and eighth centuries land ownership drifted gradually into private hands. And after the middle of the eighth century the nobles progressively usurped the powers of the king to the point where the kingship had lost all but its religious significance. The Athenian government was now an aristocracy ruled by nine archons and the council of the Areopagus. The ecclesia or assembly, to the extent that it still existed, functioned in a purely routine manner (24:55). Under the aristocratic regime the chief social classes were the eupatrids or ruling nobles whose landed estates were growing larger, the georgi or small farmers whose lands were rapidly falling into the hands of the nobles, and the demiurgi or artisans. The last two classes were free citizens, but without political rights (28:186).

By the middle of the seventh century B.C., Athenian aristocracy began to veer toward timocracy; that is, property qualifications in terms of income now became one of the determiners of civic rights. The immediate occasion for this appears to have been the reorganization of the army with the introduction of the Dorian phalanx. The heavy armed infantry now assumed greater importance than the cavalry. Shifting from birth to income as a criterion for service greatly increased the manpower available for the infantry. Its real significance, however, lay in the fact that in Athens wealth had now begun to challenge birth as a political criterion. In the end this was to pave the way to civic rights for much of the population, especially small farmers and artisans (4:168–169).

Meanwhile, social discontent increased. The labor and lower artisan classes could serve in the army in only nondescript fashion, and they had no civic rights. The same thing was true of the agricultural serfs and share-croppers. Under these circumstances resentment against the tyranny of the nobles assumed increasingly alarming proportions. The situation was aggravated, further, by the fact that there was no written code of laws. This meant of course that the law in any given case was apt to be whatever the nobles saw fit to make it. And we may rest assured that self-interest was a primary determiner in their pronouncements (24:56).

The situation reached a climax in 632 B.C. when Cylon almost succeeded in setting himself up as a tyrant. At this point the nobles reluctantly conferred upon Draco, as chief archon, the power to codify the laws. The task was completed in 621 B.C. Its main significance lay in the fact that it took the punishment of crime out of the hands of clans and families and placed it under state jurisdiction (31:140). It made no attempt to alleviate the economic distress of the masses. Their status continued to deteriorate and their lot became increasingly intolerable. "Attica," says Trever, "was fast becoming a country of large estates, while the masses were sinking into serfdom. The peasant owners were losing their land and the landless tenants their freedom. The spirit of revolution was rife, demanding a redivision of the land" (28:187).

At this juncture (594 B.C.) the crisis that was rapidly approaching its climax was resolved by the appointment of Solon—an artistocrat with large sympathies for the poor— as sole archon with complete power to effect essential reforms. The fact that the steps which he took were agreeable to neither extreme, attests the moderation of his policy. In place of the customary promise of the chief magistrate that he would protect private property, he issued a proclamation annulling all mortgages and debts involving lands or persons, freed those who had become enslaved, and limited the amount of land an individual could own (4:174–175; 29:468). On the other hand, he made no attempt to confiscate and redistribute the estates of the wealthy. Neither did he interfere with existing monetary and commercial policies apart from the adoption of Euboic coinage and the restriction of exports to oil (4:175). Industrial activities were encouraged by granting foreign artisans political privileges and requiring training in the crafts (29:468; 31:140).

More far-reaching than his economic reforms were the political reforms of Solon. In general, as Bury observes, these reforms laid the foundation and shaped the framework of subsequent Athenian democracy (4:175). They represent, as Trever adds, the first real step toward popular government (28:189). Specifically, Solon retained the classification of citizens on the basis of wealth but added a fourth class, the *thetes*. This opened the assembly to the lowest of Athenians and to many foreign artisans. A new council of four hundred, chosen by lot from the citizenry at large. This constituted determine general policies and prepare business for the as-

sembly. This deprived the council of the Areopagus of much
of its power, but without in any way lowering its dignity.
Archons continued to come from the highest class but they
were elected annually by the assembly and strictly account-
able to it. However, the most significant of Solon's reforms
was the creation of the *heliaea*—a body of six thousand jurors
chosen by lot from the citizenry at large. This constituted
the popular courts which, apart from treason and homicide,
passed upon all matters including the conduct of the magistrates. Since the citizenry now controlled both the appointment and the conduct of the magistrates, popular government
was clearly under way (4:175–178; 28:188–189; 31:141).

Since the economic and political reforms of Solon met the
expectations of neither the rich nor the poor, strife broke out
anew. Momentarily, the war with Megara, that was to put
Athens in possession of the Island of Salamis, averted another crisis. However, at the conclusion of the war, Peisistratus, the successful general, accepted the leadership of the
Hill and Shore Factions—peasants, artisans, traders—and set
himself up as tyrant. With only slight interruptions he and
his son ruled Athens from 560 to 510 B.C. Peisistratus himself
proved to be a statesman of the highest order. In place of
disrupting Solon's reform program, he built upon it and carried it to its logical conclusion. He confiscated and redis-
tributed the landed estates of leading nobles, set up and promoted large-scale public works, encouraged trade and industry, enhanced the prestige of Athens through peaceful alliances with other cities and the maintenance of a strong fleet
and army, beautified Athens and transformed it into a first-
rate city, sponsored brilliant civic festivals, and served as
patron of the arts. The Iliad and the Odyssey presumably
reached their present rendition at this time. For a time his
sons followed in his footsteps, but in the end the tyranny
degenerated and collapsed (28:189–190).

The end of the tyranny brought with it renewed disorder

and factional strife. The circumstances which placed Cleisthenes in control of the situation need not be detailed here. Suffice it to point out that, although he belonged to one of the most illustrious Athenian families, he was supported by, and championed the cause of, the underprivileged masses. As Bury observes, Solon had set up the institutions and the machinery of Athenian democracy; Cleisthenes' problem in turn was to render them workable (4:199–200). And he proved to be quite equal to the task. The situation that confronted Cleisthenes was a society torn asunder by ancient clan loyalties and sectional interests. The clan, as Hoebel observes, is the greatest source of individual security in primitive society, but, due to its intrinsically divisive tendencies, it is incompatible with the welfare of civil society, and must be suppressed if the latter is to function effectively (17:273). In Greece the rise of the city-state had weakened its influence, but it devolved upon Cleisthenes to deal it the final deathblow as a political instrument. The sectional interests—represented by the Shore, Plain, and Hill factions—revolved about economic issues, and, as in the case of the clans, tended to take precedence over the welfare of the state as a whole.

Cleisthenes' approach to the solution of the problem presented by the clan and sectional interests shows him to have been a constructive statesman of the highest order. In the constitution which he drew up he replaced the four hereditary tribes with ten new ones based on locality. In forming the latter, the *demes* or townships in the three regions—Hill, Plain, and Shore—were grouped into ten *trittyes* each, or thirty in all (20:52). Each of these ten new tribes was thereupon constituted out of three widely separated trittyes—one from each region (24:62–63). In this way the old clans and parties were so thoroughly shuffled and scattered that they lost their functional identities. All state political and military powers now had their source in the ten tribes. Local government was vested in the demes or townships. By way of compromise with traditional sentiment, membership in the demes became hereditary and could not be transferred with change of residence (28:192). All resident freemen, whether native or foreign born, automatically became citizens.

The old council of four hundred, based on the four traditional tribes, was transformed into a council of five hundred with fifty members drawn by lot from each of the ten new tribes. Since no one could serve more than twice, every citizen might presumably serve at some time or other. Choice by lot eliminated of course both birth and wealth as eligibility criteria (10:125). The council was the chief executive and administrative instrument of the government. It supervised the magistrates, and in addition served as a deliberative body to prepare business for the assembly. It left very little real initiative to the old council of the Areopagus and the archons (28:192–193).

The assembly, now greatly enlarged due to the admission of new classes, consisted of all male citizens over twenty years of age. It was the final source of authority in the state. Meeting regularly at stated intervals, it debated the measures submitted by the council, passed legislation, issued decrees, examined the records of the magistrates, and had the power to ostracize individuals whom it considered dangerous to the welfare of the state. The heliaea or popular court of six thousand citizens became differentiated into several courts and began to hear cases as well as cases on appeal. Finally, each of the ten tribes furnished an allotment of infantry and cavalry toward the formation of a national army in charge of ten generals, one from each tribe. In time the commanding general became the leader of the council and the assembly as well as of the army. Since there were no restrictions upon re-election this made him a potentially very influential official (28:193).

The constitution set up by Cleisthenes was in full operation by 502 B.C., and, with some modifications, it was to serve Athens for nearly two centuries. The most important changes were effected during and after Pericles' time, and included among other things the restriction of citizenship to the sons of Athenian parents, the removal of property qualifications for archons, the stripping of the council of the Areopagus of practically all its powers, and the institution of compensation for civic services (24:80).

The Persian Crisis and the Athenian Empire

The constitution of Cleisthenes had scarcely gone into effect when the Ionian revolt against Persia (199–494 B.C.) broke out. Due to the fact that it had rendered some assistance to the Ionians, Athens became the next target of the Persians. In the ensuing struggle—from Marathon (490 B.C.) through Thermopylae and Salamis to Plataea (479 B.C.)—the Greeks revealed both their greatest virtues and their most serious weaknesses. As Turner aptly puts it, they met the "supreme crisis—heroically but with divided counsels, hesitant actions, and treasonable connivance with the enemy" (29: 473). Historically, the significant consideration is the fact that their decisive defeat of Persia left them free to continue their elaboration of the base of Western civilization (32:221; 28:241).

A more immediate outcome of the Greek victory was the formation, in 478 B.C., of the Delian Confederacy under the leadership of Athens. This was initially a voluntary organization of some two hundred cities for the maintenance of a fleet as a weapon—both offensive and defensive—against Persia. It represented a most promising step in the direction of federal government. And, if Athens had been less provincial and selfish, it might have averted the Peloponnesian tragedy. Actually, the Confederacy rapidly degenerated into an agency for the aggrandizement of Athens (32:222). In 454 B.C. the treasury was moved from Delos to Athens, and the funds were used increasingly for improvements in Athens

(28:274). At the same time the general congress at Delos was discontinued. In place of a voluntary association of independent states the Delian Confederacy was now in essence an Athenian maritime empire (32:222). Imperial supremacy was not based on the general agreement with the allies but on special treaties in which individual states were forced to renounce their sovereign rights. Athens freely interfered in their internal politics and imposed upon them the jurisdiction of Athenian courts (28:274–275). No one could withdraw without the consent of all, and since Athens was one of them, none actually could withdraw. Revolts were ruthlessly put down (28:243, 280).

Although bitterly resented throughout Greece, Periclean naval imperialism was popular in Athens. It made for prosperity and well-being. Life in Athens had never been so tolerable. Under Pericles, democracy continued to be liberalized, and, within its limits, it functioned effectively. Although bitterly denounced by the opposition as another Peisistratus, he remained at the head of the government for more than thirty years. And this despite the fact that the assembly could have deposed him at any time. Civic strife there was, but not to any extent the bitter partisanship of earlier days (28:282–289).

In both modern and ancient perspective, Periclean Athens was a small city. Trever estimates that, before the restriction of citizenship to sons of Athenian parentage, the adult male citizens may have numbered about 40,000, and that with the inclusion of women and children the total citizen population may have ranged somewhere between 120,000 and 160,000. In addition there appear to have been about 45,000 metics, or resident aliens, and approximately 80,000 slaves. The metics, for the most part Greeks, were not discriminated against except in the matter of land ownership and citizens' rights. The lot of the slaves, mostly non-Greeks, seems to have been fairly tolerable. With only about 2,500 nobles and knights, the Zeugite or small farmers constituted the most numerous element in the adult male citizen population, the thetes—artisans, laborers, sailors—coming next with about two-fifths of the total (28:292–294).

Life in Periclean Athens was simple and unpretentious. Most of the luxuries and conveniences that we consider indispensable today were non-existent. There were no elegant dwellings and no sanitary facilities. Since men spent most of their time in public and recreational activities from which women were excluded, home life was negligible. The accumulation of wealth was a means rather than an end—the Athenian wished first of all to live. To civil, social, and recreational life he devoted himself unstintingly. These were the activities befitting a free man. By the same token, his temples, and the theatrical displays which he witnessed, were as elegant and stirring as his home life was plain and uninspiring (1:241–247; 10:291–310; 28:318–322; 32:223–225).

The Decline of the Greek City-State and the Rise of Macedon

But the Athenian maritime empire was headed for disaster. At the conclusion of the Peloponnesian War (431–404 B.C.) Athens was a physical and cultural wreck. Its fleet and empire were gone, and it was forced to join the Peloponnesian League. For a time Sparta took over, but soon proved unequal to the task of supplying a constructive leadership for the Greek city-states. Thebes followed, and likewise promptly disqualified herself. Athens then staged an almost miraculous recovery. Within a decade after its collapse it had freed itself of Spartan domination, and by 370 B.C. it had regained many of its former allies and was once more the chief power in the eastern Mediterranean (28:373; 10:463).

However, Athens failed to profit by the mistakes of the past. Despite assurances to the contrary, it began once more to infringe upon the liberties of other states. Recourse to coercion and force became commonplace. As a result, the new empire broke up, and Athens found herself, as Durant observes, without friends or allies (10:470). This situation was of course not peculiar to Athens. It was symptomatic of the Greek city-state as such. The latter, as Trever stresses, was so selfish and provincial in its orientation that it saw no contradiction whatever in demanding autonomy for itself and practicing tyranny over others (28:380). "By the middle of the fourth century B.C.," says Webster, "it had become evident that no single city-state was strong enough or wise enough to rule Greece" (32:227).

And it was in 338 B.C. that Philip II defeated the Athenian and Theban forces at Chaeronea and became master of Greece. Although treated generously, the Greeks accepted Macedonian suzerainty reluctantly, and had to be dealt with energetically both by Philip and by his illustrious son, Alexander the Great, who succeeded him upon his death two years later. With the Greeks pacified, Alexander entered upon the Asiatic expedition that was to make him master of the Persian Empire within ten years. The plans for the reconstitution of the Empire had scarcely gotten underway at the time of his premature death in 323 B.C. However, such preliminary steps as he had taken indicate that he was bent upon a fusion of the Graeco-Macedonian and Oriental cultures (24:121–122; 32:228–230).

Since Alexander left no heir, the control of the Empire passed temporarily into the hands of his generals. When the Empire subsequently disintegrated there arose in its place three leading kingdoms, each with its own royal dynasty,— Macedonia (including Greece) under the Antigonids, Egypt under the Ptolemies, and Syria under the Seleucids. During the third century B.C. the Greeks made a final unsuccessful attempt to escape Macedonian domination through the formation of two leagues—the Aetolian and the Achaean. In the kingdoms government was monarchial, but cities frequently enjoyed relatively large autonomy, and some of them—as Antioch, Seleucia, and Alexandria—attained great size and splendor.

The Hellenistic Age

The era beginning with the death of Alexander and ending with the Roman conquest is generally known as the Hellenistic Age. During this period Greek culture was diffused throughout the Orient and was itself modified and extended through contact with Oriental cultures and through new contributions. Racial fusion likewise was a conspicuous feature of the age. The Greeks left the city-states in large numbers and settled throughout the Graeco-Oriental world. As they did so, they gave up much of their provincialism, including the antagonism toward non-Greeks, and became citizens of the kingdoms in which they settled. Attic Greek, somewhat modified, became the prevailing language of the Graeco-Oriental world. Leading cities, such as Antioch, Seleucia, and Alexandria, became great cosmopolitan cultural centers.

The Cultural Achievements of the Greeks

Our concern thus far has been primarily with the political, economic, and social development of the Greeks. Their cultural achievements—in literature, art, philosophy, and science —have been touched upon only incidentally. At this point, although an adequate account of them is beyond the scope of this discussion, we must at least bring them into perspective. In any consideration or appraisal of them we must constantly bear in mind that the Greeks did not, as was long assumed, start from scratch (1:217). With Crete as the intermediary, they were the heirs of millennia. And significantly enough, the first brilliant outburst of Greek culture occurred among the Aeolian and Ionian settlers on the coast of Asia Minor where the sequence with Minoan culture had been least disrupted (28:128–129).

And we may as well discard the notion that the uniqueness

of Greek cultural achievements can be explained on racial grounds. They were an extremely mixed people, even before the coming of the Dorians. The admixture of the latter could scarcely have improved upon them, for where this was most pronounced, as in Laconia, Greek achievements were least conspicuous. That there was no cultural compulsion in the Greek racial strain is evidenced, further, by the fact that the majority of the city-states made no significant contributions to civilization (1:249).

We shall assume, therefore, that the ancient Greeks were biologically closely comparable to other ancient culture carriers. Apart from differences in physical environments, the influence of which can easily be overrated, the forces that molded these ancient peoples so very differently were cultural accidents rather than biological characteristics. Contrasting, by way of example, the Indians and the Chinese on the one hand with the Greeks on the other, we find that the Indians (Aryas), initially a jolly and extroverted people, early fell under the sway of a sacred literature and a tyrannical priesthood. The Chinese escaped the sacred and the priestly, but succumbed to the cult of the past—the worship of tradition. The results were much the same in either case. Both peoples developed cultural orientations that kept them from realizing their biological potential. They failed to face the world and nature realistically. Hence, science and free thought could not get under way consistently. The arts, being more largely intuitive, fared much better.

By way of contrast, the Greeks had no sacred book, no priestly hierarchy, and no authoritarian tradition to keep them from speculating about the nature of man and the world. Their geniuses were, therefore, relatively free to think and to speak. And the Greeks appear to have acquired this freedom more or less accidentally. As Burn stresses, it is extremely probable that Homer's rather flippant treatment of the gods may not only have precluded the development of a dogmatic Greek theology, but that it may actually have put the stamp of approval upon religious criticism (3:255–256). Homer's attitude in turn may have been appreciably influenced by Minoan antecedents.

Greek Literature

Greek literature began with the epic—Homer's *Iliad* and *Odyssey* falling in the ninth century B.C. and Hesiod's *Works and Days* and the *Theogony* in the seventh. During the next two centuries lyric poetry, both personal and choral, rose to great heights, with Sappho and Pindar as the most notable contributors. During the fifth and the early part of the fourth century the drama came into the foreground, with Aeschylus, Sophocles, and Euripides as the great writers of tragedy, and Aristophanes and Meander as the leading producers of comedy. The fifth century also witnessed the rise of prose in the form of history, with Herodotus and Thucydides (along with the fourth century Xenophon) as the chief figures. The fourth century turned to oratory, with Demosthenes as the most eloquent exponent of the art.

The Arts of Greece

The major arts of Greece were architecture, sculpture and painting. Conspicuous among the minor arts were vase-painting and gem cutting. The major arts revolved primarily about the great temples, and so were intimately tied up with religion and national life. Despite Minoan antecedents and Egyptian influences, Greek art did not get seriously under way until the seventh and sixth centuries B.C. Thereafter, it developed rapidly, reaching its climax in the fifth and fourth centuries (32:251). The basic structural features of the Greek temple appear to have been suggested by the Mycenaean megaron. Beyond this, there were Asiatic and Egyptian influences (10:223–224). The Athenian Parthenon (mid-fifth century) and the Erechtheum (late-fifth century) are generally

regarded as the supreme Greek architectural achievements—
the former Doric and the latter Ionic (28:304, 364). Phidias,
under whose direction the frieze reliefs of the Parthenon were
executed, is rated as the greatest sculptor of the ages (28:307).
Not too much is known regarding the painters and their work.

While very little of the major art creations has come
down to us, the survivals of the work of the vase-painters are
fairly numerous. In general, this minor art passed through the
same developmental stages as the major arts. To the beginning of the eighth century B.C., vase decoration was restricted to crude geometric designs. During the next two centuries
human and animal figures came into use. At first the figures
were rather stiff and conventional, and the themes were
mainly mythological. By the fifth century, when the art
reached its height, the figures had become natural and life-
like, and the representations frequently embodied scenes
from every day life (27:130–131).

The Nature Philosophers

Philosophy and science were closely tied up among the
Greeks. In fact most Greek thinkers were both philosophers
and scientists. Thales of Miletus (640–546 B.C.), sometimes
referred to as the father of Western philosophy, was the first
of a group of nature philosophers who attempted to account
for the physical universe in natural terms (12:31–33). He was
familiar with Egyptian and Babylonian astronomical developments and predicted an eclipse of the sun that took place in
May, 585 B.C. (10:137). He assumed water to be the primal
substance out of which the universe arose. Primal substances
suggested by others were air, earth, and fire (1:220). And
Pythagoras proposed number as the essence of things (29:
556–557). However naive such suggestions were, they represented, as Barnes stresses, a tremendous advance in human
thought—the transition from mythological to naturalistic explanations of man and nature (1:220).

Having posited primal substances, the nature philosophers turned to the problem of change. The question that confronted them was: How can a primal substance, such as water, become many different things—things that bear no semblance to the original? Heraclitus of Ephesus answered, at about the beginning of the fifth century B.C., by positing change and flux as the very essence of things, stability and permanence being illusionary phenomena. At a somewhat earlier date Anaximander had suggested that living beings arose from a primitive substance by gradual stages, man, for example, having once been a fish (10:139). About the middle of the fifth century B.C., Empedocles elaborated Anaximander's concept of gradual developmental stages by positing four simple and changeless elements—fire, water, earth, and air—which in varied combinations gave rise to all living things, first plants and then animals and man (12:72–75). Beyond this, Aristotle gives him credit for advancing the notion of chance variations, adaptation, and the survival of the fittest. With this, the nature philosophers had reached a rough approximation to a theory of organic evolution (12:75; 1:220).

Philosophical Skepticism

Meanwhile, philosophical skepticism had been getting under way. The Eliatics, of whom Parmenides (fl. 500 B.C.) was the leading figure, in essence ruled out the sensory approach to an understanding of the universe. They characterized the physical universe, with its apparent instability and heterogeneity, as a sensory illusion and predicated instead an eternal, changeless, and homogeneous being that could be known only through reason (29:560–561). The significance of this formulation lies, as Durant observes, in the fact that it represents the starting point of the idealistic philosophy that was subsequently to be elaborated by Plato and his followers (10:168).

Materialism

During the latter half of the fifth century B.C. the material-ists—Leucippus (fl. 450 B.C.) and Democritus (ca. 460–370 B.C.)—came into the foreground and, as Fuller puts it, "laid down the fundamental principles of the atomic and mech-anistic hypothesis which has been the basis of all scientific advance up to the present day" (12:86). They denied the ex-istence of multiple elements—such as water, air, fire—and repudiated the distinction between mind and matter. Instead, they posited an ultimate reality consisting only of space and an infinitude of indivisible atoms. The latter differ in size and shape, and are endowed with perpetual motion. By force of necessity, entirely apart from the operation of chance, like atoms combine to form objects—plants, creatures, and even the soul. The gods themselves, to the extent that they exist, are composed of atoms. Death is merely the dissolution of combinations of them. The atoms themselves persist eternally (28:348–349; 10:352–354).

The Sophists

For a variety of reasons the middle of the fifth century B.C. ushered in a period of all around doubt and skepticism. The nature philosophers had raised havoc with the gods and traditional religion. Their failure to agree on such basic issues as the trustworthiness of the senses and the reliability of reason served as a further stimulus to uncertainty. Beyond this, growing contacts with other peoples and cultures pointed to knowledge and truth as relative rather than abso-lute (12:100–101). Finally, the economic and political condi-tions of the age placed a premium upon individualism. The net outcome of it all was a new school of philosophers—the sophists—with Protagoras of Abdera (ca. 481–411 B.C.) and Georgias of Leontini (ca. 485–380 B.C.) as the chief spokes-men.

In general the sophists were wandering scholars who

taught for pay. While instruction centered primarily upon grammar, rhetoric, and oratory, it was carried on within a frame of reference that was definitely hostile to the old order and in harmony with the ideals of the new age. The gods were treated lightly; metaphysical speculation was decried; knowledge was restricted to sense impressions which reason could not transcend; truth was strictly relative; there were no universal or ultimate moral and ethical standards; man was the measure of all things. Those who patronized the sophists were primarily interested in preparation for public and private careers.

Although long condemned as a destructive and unscrupulous lot, the sophists are now regarded as significant contributors to Greek culture. They were the first to set up grammar, rhetoric, and logic. And they elaborated dialectic. They undermined endless traditions that had no basis in fact or logic. They posited institutions and laws as the creatures and servants of man, and stressed knowledge for man's sake rather than as an end in itself (10:361–362; 12:102–103; 28:351–352). And finally, as Durant observes, they prepared the way for Socrates, Plato, and Aristotle (10:364).

Socrates

Socrates (469–399 B.C.) was the first Athenian born philosopher. He saw Athens rise to greatness, witnessed its decline, and was executed during the period of confusion following the Peloponnesian War. Apart from his ethical teaching, the scope of his philosophical interests is uncertain. Due to the fact that he left no writings, his views must be inferred from Plato's works and Xenophon's Memorabilia. The problem is complicated by the fact that we do not know whether Plato in his earlier works expresses the views of Socrates or his own. If he serves as spokesman for Socrates, then the latter must be given credit for rather broad philosophical orientation; if he sets forth his own views, then Xenophon's portrayal—a portrayal which characterizes Socrates as primarily a moralist—may be accepted as fairly authentic (12:110–111).

Even so, Socrates' fame rests chiefly upon his ethical teaching. In this he differed from the sophists primarily in his insistence upon essentially universal principles of morality in place of sheer opportunism. That he erred in assuming knowledge to be a sufficient instigator of good behavior may be pardoned him. Since it is well known, we shall not at this point elaborate upon the method which he used so effectively.

Plato

Plato (ca. 429–347 B.C.) was the son of aristocratic Athenian parents, and Socrates' most distinguished pupil. The age in which he lived was chaotic and troublesome. He witnessed the Peloponnesian War and lived through the confusion and strife that followed it—a fact which may have had much to do with his penchant for the mystic and the subjective. After the death of Socrates he traveled for more than a decade. Upon his return to Athens, he founded the Academy and taught there almost continuously during the remainder of his life.

How Plato came to formulate his views is beyond the scope of our discussion. Suffice it to note that, apart from Socrates, he appears to have been appreciably influenced by Heraclitus, the Eleatics, and Pythagoras. He found the Heraclitean sensory flux an inadequate explanation of reality, and posited behind this a universal order of absolute and unchanging entities, consisting, in Pythagorean terms, of forms or ideas. The latter alone are real, the objects and experiences perceived through the senses being merely shadows of, or approximations to, them. Since the universal order thus posited exists in supreme reason alone, it can be comprehended only subjectively through contemplation and thought.

A philosophy as drastically idealistic as this was bound to have far-reaching effects upon the Western mind. "Wha

Platonism has been as an intellectual influence in the Western world," says Turner, "is well known. It established subjectivism both as the content of knowledge and as the method of arriving at it. It declared the existence of absolute truth and asserted that men, through meditation, can translate it into a just social order. In supporting the illusion that men can know absolute truth, Platonism denied them the supreme satisfaction of struggling to escape other illusions. By identifying subjective experience with reason and deity, Platonism established it as the dominant element in the high intellectual tradition of the Western world" (29:586).

Aristotle

Aristotle (384–321 B.C.), the son of a court physician in Macedon, was born at Stageirus in Chalcidice. At eighteen he was sent to the Academy in Athens where he spent some twenty years as student and assistant. Upon Plato's death in 347 B.C., he left Athens to devote himself among other things to biological research and the education of young Alexander. Twelve years later he returned to Athens and founded the Lyceum which came in time to concentrate primarily upon natural science (12:170–172; 28:439–440).

As Durant observes, if Aristotle had been less under the influence of Plato he might have developed a thoroughly scientific outlook. As it was, he went a long ways, but without ever completely freeing himself of mystical Platonic preconceptions. He retained Plato's changeless forms or ideas but considered them imminent rather than transcendent. He was a thoroughgoing teleologist, rejecting Democritus' mechanistic atomism, and clinging instead to the notion of an ideal universe dominated by eternal and changeless purposes or forms. However, these are not a thing apart from the sensible world of experience. They are an integral part of it. They cannot exist apart from matter which is likewise eternal and cannot exist apart from them (12:176). They are continually combining with matter to form the objects of the sensible world. The forms as such do not change, but matter is constantly taking on new forms. Hence, the sensible world is perpetually changing, and as it does so new forms are realizing their potentialities or purposes.

Aristotle thus found himself confronted by real phenomena —the objects and experiences of the sensible world consisting of forms and matter. These could be studied and principles deduced from them. Apart from the discovery of the principles that govern them they are chaotic and meaningless. It is the province of science or philosophy to discover and analyze such principles—to attain genuine knowledge. This called for logic, and Aristotle became the founder of it. In this, deduction and induction received their first formal recognition. The former, taking the form of the syllogism, derives the particular from the universal; the latter begins with the examination of particulars, and terminates in the formulation of universals.

Behind the perpetual motion involved in the union of form and matter, Aristotle posited God—the first cause, the unmoved mover, the unifying principle of the universe. Since he is pure actuality,—a being in whom all potentialities have been realized—he is free from all desire and striving, existing in contemplation only (26:85).

We shall make no attempt to detail Aristotle's activities. Suffice it to note that they extended over a terrific range— metaphysics, logic, psychology, ethics, aesthetics, politics physics, and biology,—so much so that he is generally known as the first encyclopaedist. However, he was no mere encyclopaedist as evidenced by the fact that he was also the first to distinguish the several sciences and to assign to each its appropriate content and method. Aristotle's supreme genera accomplishment was the development of the scientific method for the study of man and nature (29:591). His mos significant specific contributions were the setting up of systematic zoology and the foundation of formal logic.

For a variety of reasons Plato's views were channelled into Western thought appreciably in advance of Aristotle's. Augustine, the most influential contributor to early Christian doctrine, was dominated almost exclusively by Platonic and Neo-Platonic considerations (12:353). The same thing was true of scholasticism to the end of the twelfth century. Aristotelianism did not enter this apart from logic. Its basic content was Augustinian, Platonic, and Neo-Platonic (26:162–163). During the thirteenth century, however, Aristotelianism thoroughly permeated scholastic thought, and was, after careful delineation from revealed theology, reconciled with Christian doctrine. In the end this led of course to the collapse of Aristotelianism and the emergence of experimental science.

Greek Science

Greek science, as distinguished from philosophical speculation about nature, matured late. It did not reach its culmination until the third and second centuries B.C., and was thus primarily a Hellenistic product. Various factors appear to have been responsible for this: the speculative proclivity of the Greeks, along with their disdain of the practical arts, retarded the development of experimental techniques; the powerful Hellenistic monarchs were in better position to encourage and endow research than were the leaders of the small Greek democracies; and, above everything else, the Hellenistic setting gave a tremendous impetus to diffusion and communication, and in so doing made the scientists of the day not only the heirs of the past but also the participants in all that was going on in the contemporary world.

Among the greatest figures of the period under consideration were the botanist, Theophrastus (372–287 B.C.), a pupil and successor of Aristotle; Euclid (323–287 B.C.), the mathematician, who synthesized the elements of geometry; Aristarchus (310–230 B.C.), the astronomer, who first proposed the heliocentric theory; Herophilus (fl. 300 B.C.), the anatomist who first recognized the brain as the seat of the mind; Erasistratus (fl. 300 B.C.), the founder of physiology; Eratosthenes (ca. 276–195 B.C.), mathematician and astronomer, who first calculated the earth's circumference; Archimedes (ca. 287–212 B.C.), the greatest of the ancient mathematicians and physicists; and Hipparchus (ca. 160–125 B.C.), the foremost ancient student of the stars (10:627–639; 28:508–514).

Greek Religion

Thus far our references to Greek religion have been restricted largely to the Olympian state cult. This was a stately and relatively rational affair with little recourse to mysticism and emotional display. It was, as Fuller observes, an extroverted rather than an introverted religion. The Greeks were not given to introspection. They normally lived their religion through participation in family, communal, and civic affairs. Neither were they concerned with sin, redemption, or communion with the gods. Even immortality was not of vital concern to them (12:18–20).

In the course of the seventh and sixth centuries B.C., however, mystic Oriental cults that antedated the Olympians, began to assert themselves. Basically, they revolved about the primitive beliefs in the fertility of nature—the recurring cycles in the death and rebirth of vegetation. The deities associated with them were conceived of as resurrected deities —deities who had died and risen again. Through mystic initiation and the observance of appropriate sacraments their worshipers might likewise overcome earthly limitations and achieve immortality. The sacred symbols and mystic rites of the cults were revealed to the initiates at secret ceremonies known as mysteries. The two outstanding ones were the Eleusinian and the Orphic.

The central figures in the Eleusinian Mysteries were Demeter, the goddess of the soil and fertility, and her daughter, Persephone, who spent half of the year (the growing season) with her mother and the other half (the season of decay) with Hades in the underworld. This cult derives its name from the fact that the main temple of Demeter was at Eleusis. When the latter was annexed to Athens the cult was adopted by Athens and later by all of Greece. The communicants constituted a close-knit and privileged group who alone enjoyed the blessings of immortality.

The Orphic Mysteries center about the twice-born god, Dionysus. The cult derives its name from Orpheus, its purported founder. In the eighth century B.C. Dionysus appears to have been a Thracian deity of vegetation and wine whose worship was accompanied by orgiastic rites and drunkenness. In Greece the cult became more moderate and developed its own doctrines culminating in a rather complex systematic theology. The characterization of this is beyond the scope of our discussion. Suffice it to note that some of its elements seem to have been derived from Egypt and Babylonia, and that many of them appear later to have been absorbed by Christianity. Permeating the cult was a mystical and highly emotionalized sense "of the body as evil and the soul as divine" (10:191), and the necessity of purifying the former as a means to the release of the latter. Actually, escape and salvation came through repeated transmigrations accompanied by progressive purification. And the latter could of course be effected only by following the prescriptions of the cult (29:551). In the end these appear to have been for the most part mystical and symbolic, the individual managing somehow to attain salvation miraculously through symbolic participation in the death and resurrection of the deity (12:22–23).

The import of these cults has been variously interpreted. Those who harbor large sympathies for the mystic and the transcendent in contemporary life adjudge their rise as further evidence of Greek genius. Those whose outlook is basically objective and realistic regard them as among the greatest dangers encountered by the Greek mind—the danger of being swallowed up by Oriental mysticism. With rare exceptions, as in the case of Pythagoras, it was the philosophers, from Thales to Aristotle, that came to the rescue of Greece in this supreme crisis (4:296–306).

BIBLIOGRAPHY

See Chapter 6.

CHAPTER VI

Education in Ancient Greece

The Minoan Script

AS noted earlier, the Cretan script emerged in Early Minoan times in the usual pictographic and idcographic form. In the course of the Middle Minoan period it evolved into a linear script employing less than one hundred characters designating words and syllables and even some letters. This script subsequently spread throughout Crete and the Aegean world. Early writing in the Aegean, as elsewhere, appears to have served a variety of practical purposes—administrative, legal, religious, and commercial. And there are indications that literacy was widespread, in Crete at least. At Hagia Triada, for example, commonplace inscriptions were scrawled on walls in modern fashion. This leads Glotz to conclude that "the humblest folk could read and write" (13:379–380).

The Greek Alphabet

What became of the Minoan script is not known. As noted elsewhere, some of the characters may have been incorporated in the Semitic alphabet which the Greeks subsequently borrowed from the Phoenicians. However that may be, with the Achaean conquest of Crete, writing went into eclipse. The Achaeans appear to have made little use of it, except for records and commercial purposes (10:52; 28:127). And the Dorian invasion, which ushered in the Greek Middle Ages, must have made further inroads upon it.

Even so, the onetime prevalent notion that writing had almost completely disappeared for centuries is no longer tenable. It is now known that the Greeks very early borrowed the Semitic alphabet from the Phoenicians. The time when this occurred is still, within limits, conjectural. According to Greek tradition the alphabet was introduced by Cadmus, the legendary founder of Thebes, sometime during the fourteenth century B.C. Among contemporary authorities, both Kenyon and Ullman favor the fourteenth century B.C. as the probable time of its introduction (18:21–22; 30:11–12). And very few would place it later than the tenth century B.C. (28:82; 32:182; 29:488).

The alphabet which the Greeks borrowed from the Phoenicians was not a complete alphabet. It consisted of twenty-two consonant signs. The vowels had to be inferred, as in Hebrew to this day. The signs for the several consonant sounds were conventionalized word symbols which had come to represent the initial sounds of the word. Thus, the Semitic *aleph* and *beth*, whence the Greek alpha and beta, were originally the word symbols for *ox* and *house*, respectively. In the Semitic alphabet, which the Phoenicians borrowed, they became in addition the signs for the initial sounds A and B. In the Greek rendition, alpha and beta lost all significance except as signs for the sounds A and B (19:517–518).

With the Semitic consonant signs in their possession, the problem of the Greeks was to supply vowel signs. This they did in the course of several centuries. In the end they had an alphabet in which there was a sign for every sound—an alphabet that was to constitute the foundation for all subsequent European alphabets. Actually, the process of its elaboration was an exceedingly complicated one, and the Greeks displayed remarkable ingenuity in following it through. Since the technical details of the process are beyond the scope of this discussion, we shall merely note its general character.

To begin with, the Greeks did not just borrow the Phoenician consonantal alphabet and add vowel signs to it. What they actually did was to adapt the borrowed alphabet to the requirements of their language, introducing new elements only as needed. Since the Phoenician alphabet had a greater number of consonant signs than the Greek language required, they set out by selecting and adapting the consonant signs which they needed. Thereupon, they assigned vowel values to the remaining consonant signs, adding only such new signs as they needed. In this way—to use but one illustration—*aleph*, which had a well-defined consonantal value in the Phoenician alphabet, became the sign for vowel *A* in the Greek alphabet (19:518–519).

As in other matters, the Greek cities vied with each other in the elaboration of the alphabet. As a result, as many as ten different versions got under way (10:205; 13:116–117). Gradually one of these—the Ionian—gained the ascendancy. It became prevalent first in eastern Greece. In 403 B.C. Athens adopted it as its official alphabet. Thereafter, it spread rapidly throughout the rest of Greece (30:31).

Along with their elaboration of the alphabet the Greeks also changed the direction of writing. In the oldest extant inscriptions, which belong to the eighth and seventh centuries B.C., they wrote from right to left as did the Semites. In some of the sixth century inscriptions they wrote alternately from right to left and from left to right. Thereafter, they wrote consistently from left to right (10:205).

There is widespread agreement among authorities that the motives which led the Greeks to elaborate their alphabet were largely commercial and practical. The Phoenician alphabet obviously came to them through trade channels, and, as Glotz observes, when they noticed the advantages which Phoenician traders derived from records they proceeded to develop their own system (13:116–117). On the political side there was increasing need of preserving official documents for cities and temples. That literary motivation was operative to any extent is doubtful. There was of course, as Kenyon stresses, no *a priori* reason why the Homeric epics should not have been written down when composed (18:11–12). On the other hand there appears to be no valid evidence that this occurred before the beginning of the sixth century B.C. (29: 534). The Greeks were as capable of handing down their literary tradition orally as other early peoples.

Whatever the motivation back of it may have been, the significance of the Greek alphabet as a cultural contribution cannot be overstressed. Kroeber regards its elaboration as one of the most important new steps in the history of civilization, and feels that what the Greeks contributed was fully original and unique as the initial Semitic invention (19:519–520). Next to the democratic tradition it may well rank as the greatest gift of the Greeks to Western civilization.

The Greek Numerical System

The Greeks displayed no comparable ingenuity in the development of their numeral system. They had early borrowed the Egyptian decimal system of counting, and had, along with most other early peoples, set out initially by representing the units from one to nine by vertical strokes, supplemented by special symbols for ten and powers of ten (10:337–338). Later they developed two fairly elaborate systems. In one of these the numerals were represented mainly by the initial letters of their names. In the other, which proved to be the more ingenious of the two, they were represented by the accented letters of the alphabet (plus three additional letter symbols). The first nine letters were assigned to the numbers 1–9, the next nine to the numbers 10–90, and the last nine to the numbers 100–900. Numbers beyond this point were represented by letters with different accents (29:564–565).

While the alphabetic system appears to have lent itself to rather elaborate computations, it was nonetheless cumbersome due to the multiplicity of its signs, though by no means as much so as the original one which apparently prevailed down to Pericles' time (10:627).

The multiplicity of numeral signs was of course forced upon the Greeks because of their inability to conceive of the zero. Without a zero sign and position values a complex numeral system of one kind or another is, as Kroeber stresses, inevitable (19:468).

It remains to be noted finally that the Greeks drew a rather sharp distinction between the art of computation and the science of numbers. What we have said above concerns primarily the former. It was in this that the Greeks failed to distinguish themselves. To the science of numbers their contributions were much more notable.

The Rise of Formal Education

If by the rise of formal education we mean—as many historians of education apparently do—the beginning of the regular school tradition, then there is no evidence in support of it in Greece before the seventh century B.C. The Spartan code of laws, regulating education along with all other affairs of the state, and setting up what essentially amounted to a state school system, appears to have been enacted late in the seventh century B.C. And according to tradition, the first Athenian laws designed to regulate various aspects of education were enacted by Solon early in the sixth century B.C. Since legislative enactments of this kind normally follow a period of practical experimentation, it is, as both Boyd and Butts observe, reasonable to assume that formal education of one kind or another existed in Greece as early as the seventh century B.C. (2:10–16; 5:52–55).

However, this is not the definition with which we originally set out. It was our contention rather that formal education arose initially to supply training for specialists—scribes, priests, accountants. These functionaries arose with the urban revolution and were indispensable in connection with the administration of the economic surplus. The urban revolution in Greece antedated the appearance of the characteristic city-state by centuries. The centers of Mycenaean civilization were walled cities. The Dorians also developed urban centers as rapidly as they settled down. The ruling classes who lived upon and administered the economic surplus—derived from agriculture and trade—were chiefly warriors. They were expected to be speakers of words and doers of deeds, and so had little need of literacy. That probably goes far toward explaining why there are but two references to education in the Homeric epics—both of them having to do with the training of Achilles,—and only one reference to writing (2:6–7; 10:52).

However,—and this is the crucial consideration—the technical administration of the economic surplus, and its production, to the extent at least that this devolved upon the trading classes, demanded scribes and accountants, and these had to be trained. How this was accomplished we do not know, but there must have been formal education agencies of one kind or another. The best evidence in support of them is of course supplied by the development of the alphabet. That Greece should have had no facilities for the teaching of reading and writing in the ninth century B.C.—and possibly much earlier—when several local alphabets were under way is extremely unlikely (13:117). Further indirect evidence in support of such agencies is of course supplied through our observance of their rise and development in Mesopotamia and Egypt. In the face of these considerations we are justified in assuming that formal agencies for the training of specialists must have gotten under way in Greece far in advance of the rise of the regular school traditions (34:298).

When the Greek school tradition finally got under way it was, as Butts observes, with an aim that differed significantly from that of any previous school tradition—the training of citizens (5:52). The schools of Mesopotamia, Egypt, and China trained specialists for the service of the state, but left the citizenry largely untouched. The schools of India and the Hebrews were religious in their basic orientation and services. In Greece, then, for the first time in history the aim of education became civic. In Sparta it was to remain so to the end; in Athens and the other city-states decreasingly so after the middle of the fifth century B.C.

Spartan Education

Not only was the purpose of education in Sparta civic, but the educational system as such was established, maintained, and controlled by the state, with a special representative of the ephors in immediate charge (5:33). The supreme civic obligation of the Spartan male citizen was to be a brave and ruthless warrior. Hence, the content and method of education were from beginning to end determined by military considerations. A detailed discussion of these is not pertinent at this point. They have been ably characterized by numerous writers on Greek education. For our purposes, suffice it to note that the state set out by deciding upon the fitness of the child to live; that at age seven the boys were removed to barracks where, after having been organized in herds and companies, they received their basic training in physical fitness and morale; that the girls, although they remained at home, were given somewhat comparable training in their own gymnasiums; that at age eighteen the young men entered upon two years of intensive military training followed by ten years of active military service; and that finally at thirty they became full-fledged citizens and were expected to marry (5:52–54; 34:240–272). Through all these years, it should be borne in mind, the young Spartans apparently received—apart from a certain sharpening of their wits—very little in the way of intellectual or aesthetic training. Sparta had no need for such embellishments. If they learned to read and write at all it is

generally conceded that it must have been in very minimal
fashion (33:138–140; 34:241–242).

The Old Athenian Education

In contrast with Spartan education which endured for
many centuries with very little change, Athenian education—
as the instrument of a dynamic and changing society,—passed
through several well-defined stages. The Athenians themselves when they began to throw the spotlight upon themselves drew a rather clear-cut distinction between the *old* and
the *new* education (2:17). And these were of course in time
followed by the Hellenistic stage.

The old Athenian education prevailed roughly from the
earliest beginnings to the post-Persian War era. As in the case
of Spartan education, its primary aim was to develop citizens
—not, however, through military regimentation, but rather
through the all around physical, aesthetic, and intellectual
development of the individual. Although regulated to some
extent by the state, education was not—apart from the public
gymnasiums—a state or public affair in early Athens. Even
the decision whether the child should live or be exposed was
left to the father. Neither were parents required to send boys
to particular schools. About all that the state demanded was
that they give them "an elementary education in gymnastics,
letters, and music" (5:55).

There was, moreover, no highly organized educational system. In fact, as Butts observes, it would perhaps be "more
correct to speak of Athenian teachers than of Athenian
schools; where the teacher was, there was a school. Parents
selected a teacher and sent their boys to him" (5:55). Three
distinct types of elementary teachers arose by degrees—the
citharist or teacher of music, the *grammatist* or teacher of
letters (reading, writing, and arithmetic), and the *paedotribe*
or teacher of gymnastics. Of these the first appears to have
been the most ancient. In fact there is rather widespread

agreement now that the citharist long taught reading, writing and arithmetic as well as music. Just when the grammatist as such appeared is not known, but it must have been near the end of the Old Athenian period (5:66; 2:22; 22:139–140; 34: 303).

Although not a highly developed art, music played an important role in Greek life. It was intimately tied up with the great religious and civic festivals. Military training was generally carried on under the stimulus of martial airs. The great national songs and the poems of the ancient bards were customarily chanted to the accompaniment of the lyre, and, in a somewhat lighter vein, the cultured Athenian was expected to improvise his own accompaniments on the lyre to such songs as he chose to recite at social gatherings (16:83–84).

For these and other reasons the study of music was highly esteemed by the ancient Greeks. However, the citharist made no attempt to develop technical excellence. Music was for him primarily an instrument for the molding of character. It developed rhythm, harmony, and balance, and instilled the proper ethos in the young (8:40–41; 11:243–244; 22:139–140).

The methodological details of the teaching of letters need not detain us here. Suffice it to note briefly the content employed and the outcomes achieved. The most significant feature of the teaching of reading and writing was the fact that it revolved so largely about the great national literature— Homer and the lyric poets. As soon as the boys had mastered the bare technical elements of reading and writing they began to read and write and to memorize and recite selected passages from the poets and from the Iliad and the Odyssey. And they continued to do so with ever-increasing tempo as they grew older (21:49–50; 22:135–137; 34:304–305). In the end some of them appear to have been able to recite the Iliad and the Odyssey in their entirety (7:68–69). As a result, the Athenians not only learned to read and write rather well, but they became thoroughly impregnated with the traditions and

ideals of Athens and Greece generally. On the technical side
this program appears to have worked so well that illiteracy
was extremely rare among the citizen class.

Due to the cumbersomeness of their numeral system and
their antipathy to commercial and other practical occupational pursuits, training in arithmetic appears to have been
very meager, extending probably not appreciably beyond
simple counting with the aid of the fingers and an abacus (8:
36–37).

With the Greeks' pride in physical excellence, gymnastics
may have been the most esteemed of the three studies pursued by Athenian boys. In any event, parents appear to have
selected the paedotribe with more than ordinary care (11:
127). And he may actually have been somewhat more accomplished than his co-workers (34:307). Gymnastics like
music was not specialistic in its aims (7:73). It was designed
rather to promote all around bodily development, physical
strength and endurance, ease and grace of movement, and
skill in expression. The palaestra, where the boys received
their gymnastic training, appears to have represented a gradual elaboration of the playground. "When fully developed,"
says Woody, it "furnished privacy, protection against bad
weather, a dressing room, storage space for oil, sand, specially
constructed baths, perhaps also a place for dust with which
to sprinkle and rub the body, and a *dromos* or racecourse,
though some lacked this feature" (34:307).

Since the ages of the boys who frequented the palaestra
extended over a considerable range—normally from seven to
fifteen—a distinction appears to have been made between the
exercises designed for the younger (ages seven to eleven) and
the older (ages eleven to fifteen) boys. Those for the former
seem to have been restricted to a varied assortment of plays
and games, and to running and jumping; while those for the
latter included, in addition to running and jumping, also such
heavier exercises as wrestling, boxing, throwing the discus

and the javelin, and, in some cases, pancratium. Swimming may likewise have been taught quite generally (22:141–143; 34:307–309).

At age fifteen, and probably appreciably earlier in the case of the poorer classes, the Athenian boy's elementary education came to a close. From age seven on he had regularly frequented the several teachers, always in the company of the proverbial pedagogue. His teachers, mostly metics, had been people who ranked low on the social scale. The school day had been long and discipline strict. He had ostensibly pursued only three subjects but somehow managed to emerge as a well-rounded and integrated individual (5:66–67). Now for the first time he was free from the surveillance of the pedagogue (6:73). What he did during the next two or three years—that is, until age eighteen—depended upon his economic status. If he belonged to the poorer classes he engaged in some remunerative occupation; if he belonged to the well-to-do he spent most of his time in one of the public gymnasiums perfecting himself in the physical exercises begun in the Palaestra, and undertaking new ones (2:20; 22:148). He was now free, if he wished, to specialize under the direction of gymnasts and thus prepare himself for participation in athletic contests. For this he had of course to pay a fee. Apart from such special coaching services, the facilities of the gymnasium were free to Athenians—adults as well as youths. And they appear to have made generous use of them (11:141–142).

The gymnasium was supported and controlled by the state. The chief official in charge of it—the Gymnasiarch—was one of the wealthiest and most respected citizens (34:312). Provided with spacious parklike grounds and buildings, it carried on a broad and varied program ranging from the basically athletic to free discussions and public lectures (7:159–162; 11:135–141; 34:312–315). As a result, the boys who were receiving their advanced gymnastic training were exposed to many broadening influences. This, together with the fact that they were now free to attend the popular assembly, the theatre, and courts, probably explains in a large measure the absence of provisions for direct intellectual instruction (6:74–75).

"How effective might be the informal education got from this participation in adult affairs," says Boyd, "will be evident when the character of the Athenian youth's environment is considered. As he went along the streets he saw on every side products of the noblest art the world had known. Day by day he might hear the discussions of men of apt speech and wide experience on political questions, in the settlement of which they had a personal share; and in the springtime he might take his appointed place in the theatre of Dionysus, and witness from morning till night the performance of the tragedies presented in competition for the prize given annually for tragic poetry. Surely there never was an age that made a richer or more varied appeal to the adolescent" (2:20).

Not too much is known about the last two years of the Athenian youth's education—as far as the Old Athenian period is concerned. It was presumably designed to prepare him for military duties and for initiation into full-fledged citizenship. Until rather recently most writers on Greek education assumed that the Ephebic College program was ancient and had been in effect during the Old Athenian period. According to this—to mention only the bare essentials—the young Athenian became an *ephebus* at age eighteen. Upon the establishment of the authenticity of his age and parentage, his name was inscribed in the register of his *deme*. He now had ahead of him two years of military training at government expense—one devoted to drill in the use of arms and in military tactics near Athens, and the other given over to garrison and patrol activities on the frontiers of Attica (9:24; 22:151).

During these two years the ephebi worked under the supervision of carefully selected guardians and trainers, and they received in addition to basic military training, a certain amount of instruction in religion and patriotism, primarily through a visitation of temples and participation in religious and national festivals (34:319–320). At the beginning of the second year of their training the ephebi paraded through the streets of Athens and appeared before the assembled citizens, and upon being armed with a shield and a spear, they took the following oath:

"I will never disgrace these sacred arms, nor desert my companions in the ranks, but will fight for the temples and public property, alone and with others. I will leave my fatherland, not less, but greater and better, than I received it. I will obey those who may at any time be in power, and both the existing laws and those which the people may unanimously make, and, if any one seeks to annul the laws or does not obey them, I will not allow him, but will defend them both alone and with others. I will honor the religion of my fatherland; let the gods, Agraulos, Enyalios, Ares, Zeus, Thallo, Auxo, and Hegemone bear witness" (34:319).

Actually, as Woody shows in some detail, a variety of considerations force the conclusion that the Ephebic College system did not exist before 335 B.C. (34:315–316). Some features of it—the oath, for example—may be ancient, and the system may have evolved by degrees over a long period of time. However, be that as it may, there are strong indications that military training, to the extent that it may have been carried on in advance of the ephebic system, was a private responsibility and not a state function. Indeed, the introduction of the compulsory ephebic program appears to have represented more than anything else a deliberate attempt on the part of Athens to check its military decadence after the defeat at Chaeronaea. The setting up of compulsory ephebic training by the state, says Woody, "marked the termination of reliance upon strength and loyalty developed through individual freedom, initiative, and choice. What life in a corrupt, selfish society no longer could confer, was now to be attempted by state officials" (34:317).

The New Athenian Education

The old Athenian education, with which we have been concerned thus far, did not make way for the *new* in sudden or abrupt fashion. It had served the Athenians well as long as they remained a provincial and self-sufficient people—a people committed to action rather than to reflection. When, in the post-Persian War era, and in some respects appreciably before that, new conditions over which the Athenians had no control induced a far-reaching cultural reorientation, the old educational practices lost much of their relevancy and had to be revised and supplemented. While these changes were effected by degrees, the new education as such was certainly, as Woody observes, well under way by the middle of the fifth century B.C., and it was to remain in force to the Macedonian conquest in 338 B.C. (34:285).

The conditions which were primarily responsible for Athenian cultural reorientation were fundamental, philosophical, political, and economic developments. As already noted, Athens was traditionally given to action rather than to reflection and speculation. The first native born philosopher was Socrates (469–399 B.C.), and he was executed in a frenzy of post-war hysteria. Even so, Athens could not in the long run ward off the influence of the philosophical developments that had gotten under way in Ionia and elsewhere beginning with the late seventh century B.C. And the philosophers, it must be borne in mind, were generally skeptical of the orthodox theology and critical of the traditional mores (12:97). The most outspoken of them—Xenophanes, born about the middle of the sixth century B.C., and Empedocles, born some sixty years later—openly declared that men had created the gods in their own images (12:38, 71). Xenophanes further took particular delight in hurling invectives against such cherished Greek idols as the athletic cult with its attendant worship of physical strength at the expense of intelligence (12:37). To complicate the situation, the philosophers failed to agree on such basic issues as the trustworthiness of the senses and the reliability of reason. The net outcome of all this was that Athens began to lose its old moorings and drifted increasingly toward skepticism and doubt.

The political and economic developments of the post-Persian War period strongly reinforced this trend. At the close of the war, Athens emerged as the leader of Ionian Greece, and shortly thereafter became the Mecca of the Greek world. Trade and commerce increased phenomenally. Foreigners came to Athens in large numbers, bringing with them diverse customs and beliefs. Democracy was extended to the limit, and opened up new opportunities for individual careers (9:25–26). For the first time in history philosophers were welcome. Pericles' Athens, as Durant observes, was captivated by philosophy, and discussion ran riot. "No age until the Renaissance would know such enthusiasm again" (10:349). In the wake of all this, emerged a pronounced sense of relativity. Different standards, beliefs, and institutions seemed to be working equally well in different settings and backgrounds—there appeared to be nothing ultimate or absolute about any of them (12:100–101).

By the middle of the fifth century B.C. the Athenians had thus drifted far from their ancient moorings. Much of their traditional solidarity was gone, and with the passing of this, there was, as Davidson stresses, no escape from individualism (6:80–81). And a rampant individualism was bound to have far-reaching effects upon education. "The dominant art," says Fuller, "was now the art of worldly success, and instruction in this became the Alpha, and only too often the Omega, of Education" (12:101).

As might be expected, the new individualistic order affected education on the advanced and higher levels much more than on the elementary. In fact, higher education emerged for the first time as a direct consequence of it. On the elementary level the most conspicuous change appears to have called for a rather clear-cut differentiation between the teaching of music and the teaching of letters. Under the old regime the teacher of music—sometimes possibly with an assistant—had been responsible for both subjects. Now, each was placed in charge of a different teacher. The significance of this change lay in the fact that it prepared the way for different emphasis upon these subjects. And, due to the fact that the new conditions placed a premium upon literary achievements, the emphasis shifted increasingly from music to letters. When as a further result of changing conditions, gymnastics began to lose much of its onetime appeal, the teaching of letters—reading, writing, and counting—came to be the primary function of education on the elementary level (2:22–23; 5:66, 70).

As noted earlier, during the old Athenian period elementary education terminated at age fifteen. At this point the sons of the poorer classes went to work, while those of the well-to-do continued to improve themselves at the gymnasiums. There were no provisions for intellectual training apart from public lectures and free discussions. It was on this level, and beyond it, that the new education was to make its first great inroads upon the traditional order. Its protagonists were of course the sophists. The latter, as already noted, were wandering scholars—mainly from the colonies in Asia Minor and Magna Graecia—who came to Athens and gave instructions for fees. Their chief purpose was to prepare young men for public careers. While such preparation naturally called for extensive training in speech—grammar, rhetoric, and oratory,—the sophists were anything but coaches in the technicalities of speech. They were for the most part keen and critical students of the changing social order in which they

found themselves (34:425), and as such desirous of imparting
a sound basic education (8:49–50). Accordingly, their instruction—even though no two followed the same program—extended over a wide range of subjects. Although admittedly
thoroughgoing skeptics and individualists, "they were not,
however," as Dobson puts it, "conspirators against morality:
they merely professed to teach what they described as 'virtue,'
that is, the quality which will enable a man to make a success
in life, especially in public life" (8:52).

"Essentially," says Woody, "the new learning represented
an extension of education on a higher and broader plane than
had been known by the old order. It was informative, critical,
destructive, and constructive. The sanctions of the old mores
that comfortably fitted the old city were giving way. Athens
was coming of age intellectually" (34:425).

As might be expected, this type of education made a deep
appeal to young Athenians. They deserted the gymnasiums
and eagerly sought out the sophists (8:50). Only the guardians of the old order expressed fear and apprehension (5:68).
As a result, the sophists' conquest of Athens was rapid and
thoroughgoing. Protagoras, the first and ablest of them, arrived in Athens about 450 B.C. and promptly became a conspicuous figure in the Periclean circle. Georgias, his closest
rival from the standpoint of ability, arrived in 427 B.C., just
in time to become a brilliant participant in the closing phase
of the Periclean age (12:105). By the close of the fifth century
B.C. the sophists had completed their conquest of Athens. As
Boyd puts it, "the new studies introduced and developed by
them had become an accepted part of Athenian education,"
and the Athenians were now ready to launch their own system of advanced and higher education (2:23). In fact, Socrates
(469–399 B.C.), the first native-born philosopher, who is himself often classed as a sophist, had already practically arrived
at the end of his teaching career.

In contrast with the sophists who had carried on their instruction informally without any attempt to institutionalize it, the new Athenian system took the form of systematic schools. Two rather separate and distinct types of these— which incidentally were to persist for centuries—got under way at the beginning of the fourth century B.C.—the rhetorical and the philosophical. The former was to continue, on a higher plane, the sophist tradition of preparing young men for public careers; the latter was to elaborate the philosophical tradition initiated by Socrates (9:43–44).

The first of the rhetorical schools was established by Isocrates near the Lyceum about 390 B.C. He had studied with Georgias and had so much in common with the abler sophists that he has frequently been classed as a sophist (2:25; 21:92). Be that as it may, authorities generally rate him as a man of remarkable talent, vision, and integrity. He was not only a brilliant teacher of rhetoric and oratory, but also a keen student of the political and social problems of this time, and with it all a pan-Hellenic figure of note (4:568–569). His instructional program was well organized and extended over some four years (2:25). He considered its influence upon the soul to be comparable to that of gymnastics upon the body (8:84). He drew his students—among whom were the foremost future politicians and statesmen—from the entire Greek world (11:186, 190; 21:93). The rhetorical school tradition which he founded was to persist through Hellenistic times and exert a strong influence upon subsequent Roman education.

The first of the philosophical schools growing out of the Socratic tradition was the Academy founded by Plato about 386 B.C. (9:45). Its instructional program, given over largely to philosophy and mathematics, was no less thorough and exacting than that of Isocrates' rhetorical school (5:72). However, its purpose differed strikingly—it was not preparation for public service, but rather the discovery of truth. As Boyd observes, due to the abstract and speculative character of the work carried on by Plato, his students must have been both more mature and fewer in number than those of Isocrates (2: 25–26).

Three additional philosophical schools were established toward the close of the fourth century B.C.—the Lyceum founded by Aristotle in 335 B.C., the Stoa founded by Zeno in 308 B.C., and the school of Epicurus founded in 306 B.C. The instructional program of the Lyceum, although by no means excluding philosophy, placed tremendous emphasis upon natural science, the study of which was initially at least greatly facilitated by grants from Alexander the Great (5:72). That the Lyceum achieved early and great success is, as Boyd observes, attested not only by the vast amount of scientific work which it turned out but also by the fact that its enrollment presumably reached two thousand under Theophrastus, the immediate successor of Aristotle (2:48). And it had of course a long period ahead of it.

In their organization, the Stoic and the Epicurean schools did not differ appreciably from the Academy and the Lyceum. In their instructional emphases, however, they were more concerned with human conduct and less with logic and metaphysics. In their general philosophical orientation the two groups differed rather sharply, the Stoics leaning heavily upon Socrates and Plato, and the Epicureans upon Democritus. The Stoics stressed the reasonableness of nature and urged conformity to its dictates (5:73). The Epicureans, by way of contrast, looked upon the universe as mechanistic and governed by chance rather than by reason, and in keeping with this, stressed the avoidance of pain (including fear) and the quest of happiness (of which understanding is the highest). To this end, philosophy should be man's chief guide (5: 73; 10:646–648). Both of these schools persisted for centuries, and were destined to play conspicuous roles in Roman times.

The Rise of Educational Theory

One of the extremely significant outgrowths of the new Athenian education was the rise of educational theory. As Boyd observes, "theorizing about education is uncommon" (2:26). Most societies content themselves with the rationalization of their practices. When theorizing actually does get under way it is usually instigated by major cultural changes that call for far-reaching readjustments. Boyd feels that this happened only three times in the history of European civilization—in the Greek period, during the Renaissance (following the Middle Ages), and immediately before and after the French Revolution (2:26).

As noted earlier, by the middle of the fifth century B.C. Athens had drifted far from its ancient moorings. It was deluged with skepticism and individualism. To make matters still worse, the loss of its empire by the close of the century wrecked its political prestige and threatened its economic security. By the opening of the fourth century B.C. it was confronted by a crisis of the first order. Politically and economically it managed to stage, for the time being at least, an almost miraculous recovery. A thoroughgoing moral reorientation presented a more difficult problem.

And this was the problem that called the educational theorists into action. Significantly enough, both of the two major theorists—Plato and Aristotle—betook themselves to Utopia instead of confronting the actual situation (34:421). And neither of them had admittedly any influence upon the contemporary scene (9:42–43). Socrates before them had been more realistic. The same thing was true of Isocrates (5:79). Xenophon scarcely deserves mention since he was little more than a special pleader for the Spartan system (5:78).

An analysis of the educational proposals set forth by Plato in the Republic and the Laws and by Aristotle in the Ethics and the Politics is beyond the scope of this discussion. Suffice it to note their approaches to the solution of the basic problem that confronted Athens at this time—"the reconciliation of individual liberty with social stability and welfare" (9:32). Socrates had accepted the sophist pronouncement that man is the measure of all things, but as Duggan points out, with the reservation that this is true of what is universal, rather than individual, in man. In other words, he had found the solution to the problem under consideration "in a morality based upon knowledge, the elements of which exist in the consciousness of every man," and he had elaborated a method for the discovery and formulation of such knowledge. "Knowing the right," he assumed, would "be followed by doing the right" (9:31–32).

Plato accepted Socrates' position regarding the relationship between knowledge and virtue, and then proceeded to modify it through a critical examination of the nature of knowledge. As noted earlier, Plato found the Heraclitean sensory flux an inadequate explanation of reality, and posited behind this a universal order of absolute and unchanging entities consisting of forms or ideas. The latter alone were real, the objects and experiences perceived through the senses being mere shadows of, or approximations to, them. The universal order of absolute and unchanging entities lay beyond the reach of sense perception and could be apprehended only subjectively through contemplation. Moreover, only philosophers were capable of such contemplation. The rank and file of individuals—such as Socrates had questioned—could do no more than form opinions, and the concepts derived from such questioning would be no more than generalized opinions.

There thus existed for Plato an absolute and changeless moral order that had only to be apprehended and put into effect by philosophers. To apprehend this order and put it into effect would solve the basic problem of Athens and the Greek states generally, namely: "the reconciliation of individual liberty with social stability and welfare" (9:32). Plato attempted it—in Utopia.

Aristotle rejected Plato's theory of reality. He accepted his changeless forms or ideas, but not as things apart from the sensible world of experience. On the contrary, he regarded them as an integral part of it. They could not exist apart from matter any more than matter could exist apart from them (12: 176–177). Aristotle thus found himself confronted by real phenomena—the objects and experiences of the sensible world consisting of forms and matter. These could be studied and governing principles deduced from them. It was the province of science and philosophy to discover such principles—to obtain real knowledge.

Aristotle also rejected Socrates and Plato's position regarding the relationship between virtue and knowledge. For Aristotle virtue was an accompaniment of action rather than of knowledge (9:40). Everything has its peculiar function, and its well-being depends upon the extent to which it acts in conformity with that function. The greatest good is happiness, and man may achieve it by acting in accordance with his peculiar function—reason. Action in accordance with reason is characterized by moderation; hence, the doctrine of virtue as the golden mean (12:209).

Ethics embodies the principles of individual happiness, and politics those of collective happiness (10:534). The greatest good for the individual is self-realization, but not in terms of rank individualism. Self-regard, to the extent that its goal is rational self-realization, is indispensable, but it must be balanced by regard for the interests of other individuals and the state (26:91). Since man is a social creature that can realize its potentialities only in society, and the state is the goal of human social evolution, the individual and the state are so inextricably intertwined that there can be no conflict between the interests of the two.

Aristotle thus would solve the problem of reconciling individual liberty with social stability and welfare by an appeal to reason.

Hellenistic Education

In dealing with the educational developments of the Hellenistic period we shall merely touch upon a few highlights. As Butts observes, by the close of this period elementary education was largely in the hands of the *grammatist* who taught reading and arithmetic. Music and gymnastics played negligible roles. Elementary education was thus basically literary, and it was to remain such for a long time to come. Advanced or secondary education in turn was in charge of the *grammaticus* who taught grammar and rhetoric, and occasionally arithmetic and geometry. Music and gymnastics had lost their onetime popularity (5:70–71).

The Ephebic College which had been established in 335 B.C. also was losing its original status. Even before the close of the fourth century B.C. the program was reduced to one year and was no longer compulsory. With this, the enrollment dropped from approximately one thousand to some twenty or thirty. And presently foreigners were to be admitted. The program as such experienced significant changes. Physical training for military purposes became increasingly perfunctory, and the gymnastic exercises lost their onetime rigorousness. Moreover, literary and philosophical studies were making increasing inroads upon the program (34:325–326).

The philosophical schools—sometimes rather loosely referred to as the University of Athens—persisted under varying vicissitudes not only through the Hellenistic age, but far beyond into the Christian era. Hadrian (A.D. 76–138) recognized and endowed all of them. In the end they succumbed by degrees to the growing popularity of the rhetorical schools. The Academy, however, continued to function until its suppression by Justinian in A.D. 529 (2:48–49; 5:74).

Meanwhile, other centers of higher learning had arisen in various parts of the Hellenistic world—notably at Alexandria, Pergamum, Antioch, and Rhodes. While these at no time threatened Athens' supremacy as a teaching center, they surpassed it by degrees in research activities. The most illustrious of them was of course the one at Alexandria which was founded by the Ptolemies at the beginning of the third century B.C. It included the library and the museum. The former —the greatest library of ancient times—may ultimately have comprised as many as 700,000 manuscripts of various kinds (2:50). The latter—a brotherhood of scholars—included in its roster the names of the foremost scientific, literary, philosophical, and mathematical geniuses of the age (2:51).

BIBLIOGRAPHY

1. Barnes, Harry E., The History of Western Civilization, Volume I. New York: Harcourt, Brace and Company, 1935.
2. Boyd, William, The History of Western Education. London: Adam and Charles Black, 1947.
3. Burn, A. R., Minoans, Philistines, and Greeks. New York: Alfred A. Knopf, 1930.
4. Bury, J. B., A History of Greece, Second Edition. New York: Modern Library, Random House, 1913.
5. Butts, R. Freeman, A Cultural History of Education. New York: McGraw-Hill Book Company, 1947.
6. Davidson, Thomas, The Education of the Greek People. New York: D. Appleton and Company, 1894.
7. Davis, William S., A Day in Old Athens. Boston, New York: Allyn and Bacon, 1914.
8. Dobson, J. F., Ancient Education and Its Meaning To Us. New York: Longmans, Green and Company, 1932.
9. Duggan, Stephen, A Student's Textbook in the History of Education. Third Edition. New York: Appleton-Century-Crofts, 1948.
10. Durant, Will, The Life of Greece. New York: Simon and Schuster, 1939.
11. Freeman, Kenneth, Schools of Hellas. London: Macmillan and Company, 1912.
12. Fuller, B. A. G., A History of Philosophy, I. New York: Henry Holt and Company, 1945.
13. Glotz, Gustave, The Aegean Civilization. New York: Alfred A. Knopf, 1925.
14. Glotz, Gustave, Ancient Greece at Work. New York: Alfred A. Knopf, 1926.
15. Graves, Frank P., A History of Education—Before the Middle Ages. New York: The Macmillan Company, 1914.
16. Gulick, C. P., The Life of the Ancient Greeks. New York: D. Appleton and Company, 1902.

17. Hoebel, E. A., Man in the Primitive World. New York: McGraw-Hill Book Company, 1949.

18. Kenyon, F. G., Books and Readers in Ancient Greece and Rome. Oxford: at the Clarendon Press, 1932.

19. Kroeber, A. L., Anthropology. New York: Harcourt, Brace and Company, 1948.

20. Langer, W. L. (Editor), Encyclopedia of World History. Boston: Houghton Mifflin Company, 1948.

21. Mahaffy, J. P., Old Greek Education. New York: Harper and Brothers, 1901.

22. Moore, Ernest C., The Story of Instruction. New York: The Macmillan Company, 1936.

23. Robinson, C. E., A Short History of Greece. New York: Pantheon Books, 1948.

24. Smith, C. E. and Case, M. L., A Short History of Western Civilization. Boston: D. C. Heath and Company, 1948.

25. Swain, Joseph W., The Ancient World, Volume One. New York: Harper and Brothers, 1950.

26. Thilly, Frank, A History of Philosophy. New York: Henry Holt and Company, 1914.

27. Thorndike, Lynn, A Short History of Civilization. New York: F. S. Crofts and Company, 1926.

28. Trever, Albert A., History of Civilization, Volume I, The Ancient Near East and Greece. New York: Harcourt, Brace and Company, 1936.

29. Turner, Ralph, The Great Cultural Traditions, Volume I, The Ancient Cities. New York: McGraw-Hill Book Company, 1941.

30. Ullman, B. L., Ancient Writing and Its Influences. New York: Longmans, Green and Company, 1932.

31. Wallbank, T. Walter and Taylor, A. E., Civilization—Past and Present, Volume I. New York: Scott, Foresman and Company, 1949.

32. Webster, Hutton, History of Civilization—Ancient and Medieval. Boston: D. C. Heath and Company, 1947.

33. Wilkins, Thomas, Life and Education in Greece. London: Strahan and Company, 1873.

34. Woody, Thomas, Life and Education in Early Societies. New York: The Macmillan Company, 1949.

CHAPTER VII

The Rise of Roman Culture

Prehistoric Peoples and Cultures

SKELETAL remains and artifacts attest the presence of both Paleolithic and Neolithic peoples throughout much of Italy. The latter were appreciably more prevalent than the former. They were to supply the Mediterranean base of Italy's subsequent population (22:15; 25:13–14). Near the beginning of the second millennium B.C. successive waves of Indo-European peoples began to enter Italy from the northeast. The earliest ones settled in the northern lake regions. They were lake-dwellers whose culture came to be known as the Palafitte. The group which followed them settled in the Po Valley. They were farmers and herdsmen who lived in pile-supported villages, used bronze, and cremated the dead. In their social organization they had already advanced beyond the family to the clan. Their artifacts and remains are known as the Terremara culture (25:14–15).

Near the end of the second millennium B.C. additional Indo-European invaders—the so-called Italic peoples—began to enter Italy from the northeast. They spread throughout most of the Italian peninsula and Sicily, and, as they did so, absorbed the earlier immigrants and the Mediterranean peoples. They, too, were farmers and herdsmen. Their settlements were fortified villages. Although bronze was in extensive use, they smelted iron and fabricated improved tools. Their culture is known as the Villanovan. By the beginning of historic times the Italic peoples had split into three fairly

150

distinct groups, each with its own dialect—the Samites to the south, the Latins near the center, and the Umbrians toward the north and center (2:256–257; 23:131–132; 25:15–16; 26: 498–501).

The Etruscans and the Greeks

Meanwhile, by the beginning of historic times two additional peoples—the Etruscans and the Greeks—had established themselves in Italy. Both brought with them eastern Mediterranean cultures that were to have far-reaching effects upon Italian cultural developments. The Etruscans—still a rather obscure people (11:5; 24:11)—appear to have migrated from Asia Minor about 900 B.C. (18:68). Subsequently, they gained control of the entire Po Valley and expanded southward into Latium and Campania. With the beginning of the fifth century B.C. they went into rapid decline (25:18; 24:13). However, despite their relatively brief dominance, they made an abiding impression upon Italian culture. Among other things, they introduced the strong city-state, and made significant contributions to architecture, engineering, metallurgy, agriculture, industry, trade, and the arts (12:25; 11:6; 25:22–23). Before 700 B.C. they borrowed the Greek alphabet and by degrees passed it on to the Italic peoples (24:12; 26: 522). And they were of course the rulers of early Rome for a century or more. As evidenced by representations in their elaborate tombs, life among them appears to have been both strenuous and gay (11:6–7). Their script has not yet been deciphered but the content of the numerous brief inscriptions that have come down to us seems to be clearly associated with burial practices (25:19).

Greek colonization of southern Italy and Sicily began early in the eighth century B.C. and continued to the end of the sixth. On the coast of Italy the settlements extended from Cumae on the west to Tarentum. In Sicily they reached around the eastern two-thirds of the island, with Syracuse as the chief center. Further expansion was blocked, partly by the Samites, the Etruscans, and the Carthaginians, and partly by internal dissension. With Rome, Greek relations were generally friendly—in fact they assisted Latium in ridding itself of Etruscan rule. And with the setting up of the republic, Greek, rather than Etruscan, cultural influences were to mold Roman culture (25:23–24; 24:14–16).

The Rise of Rome

The site on which ancient Rome arose was on the south bank of the Tiber some fifteen miles inland. When the Latins took over the plain of Latium—which extended from the lower Tiber to the Alban Hills—in early Villanovan times, they settled in villages on scattered hilltops and farmed the surrounding regions. From time to time groups of such villages coalesced to form cities. Seven of these so-called hills stood in fairly close proximity on the south bank of the Tiber, and on one of these—the Palatine—Rome appears to have originated (26:499).

According to tradition, Rome was founded in 753 B.C. However, the Roman account of the founding and early history of Rome is so enmeshed with legend that it is impossible to set an accurate date for the founding of the city (4:33). Archeological evidence shows that there were permanent settlements by different peoples—Latins, Sabines, Etruscans— well in advance of 1000 B.C. It further appears to confirm the contention of the later historians that the first important settlement was made on the Palatine hill. The settlement seems to have been made in the tenth century by Latins. Subsequently, other hills were settled by different peoples. In the course of the eighth century B.C. several villages, including the one on the Palatine, appear to have formed a loose confederation known as the *Septimontium*. The first real city to bear the name Roma (Roma Quadrata) appeared late in the seventh century. It included all but one of the seven hills, and was surrounded by a stone wall (25:26–27; 4:33–35).

Toward the close of the seventh century Rome became a monarchy, and was for a century or more presumably ruled by Etruscan kings—the so-called Tarquins. Like all else in early Roman history, the accounts of this period are so involved with legend that historians are extremely guarded in their generalizations. However, there seems to be no doubt about the existence of Etruscan suzerainty during this period and the Etruscan origin of some of the later kings. It is also generally conceded further that this was an era of marked growth and expansion, of growing contact with the eastern Mediterranean and the Orient, and of far-reaching internal improvements. Socially, the differentiation between *patricians* and *plebeians* appears to have gotten well under way. The political organization, calling for an elected king, a council of nobles, and a popular assembly, was closely comparable to that of the Greek city-state (26:502–503).

The Early Republic

Late in the sixth century B.C.—according to tradition in 509 B.C.—the patricians expelled the Tarquins and set up a republic. At the head of this were two consuls elected annually from the patricians. They had equal powers, as in the case of the Spartan kings. There was provision, further, for the appointment of an emergency dictator for a period not to exceed six months (23:134–135). Next to the consuls stood the senate, consisting of three hundred patricians chosen by the consuls for life. Although initially an advisory body, the senate soon became the chief power in the state (25:59). Beyond this, there were two assemblies—the *comitia curiata* and the *comitia centuriata*. The functions of the former were negligible; those of the latter very important. Among other things, the comitia centuriata elected the consuls, passed upon their proposals, and had the power to declare war. Theoretically, every citizen was free to vote in the comitia centuriata. However, the voting arrangements were such that the casting of plebeian votes was reduced to a meaningless formality (23:136; 25:60–61). Since the patricians also controlled the influential priesthoods, the republic was at the outset a strictly aristocratic affair in which the plebeians had little or no voice (24:26).

Down through the early part of the third century B.C., the development of the republic revolved primarily about the conquest of Italy and the struggle for democracy. By 265 B.C. all of Italy south of the Po Valley was under Roman control, and by 287 B.C., with the passage of the Hortensian Law, the plebeians had gained substantial political and social equality with the patricians (23:134; 24:30–31; 28:157).

The details of the conquest of Italy need not detain us here. Suffice it to note that the conquest involved a long series of wars, and that it was in no way a planned affair. Rome simply fought for its existence. It repeatedly faced extinction, and hit in each case upon what seemed to be the next best course of action (24:23; 28:159–160). During the fifth century it barely managed to hold its own. Early in the fourth century, after the destruction of the Etruscan city of Veli, it was sacked and burned by the Gauls. After the dissolution of the Latin League in 238 B.C. it had the great advantage of being able to deal with each conquered group individually (23:140). Much of its subsequent success depended upon the strategic manner in which it handled this problem. After the defeat and final surrender of the Samites in 290 B.C. only Magna Graecia remained. By 270 B.C. this had yielded to Rome in its entirety. Five years later the last vestiges of Samite and Etruscan opposition had been subdued, and Rome was master of the Italian peninsula from the heel to Cisalpine Gaul (25:47).

As noted above, in the early days of the republic the patricians were in rather complete control of Roman affairs. The plebeians enjoyed few, if any, political and social rights. They had no protection against oppressive acts on the part of the patrician magistrates; they could be sold into slavery for debts, even when incurred in connection with compulsory military service; they had no share in making laws, and their voting in the assembly was a meaningless formality; the laws were written and administered at the caprice of the magistrates; admission to the senate, the magistrates, and the priesthood was denied them; they could not intermarry with the patricians; and they had no share in the public lands acquired through war (4:62–68; 26:504–512).

The struggle to correct these inequalities closely paralleled the campaigns for the conquest of Italy, and it probably would not have gotten very far without the latter. The patricians needed the fighting strength of the plebeians in these campaigns, and the plebeians made good use of the patricians' predicament. They repeatedly figuratively or literally walked out on them until they gained the concessions they wanted. Fortunately, as Cary observes, both sides usually displayed remarkably sane political judgment so that it was possible to carry the struggle through without civil war (8:117).

In any event, by 287 B.C. the plebeians had gained substantial equality with the patricians. The details regarding the successive concessions achieved by the plebeians are beyond the scope of this discussion. Suffice it to note some of the major gains. Early in the fifth century B.C. the plebeians succeeded in setting up their own extra-legal governmental agencies. These consisted first of several tribunes. Later they were augmented to include the tribal assembly (*comitia tributa*). The functions of the tribunes was to protect the plebeians against oppressive acts on the part of the patrician magistrates. The tribal assembly in turn had the power to draw up resolutions (plebiscites). At first these had the force of law only when approved by the senate; in the end they became mandatory without senate approval (2:270–271; 4:65, 67; 23:

137–138; 24:27–28). By the middle of the fifth century B.C. the plebeians succeeded in having the laws codified and published in the form of the now famous Twelve Tables. Shortly thereafter, the passage of the Canuleian Law legalized marriages between patricians and plebeians (25:70–71). In the course of the fourth century B.C. the plebeians by degrees gained access to various magistracies—the number of which had by this time reached considerable proportions,—and with these open to them, they could now make their way into the senate (2:271). By the end of the century they had been admitted to the chief priesthoods. Their greatest triumph came of course in 287 B.C. with the passage of the Hortensian Law which allowed measures (plebiscites) passed by the tribal assembly to become law without the approval of the senate or the *comitia centuriata*. This, as Trever puts it, made the *comitia tributa* the chief assembly for legislative purposes (25:73–74).

Rome was now, as Webster observes, a republic—a city-state in which the "citizens made the laws, elected the magistrates, disposed of the revenues, and decided questions of war and peace," but it was scarcely a democracy in the Greek sense. The citizens could not meet in assembly except upon the call of a magistrate, and when they did meet, they could not discuss the issues placed before them—they could only approve or disapprove (29:268).

The Conquest of the Mediterranean

Rome had no sooner conquered the Italian peninsula than the struggle with Carthage broke out. The First Punic War (264–241 B.C.) was the initial round in a contest that was to make it the undisputed master of the Mediterranean world in a little more than a century. As on earlier occasions, it appears to have entered upon this course of action without any deliberately formulated plan (23:143). The immediate objective was of course to gain control over Sicily. The close of the war found Rome in possession of Italy and in position to impose harsh peace terms. Shortly thereafter Rome conquered the Gauls in the Po valley and seized both Corsica and Sardinia (23:146). The Second Punic War (218–201) ended even more disastrously for Carthage, depriving it of Spain and leaving it virtually a vassal state (23:150). Its final destruction was to be deferred to the end of the Third Punic War (149–146 B.C.) when Rome had conquered the eastern Mediterranean.

Meanwhile, Rome—disturbed by the feuds and intrigues among the rulers of the Hellenistic states—turned eastward, and in 197 B.C., inflicted a decisive defeat upon the forces of Philip V of Macedon at Cynoscephalae. Philip now became an ally of Rome (25:105). In 148 B.C., after two more wars with Rome, Macedonia was organized as a Roman province (25:118).

With the defeat of Philip at Cynoscephalae the Greek city-states regained their freedom and became autonomous allies of Rome. However, they soon proved themselves quite incapable of abstaining from intrigue and strife. After repeated clashes, Rome lost patience, captured and burned Corinth, and made Greece—with the exception of Athens and Sparta both of which had cooperated—a dependency of Macedonia (4:115).

Shortly after the initial defeat of Philip, Antiochus III of Syria, the Seleucid king, provoked war with Rome (192–189 B.C.). After his final decisive defeat in the battle of Magnesia he was excluded from the Aegean and Asia Minor and became increasingly subject to Roman dictation (25:106). In 168 B.C. Egypt became a vassal of Rome. Somewhat later (133 B.C.), the King of Pergamum willed his kingdom to Rome. "By taking over Pergamum," says Trever, "the Romans had now established themselves firmly on both sides of the Aegean, and had secured a foothold for further eastward advance. The Aegean was henceforth a Roman lake. In the

course of a little over half a century, Rome, almost in spite
of herself, had expanded to three continents, and advanced
from sporadic intervention to the supreme control over the
East Mediterranean and the recognized dictator of policies
in Greece and the whole Hellenic East. The list of Roman
provinces was now Sicily (227), Sardinia and Corsica (227),
Hither and Farther Spain (197), Macedonia (148), Africa
(146), and Asia (129). Additional territories held by Rome,
but not yet provinces, were Greece (under Macedonia), Cisalpine Gaul, and Illyricum" (25:121).

From Republic to Empire

When Rome emerged from the protracted period of conquest it was quite unprepared to cope with the new conditions that confronted it. This was due to a variety of factors—
political, economic, and social. Politically, Rome was handicapped by its city-state outlook and the monopolization of
governmental powers by selfish senatorial oligarchy. Although
faced with the necessity of administering a vast empire, the
Romans developed little, if any, real notion of representative
government and large-scale federation (2:290–291; 25:156).
The treatment of the Italian allies, which had at first been
fairly liberal, actually deteriorated in the course of the conquest. They served in the Roman armies, but failed to share
appreciably in the spoils of war. The senate stubbornly refused to grant them citizenship until a serious revolt (90–88
B.C.) finally forced it to do so   (26:867, 878; 6:539). The
administration of the provinces was in the hands of irrespon-
sible governors and vicious tax-collectors. This in turn gave
rise to repeated rebellions and wars that helped to undermine
the foundations of the republic (4:122–126; 6:514–515; 26:
868; 29:277–278).

The senatorial oligarchy which was in large part responsible for these conditions was itself a product of the conquest.
The patrician senatorial aristocracy of the early republic had

on the whole been a high-minded and patriotic body. Although there were repeated clashes between this patrician body and the plebeians they managed somehow to iron out their differences without recourse to revolution, and, as noted earlier, by 287 B.C. the plebeians had won substantial equality with the patricians. During the conquest of the Mediterranean —due to the fact that the emergency demanded a unified central government—the senate took over most of the political powers of the plebeians. With the termination of the conquest it was not only unwilling to surrender them, but had undergone radical changes in composition and orientation. The patrician-plebeian senatorial nobility of the late republic was made up of families that traced their descent from magistrates. It was, as Trever observes, "a nobility of wealth and office-holding" that had by degrees degenerated into "an exclusive oligarchy interested only in preserving its own special privilege" (25:122–123). It monopolized all offices and controlled, along with the equestrian order—the businessmen and capitalists,—most of the wealth of Rome, including of course the spoils of war and the public lands (26:865–866).

The shortsighted and selfish orientation of the all-powerful senate was to have serious and far-reaching economic and social consequences. The spoils of war and the public lands naturally drifted into the hands of the privileged. Great landed estates, tilled by slaves, became the order of the day. The one-time ubiquitous small farm disappeared and its owner joined the swelling city proletariat. The latter was further augmented by native urban craftsmen and artisans replaced by slaves, and by hordes of freedmen from the provinces.

The political and social changes referred to above inevitably affected the structure of Roman society. In early republican times there were, apart from a limited number of slaves, only two classes—the patrician senatorial aristocracy, and the plebeian farmers and craftsmen. By the middle of the second century B.C. Roman society was headed by the powerful patrician-plebeian senatorial nobility. Immediately below this was the equestrian order—the businessmen and capitalists of Rome. These two classes owned and controlled most of the wealth. At the base, above the great horde of slaves, was the urban proletariat consisting primarily of dispossessed Romans, legionnaires, and freedmen from the provinces (25: 134–136, 155; 26:871–874).

The revolution that was now getting under way (133 B.C.) was basically a struggle between the people and the senatorial oligarchy. The latter monopolized the governmental powers so completely, and so thoroughly in its own interests, that they could no longer serve as instruments of the general welfare. The senatorial oligarchy was of course a much more clearly defined group than the people. After the time of the Gracchi the two contending factions became generally differentiated in terms of the *populares* and the *optimates*, the former comprising the proletariat and its sympathizers and the latter the senatorial oligarchy and elements temporarily allied with it. The leadership of the populares came, however, usually, from liberal optimates, and the populares were normally helpless without the cooperation of the equestrian order. As the revolution progressed, other elements became operative, among them ambitious individuals and military leaders (24:64–65).

The revolution began in 133 B.C. when Tiberius Gracchus was elected tribune on a platform of social reform. It ended in 31 B.C. with Octavian's defeat of Anthony in the battle of Actium (11:208). Since the details of it are beyond the scope of this discussion, we shall merely bring a few of the major episodes into perspective. Tiberius Gracchus' measure—in so far as it concerned agrarian reform—appears to have represented little more than an attempt to put into effect the provisions of the Licinian laws of 267 B.C. Yet it aroused such violent opposition that he was speedily put to death by a sen-

atorial mob (18:91; 26:875). Gaius Gracchus, elected tribune
in 123 B.C., re-elected in 122, and defeated in 121, submitted
a stronger and more comprehensive reform program including his brother's earlier agrarian measure. In the end he, too,
was either slain or driven to suicide (18:92; 25:162–168).

Among other things, the Gracchi had taught the people the
need of a leader in their struggle against the senate. This, as
Breasted observes, presently led to the notion of one-man
rule for Rome (6:536). And before long Rome was actually in
the grip of a civil war led by rival contenders for power. The
struggle between Marius and Sulla—both of them successful
generals, the former representing the populares and the latter
the optimates—was set off by the necessity of appointing a
general to lead an army against Mithridates VI, King of
Pontus, who was endangering Roman security in the East. In
88 B.C. Sulla was elected consul and entrusted with the command of the army. Thereupon, the Marian faction secured
the passage of a law by the assembly transferring the command to Marius. When Sulla returned from an enforced absence, he challenged the legality of the act, marched upon
Rome, banished Marius, and introduced reforms which
greatly strengthened the position of the senate (4:158).

Shortly after he had left for the East, the Marian faction
returned to power. Marius was recalled and elected consul for
the seventh time. Sulla's reform measures were revoked, his
property confiscated, and many leading senators murdered.
Marius himself died shortly after his re-election as consul (4:
160).

When Sulla finally returned to Italy in the spring of 83 B.C.
with an army of seasoned veterans he speedily annihilated the
opposing forces one after another, and then marched upon
Rome which he took over toward the end of the following
year (18:94). The revenge which he inflicted upon his political
opponents by way of proscriptions beggars description (23:
166; 4:161). Then, he managed to have himself appointed

dictator for an unlimited period—ostensibly to enact needed legislation. The measures which he enacted were of course designed to re-establish and perpetuate the moribund senatorial order (4:162; 23:167). He resigned his dictatorship in 79 B.C. and died a year later.

Agitations against Sulla's obnoxious laws began shortly after his death, and within less than ten years all of them had been nullified (24:68). With the populares once more in power, the question of leadership became a burning issue. Whatever other qualifications a leader might now need, it was clear that he would have to be an able military commander (6:542). The major contenders for popular leadership turned out to be Pompey, Crassus, and Caesar. Pompey—who had formerly been allied with Sulla, but later embraced the cause of the populares—had several brilliant military victories to his credit (6:542–543; 24:68–69). Crassus had been in command of the final campaign against the slave insurrection led by Spartacus. He had amassed great wealth and was politically ambitious (23:169; 25:193–194). Caesar's career had not been particularly noteworthy thus far. He had held certain offices, was elected *pontifex maximus*, and then became governor of Farther Spain (24:70).

Circumstances now united the three into what is generally known as the First Triumvirate. When Pompey returned to Italy in 62 B.C. and dismissed his army he needed strong political support because the senate declined to confirm his plans for the East and refused to grant lands for his veterans. Crassus was in need of assistance to gain an important military command. And Caesar needed support for the consulship of 39. By pooling their resources the three became masters of Rome and each gained his own objective (23:172; 24:70; 25:207–208).

At the end of his consulship Caesar received the governorship of Cisalpine and Transalpine Gaul. He was to spend the next eight years (58–50 B.C.) in the conquest of this region, and thereby to become the military rival of Pompey. Meanwhile, factionalism became so rampant in Rome that the Triumvirate was in danger of dissolution. However, in 56 B.C. the triumvirs met at Luca and managed to renew it. Caesar's term as governor of Gaul was extended five years with the promise of the consulship immediately upon its expiration. Pompey and Crassus were to serve as consuls for another year. Thereafter, the former was to be in command of operations in Spain, and the latter was to direct the campaign against the Parthians. After the rout and death of Crassus in 53 B.C., Pompey and Caesar began to drift apart, and open conflict was imminent. Instead of assuming direct command in Spain, Pompey governed indirectly through his legates. This left him free to plot against Caesar in Rome (23:174). Moreover, he allied himself with the senate which had by this time become thoroughly apprehensive regarding Caesar's designs. Meanwhile, social chaos and political corruption had reached alarming proportions in Rome (25:222).

In 52 B.C. the senate illegally appointed Pompey as sole consul. This made him the first citizen—the supreme power in the state (25:223). His main problem now was to eliminate Caesar. This he hoped to achieve through his arrest and prosecution during the interval between the termination of his Gallic command (March, 49 B.C.) and the assumption of the consulship (January, 48 B.C.). Caesar did not want civil war and urged Pompey for legislation that would extend his command in Gaul to the time when he would be eligible to assume the consulship. Pompey refused, and shortly thereafter, in January 49, the senate declared Caesar a public enemy. Upon this, Caesar promptly crossed the Rubicon, marched southward, and entered Rome without opposition. Pompey and most of the senators fled to Greece (6:548; 18:97; 24:72; 25:224–226). After taking over the treasury and the machinery of government, Caesar defeated Pompey's commanders in Spain. Returning to Rome, he was elected consul for 48, and then set out in quest of Pompey whom he defeated at Pharsalus in 48 B.C. The latter fled to Egypt only to be slain upon his arrival. Caesar had followed him to Egypt, and then spent the winter of 47 with Cleopatra. Before returning to Rome in 46, he put down revolts in the East and in Africa (18:97–98; 23:176).

The Triumph and Dictatorship of Caesar

In July 46 Caesar celebrated a great triumph. The senate had voted him the dictatorship for ten years—in 44 it was to be extended for life (11:190–191). He was now a virtual monarch with powers comparable to those of any historic tyrant or dictator (25:233). However, in contrast with many who had gone before him, he was to use them humanely and intelligently. There were no proscriptions, and no discriminations against political opponents (25:231–232). His grasp of the problems confronting him was remarkable. He was, as Starr observes, above all else a logical and rational person (24:74–75). His executive capacity, likewise, was remarkable. He lived only five years after seizing Rome, and the bulk of his time was spent in campaigns. Yet the array of reforms which he achieved and planned was little short of miraculous (6:551; 11:192–194). Among other things, he took up agrarian reforms where the Gracchi had left them, undertook the economic rehabilitation of the urban proletariat, ameliorated the lot of the slaves, endeavored to revive Italian agriculture, encouraged industry and trade, promoted large-scale colonization projects, took steps to relieve debtors and check usury, stamped out political violence and lawlessness in Rome, set up a uniform system of municipal administration for Italy, placed the administration of the provinces on an honest and efficient basis, greatly extended the franchise wherever feasible, and reformed the calendar which was badly out of adjustment with the solar year (11:190–193; 25:235–238).

Caesar achieved his reforms without any overt modification

of the constitution. As Turner puts it, "no republican institutions were abolished, and no new institutions were created." He simply concentrated the various offices in himself and stretched the constitution to meet the exigencies of the situation in any given case (26:889). What Caesar's plans for the future may have been is not known. However, it is clear that he had no intention of restoring the republic. And he may have had in mind the establishment of a comprehensive world state (23:178; 24:75; 25:233; 26:889).

Be this as it may, his assumption of absolute power was not to go unchallenged by the vested interests. And it must also be borne in mind that Rome had a long republican tradition that was difficult to uproot. In any event, Caesar was assassinated on March 15, 44 B.C. That his short rule had brought relief to vast numbers is evidenced by the fact that his assassination was met by ominous silence rather than by popular acclaim as had been anticipated (23:179; 24:76).

The first result of Caesar's assassination was confusion—the conspirators had no immediate program of action. Then, Mark Anthony, Caesar's best friend and the remaining consul, stepped into the picture, seized Caesar's papers and funds, and prepared to act as his successor (25:243). However, he was shortly to be challenged by young Octavian,—Caesar's grand nephew, whom the latter had designated as his adopted son and chief heir. Octavian, although at first scorned and rebuffed by Anthony and the senate, quickly raised an army, marched on Rome, and had himself elected consul (23:180; 25:247).

Anthony, who had been in Gaul, now likewise prepared to march on Rome. Meanwhile, before hostilities actually broke out, the two commanders, along with Lepidus, met in conference near Bononia (November, 43), ironed out their differences, and formed what is known as the Second Triumvirate. The triumvirs took over the government of Rome in January 42. Partly to avenge the assassination of Caesar, and partly to raise funds to finance the campaign that lay ahead of them, they promptly inaugurated an orgy of proscriptions that rivaled Sulla's. Some three hundred senators and several thousand equestrians were murdered (25:248–249).

Later in 42 B.C., Anthony and Octavian crossed the Adriatic to put down the armies of the conspirators—Brutus and Cassius—who were rapidly gaining control over the East. The latter were defeated near Philippi, and thereupon committed suicide (25:251–252).

The triumvirs now divided the control of the Roman world between themselves. Anthony received the East, Octavian the West, Lepidus Africa. And Rome was held in common. Anthony, who had received by far the best deal, soon proved thoroughly incompetent and gradually lost the confidence of the West. Lepidus was eliminated shortly after the removal of the Triumvirate in 37 B.C. (23:181). Octavian, who had received the most difficult assignment, rose rapidly and by degrees became supreme in the West. Meanwhile, Anthony's entanglements, and subsequent marriage, with Cleopatra, along with the assignment of eastern provinces to her and her children, raised the suspicion that she might have designs upon Rome. Under these circumstances, Octavian—who had been at the breaking point with Anthony for some time—had no difficulty in persuading the senate to declare war against Cleopatra, and to use this as an excuse for a final showdown with Anthony. The two met in a naval engagement at Actium in 31 B.C. Anthony was defeated and fled to Egypt. The following summer, after the surrender of Greece and the East, Octavian invaded Egypt, and, upon the suicide of both Anthony and Cleopatra, annexed it to Rome. He was now in sole control of the Roman world (23:181; 24:78–79; 25:261–264).

The Early Empire

When Octavian returned to Rome in 29 B.C., the senate bestowed upon him the title *princeps*—first citizen of the state. As a result, the Roman government now became known as the Principate. A year later he was re-elected as consul. The following year (27 B.C.) he voluntarily resigned his powers to the senate and asked for the restoration of the republican constitution. The senate declined, and invested him instead with pro-consular powers for life. It further bestowed upon him the designation *Augustus* by which he was known thereafter. In 23 B.C., when he ceased to be consul, the senate granted him tribunician powers for life. As Pro-consul he was now commander of all the armies, and as tribune he had the veto power over all actions of the magistrates, the senate, and the assemblies. Beyond this, he was head of the state religion (23:186–187; 24:95–99; 25:307–310; 26:892–893).

There were thus no real limits to the powers of Augustus. However, he had the good sense to exercise them discreetly and under a constitutional guise. The governmental machinery remained intact, and to all appearances continued to function as usual. Nominally, the senate continued to exercise considerable power. It governed Italy and the provinces that were not under the direct jurisdiction of the *princeps*. The consulship, too, retained considerable dignity and honor. All in all, then, Augustus managed to function, superficially at least, within the republican framework and tradition—partly because of his own wishes, and partly for diplomatic reasons. This course of action won for him large-scale recognition and support (23:187–188; 24:96–98).

The era inaugurated by the Principate was to bring the Mediterranean world more than two centuries of practically uninterrupted peace and prosperity—an unprecedented state of affairs.

The reforms and constructive measures undertaken by Augustus cannot be detailed here. Suffice it to note that he reconstructed the Roman state in such masterly fashion that it was to endure in essentials for several centuries, concentrated on internal improvements and the strengthening of the frontiers rather than upon the further extension of the Empire (25:344), set up for the first time an efficient civil service system that proved to be a tremendous asset in the administration of the Empire (25:318), put the administration of the provinces on an honest and efficient basis (23:187–188), placed the army on a footing that was essentially professional and permanent (25:328–333), sought to revive agriculture and build up industry and trade (23:190–191), sponsored vast building and communications projects (23:193), gave a great impetus to literature and the arts (23:192), and tried almost fanatically to arrest a decadent moral order (11:221–227).

As Augustus approached the end of his long reign the problem of succession presented itself—a problem that was to plague Rome repeatedly in the future. Since Augustus' power represented, theoretically at least, a grant of the senate, he could not, as Trever observes, legally transmit it hereditarily (25:348). Moreover, he had no direct heir. Wishing, nevertheless, for a variety of reasons to keep the succession within the family line he hit upon the principle of nomination by the *princeps* and confirmation by the senate. Accordingly, he nominated his adopted stepson Tiberius who was promptly accepted by the senate (25:349–350).

Together, the four rulers who followed Augustus, either through descent or adoption,—Tiberius (14–37), Caligula (37–41), Claudius (41–54), and Nero (54–68)—are known as the Julio-Claudian emperors. Tiberius and Claudius were able rulers. Caligula and Nero, on the other hand, proved to be tragic failures. Nevertheless, the Principate was sufficiently strong to weather both of them without serious consequences.

With the death of Nero and the passing of the Julio-Claudian dynasty, the frontier legions seized control of the succession. As a result, the year 68–69 witnessed the accession of four emperors. Vespasian (69–79), the last of these, and his two sons—Titus (79–81) and Domitian (81–96)—are generally known as the Flavian emperors. Domitian proved to be an intelligent and able ruler. Titus' fame rests chiefly upon his generosity and popularity. Domitian was thoroughly despotic but exceptionally competent (11:285–294).

Upon the death of Domitian, the senate forestalled a repetition of earlier succession disorders by naming one of its own members—Nerva (96–98)—as emperor. Nerva and his successors—Trajan (98–117), Hadrian (117–138), Antoninus Pius (138–161), and Marcus Aurelius (161–180)—are known as the Antonine emperors (29:289; 26:901). Beyond Nerva, succession was regulated by the principle of adoption, which, as Trever observes, had much to do with the high caliber of these rulers (25:502–503).

Nerva's reign was brief, and, as Durant observes, the greatest service that he rendered Rome was the adoption of Trajan as his successor (11:408). Trajan and Hadrian were both exceptionally able men who put the welfare of the Empire above their own interests; both enjoyed pleasant relationships with the senate; and both were great builders. In their orientations they differed appreciably. Trajan was at heart a general and an imperialist. It was during his reign that the eastern frontiers were being extended beyond the Euphrates, and Dacia (Roumania) was conquered and annexed as a Roman province. Hadrian's interests were broad—intellectual, aesthetic, humanitarian, and cosmopolitan. In addition, he had a genius for practical administration. He abandoned Trajan's imperialistic policy, and concentrated instead upon internal improvements and frontier fortifications. He knew the provinces first hand and turned out to be Rome's ablest imperial administrator.

By way of contrast, his successor Antoninus Pius, although likewise an able ruler, remained at home. His neglect of the frontier problems was to have serious consequences during the reign of Marcus Aurelius—a true Stoic, and perhaps the most superb personality among ancient rulers. The latter, despite his strong inclinations for peaceful pursuits, had to spend most of his time defending the Empire against barbarian inroads (11:407–432; 23:202–209; 25:503–505). His son, Commodus (180–192), who succeeded him on a hereditary basis, proved to be thoroughly incompetent and vicious. With him, the Roman Empire entered upon its decline—an event to which we shall have occasion to refer only casually and incidentally (25:625–627).

Roman Cultural Achievements

With limited exceptions—as in law, to some extent in architecture, and in literature,—the Romans made no original contributions to culture. Their role was rather to assimilate, synthesize, and disseminate the cultural achievements of other peoples (2:258). How shall we account for their obvious lack of creativeness in philosophy, science, and art—areas within which the Greeks made their monumental contributions? Obviously not in biological terms, for the racial compositions of the two peoples were strikingly comparable (2:256). Nor will a geographic explanation suffice—the Greeks were as creative in the western Mediterranean as in the eastern. And we cannot of course place the blame upon a fanatical priesthood and a sacred book—the Romans had neither in the strict sense of the term (11:63; 20:113; 25:60).

The explanation must obviously be sought in cultural circumstances—in the forces that molded the core of Roman culture and gave it its basic premises. As Ruth Benedict observes, the leads which a people may follow and the interests which it may stress in the elaboration of its culture are extremely numerous and varied. Hence, choice and selection become imperative and inevitable—no culture would make sense without them. The forces or motives which may determine the leads to be followed and the interests to be stressed are themselves varied and unpredictable. But once a people has made its choice, once it has hit upon the basic premises of its culture, change is exceedingly difficult—the culture tends to maintain its integrity despite changing circumstances (3:23–24, 36).

The Romans started out as practical farmers, with no speculative, scientific, or artistic interests, and with not even enough imagination to develop a respectable mythology. And at heart the Romans remained farmers to the end (11:72; 26:907, 933–939).

Aside from being farmers, the Romans early became, by force of necessity, soldiers. From the beginning they were surrounded by hostile competitors and had no alternative but to fight or perish. In time they stumbled more or less inadvertently into conquest and became a ruling and plundering, rather than an industrial and mercantile, people. The farming and warfare orientation of the Romans was not conducive to the development of intellectual and artistic interests. It tended rather to promote an austere and practical outlook upon life. Their early family organization and their religious practices bear eloquent testimony to this. The same thing is true of Roman character as traditionally delineated.

The extended patriarchal family was the basic unit in early Roman social structure. It was really, as Durant puts it, a "miniature society," embracing "the father and the mother, their house and land and property, their children, their married sons, their grandchildren by these sons, their daughters-in-law, their slaves and clients," and containing within itself "the functions of family, church, school, industry, and government" (11:58). Within this group the authority of the *paterfamilias* was, except as gradually checked by evolving tradition, unlimited. Indeed, as Webster observes, among the societies featuring the patriarchal family system none has approximated Rome in the extreme subordination of wife and children to the father (29:264). With the development of the republic the extreme powers of the father declined of course and were gradually taken over by the state (2:260).

Roman Religion

The religion of the early Romans had reached the animistic stage—the stage embodying among other things the belief in spirits with which man needs to be on good terms,—and it was in transition to polytheism (2:312–314). The spirits, or numina, that invited propitiation were potentially legion. However, as might be expected, the practical Roman's first concern was with those having to do with family life and agricultural pursuits. Within the home religious rites centered particularly about the *hearth* presided over by Vesta, the storeroom guarded by the Penates, and the threshold under the protection of the two-faced Janus. The *paterfamilias* himself was the ward of a special Genius that promoted the welfare and continuity of the family (2:313). Then there was of course not a single event in the life-cycle of the members of the family that was not presided over by some spirit.

Other spirits that needed propitiation had to do with the family plot of land, especially in respect to its boundaries and productiveness. Beyond this, numerous rites and festivals were seasonal, and as such revolved about the agricultural cycle—from the preparation of the soil to the harvesting of the crops (2:312–314).

Very early, too, the scope of the spirits to be propitiated was extended to include those concerned with affairs of the state. As a result, a state cult sprang up alongside the family and farming cults. With this, there emerged by degrees a pantheon of major national gods and goddesses—among them, Jupiter, Mars, Saturn, Juno, Minerva, Venus, and Diana. In addition, there were such minor deities as Hercules, Mercury, Ops, and Bellona (11:61–63). In time, too, Rome borrowed and adapted to its needs most of the Greek gods. With the Empire came emperor worship, and a whole congeries of Oriental mystery cults.

The relationship between Romans and their deities was strictly practical—somewhat analogous to a contractual agreement between two parties (29:266; 24:21). Specifically, the Romans assumed that if they rigidly observed their obligations to the deities—in such matters as rituals, sacrifices, and festivals—the latter would reciprocate by granting them the favors they needed. Since all religious observances had to be conducted with meticulous care, priests were needed. In the family the *paterfamilias* served in this capacity. The administration of the state religion on the other hand was in the hands of priestly colleges which functioned under the leadership of the *pontifex maximus*. The constituents of these colleges did not, however, constitute a special class as in the ancient Orient, but were chosen from the citizenry as in the case of the magistrates (25:60; 29:265). Especially influential was the college of the nine *augurs* which determined the will of the gods through divination and auguries (2:315; 11:63–64).

Roman Character

Much has been said regarding early Roman character— some of it in praise and some in criticism. While the Roman patriotic tradition probably delineates it in far too glowing terms, there seems to be no doubt about certain homely virtues of the early Romans,—among them, industry, integrity, patriotism, piety, and seriousness. Some of their alleged shortcomings may likewise have been exaggerated. However, in the light of historic evidence it seems difficult to escape the conclusion that the early Romans were unduly conservative, lacked imagination, frowned upon freedom and individuality, and had little in the way of aesthetic taste (24:22–23; 25: 31–32).

In his generalization regarding Roman character during the first three centuries of the republic, Durant aptly observes: "The typical educated Roman of this age was orderly, conservative, loyal, sober, reverent, tenacious, severe, practical. He enjoyed discipline, and would have no nonsense about liberty. He obeyed as a training for command. He took it for granted that the government had a right to inquire into his morals as well as his income, and to value him purely according to his services to the state. He distrusted individuality and genius. He had none of the charm, vivacity, and unstable fluency of the Attic Greek. He admired character and will as the Greek admired freedom and intellect; and organization was his forte. He lacked imagination, even to make mythology of his own. He could with some effort love beauty, but he could seldom create it. He had no use for pure science, and was suspicious of philosophy as a devilish dissolvent of ancient beliefs and ways. He could not, for the life of him, understand Plato, or Archimedes, or Christ. He could only rule the world" (11:71–72).

Roman Law

As noted earlier, the greatest Roman contribution to culture was law. Roman law began with custom and arose by degrees to the level of reason. Originally there was practically no distinction between religion and law. Primitive custom was largely a matter of religious ritual, and the regulation of custom was in the hands of the priests. It was not until the middle of the fifth century B.C. that the *decemvirs* drew up the Laws of the Twelve Tables (2:271, 285). With this, the *jus divinum* or religious law made way for the *jus civile* or civil law, and the lawyer took the place of the priest (11:32). In 362 B.C. an elective magistrate, the praetor *urbanus*, was placed in charge of the administration of the judicial system (4:60). Shortly after the middle of the third century (242 B.C.), another magistrate, the praetor *peregrinus*, was designated to look after disputes between Romans and foreigners (4:116).

Although the Laws of the Twelve Tables were relatively crude and primitive in character, they were sufficiently flexible to serve as the foundation for subsequent legal development. The latter proceeded largely on an empirical basis—there were no *a priori* guiding principles to begin with. Beyond the Twelve Tables, the sources of the growing body of laws were, as Barnes observes, varied—among them, statutes, plebiscites, decisions and edicts of magistrates, and interpretations by lawyers (2:284). Due to the flexibility of the Laws of the Twelve Tables, it was possible to modify and expand them in keeping with the demands of new conditions. As a result, interpretations by jurists played a very important role in the development of the Roman legal system (2:285).

Specifically, as Boak puts it, "the main channels for the growth of the Roman law and the introduction of innovations in legal procedure were the annual edicts of the urban praetor and his colleague, the *praetor peregrinus*. In these edicts the praetors stated for the public benefit the principles which they would observe in enforcing the laws and the conditions under which they would admit prosecutions. In this way both new legal principles and new forms of action found their way into the civil law, broadening its scope and emphasizing equity rather than legal formality" (4:135).

The edicts of the praetor peregrinus, together with similar edicts by the provincial governors, soon led to the discovery that different legal systems comprised certain common principles—principles that applied to all peoples under Roman jurisdiction. This body of principles or laws came to be known as the *jus gentium*—the law of all nations in the Empire—as contrasted with the *jus civile* of the Romans themselves. Subsequently, it became increasingly a part of Roman law itself. With this, many of the cruder elements of the Laws of the Twelve Tables were discarded, and Roman law reached an abstract and reasoned level (26:1004–1006).

With the Empire, centralization and universalization gained momentum. In Hadrian's reign (A.D. 131) the annual edicts of the praetors were replaced by a perpetual edict as

a permanent basis of imperial law (26:1009). When Cara-
calla subsequently (A.D. 212) granted citizenship to all freedmen, he extended Roman law to the whole Empire. Finally,
under the influence of Stoic philosophy there emerged by
degrees, from the concept of *jus gentium,* a more comprehensive principle—the notion of *jus naturale* or natural law
which applies to all mankind everywhere. The work of the
later jurists was carried on largely under the influence of this
principle (26:1009; 25:286). In the end, says Turner, "the
Roman legal system became systematic and abstract and,
under the influence of Greek philosophy rational, i.e., the
law was conceived as grounded in a fundamental order of
justice which was worked out in practice by reason" (26:
1018).

Roman Architecture and Sculpture

Although they became liberal patrons of the arts, the Romans manifested little creative ability in art apart from architecture and sculpture. This was probably, as noted earlier,
due to the orientation of their culture—the fact that they
early selected and stressed for elaboration other cultural interests. As Durant observes, the life pursuits which they
looked upon as honorable were political and legal, and within
the manual arts, agriculture (11:338). Further evidence in
support of a general lack of artistic interest is, as Trever notes,
adduced by the fact that few, if any, outstanding Roman
writers of poetry and prose have shown any real concern in,
or knowledge of, art (25:588). Equally revealing is the fact
that the individual is almost completely submerged in so-
called Roman art—there are no outstanding personalities, no
great names (11:338).

In architecture and sculpture, although they set out by
borrowing, the Romans early began to assert their own peculiar genius. In the end they achieved an enviable distinction,
especially so in the case of architecture. They borrowed the

principles of their architecture from the Greeks and the Etruscans. The former supplied the column and the colonnade, and the latter,—who may in turn have obtained them from the East,—the arch and the vault. The arch and vault, to which they later added the dome, became in time the chief features of their architectural style (16:482). Aside from the ingenious ways in which they combined these various elements, the supreme architectural achievement of the Romans lay in the solidity and colossal size, and in the magnificence of conception, that characterized their structures. And the architects that designed them, we must bear in mind, were Romans rather than Greeks (11:356).

Although appreciably influenced by Greek models and Etruscan antecedents, the Romans developed before the end of the Augustan age a portrait and relief sculpture that was distinctly their own. Its chief characteristic was a superb and dignified realism. No other people had succeeded in portraying individuals and events so vigorously and so truthfully (11:347–351).

Roman Literature

Despite slow and humble beginnings, the Romans produced one of the world's great literatures—a literature qualitatively closely rivaling that of their brilliant predecessors, the Greeks (17:509). If the Etruscans had literary achievements to their credit, they must have left the Romans untouched, for, as Durant points out, the literature of the first three centuries of the Republic was almost wholly restricted to religious hymns, historical lays, official records, and a varied assortment of lighter materials, some of it bordering on the burlesque (11:73–74).

The publication of the Laws of the Twelve Tables in the mid-fifth century B.C. points to widespread literacy at the beginning of the Republic. However, the fact that the language of the Tables themselves was crude and stilted shows that Latin was as yet in no way a suitable medium for literary expression (25:57, 69).

Roman literature got under way in earnest during the latter half of the third century B.C. under the tutelage of Greek literature. After the fall of Tarentum (272 B.C.) Livius Andronicus—along with other educated Greek slaves—was brought to Rome to teach Latin and Greek in the household of his master. After translating the Odyssey into Latin Saturnian verse to be used as a textbook, he gained his freedom, and was commissioned to produce a tragedy and a comedy in connection with the celebration, in 240 B.C., of the Roman victory in the first Punic War. These were based upon Greek models and proved so popular that similar presentations became a regular feature at subsequent festivals (11:74; 25:145).

A few years later, Cnaeus Naevius (ca. 270–199 B.C.) began to produce comedies and tragedies based upon Greek plots. He was followed in turn by the poet, Quintus Ennius (239–169 B.C.), who adapted some of the best Greek comedies and tragedies to Latin, and wrote a Roman epic, Annales, in which the Saturnian verse was replaced by the flexible hexameter verse of the Greek epic. Plautus (ca. 254–184 B.C.) and Terence (190–159 B.C.) concentrated upon the further elaboration of Roman comedy along Greek and Hellenistic lines. The latter, especially, exerted a tremendous influence upon the further development of the Latin language as a medium of literary expression (11:99–102). Gaius Lucilius (180–103 B.C.) founded literary satire—the only native literary type (25:147). Artistic Latin Prose developed slowly. Such early historians as Fabius Pictor (fl. end of third century B.C.) and Polybius (ca. 205–123 B.C.) wrote in Greek. Cato (234–140 B.C.)—the arch foe of all things Greek—was the first to use real Latin Prose in his Origines and the agricultural treatise (18:91).

The revolutionary character of the last century of the

Republic did not seriously disrupt literary developments. The outstanding contributors of this period were: Varro (116–26 B.C.)—a prolific writer on numerous subjects; Nepos (100–25 B.C.)—among other things, the author of the Lives of Illustrious Men; Sallust (86–35 B.C.)—writer of several historical treatises; the great Caesar (111–44 B.C.)—noted for his finished narrative and descriptive prose style as exemplified in his Commentaries on the Gallic and Civil wars; Catullus (ca. 87–54 B.C.)—the greatest writer of lyric verse in any age; Lucretius (95–55 B.C.)—whose poem on De Rerum Natura marks him as the foremost philosophic poet in any language; and the illustrious Cicero (106–43 B.C.)—in whose orations and letters Latin prose reached the height of its development (25:290–299; 11:146–166).

The Augustan Age (together with the preceding Ciceronian period) is generally known as the Golden Age of Roman literature. The chief writers of the Augustan phase of this age were: Virgil (70–19 B.C.)—the supreme Roman poet whose masterpiece was the Aeneid, the immortal epic on the founding of Rome; Horace (65–8 B.C.)—whose odes raised poetic expression to a level that has never been surpassed; Tibullus (54–19 B.C.), Propertius (50–15 B.C.) and Ovid (43 B.C.–A.D. 17)—the rebellious elegists, of which Ovid was by far the greatest; and Livy (59 B.C.–A.D. 17)— the historian, whose History of Rome represents a prose glorification of Rome comparable to that of the Aeneid (11:233–258; 18:112; 23:192–193; 25:354–374).

The Silver Age, paralleling the Julio-Claudians, Flavians, and Antonines, has more writers to its credit, but few of them as eminent as those of the preceding period. The writers of this age tended to stress form at the expense of content. Outstanding among them were: Juvenal (55–138 A.D.)—the puritanical exponent of Roman satire; Seneca the Elder (54 B.C.–39 A.D.)—writer on rhetoric; Quintilian (A.D. 35–100)—teacher of rhetoric and author of the Institutes of Oratory;

Petronius (d. ca. A.D. 66)—the probable composer of the picaresque novel, the Satyricon; Tacitus (A.D. 55–117)—the brilliant historian and author of the Histories and Annals; Pliny the Elder (A.D. 23–79)—writer on science and author of the Natural History; and Suetonius (ca. A.D. 70–121)—author of the Lives of the Twelve Caesars and Illustrious Men (11: 295–318; 18:112–113; 25:601–616).

Roman Philosophy

The practical Romans had no penchant for philosophy in the Greek sense of the term. Metaphysics and epistemology in particular were meaningless to them. Quite the opposite was true of ethical and political theorizing. They were deeply concerned with human happiness, and knowledge was to them a means to such happiness. Accordingly, both the Epicureanism and the Stoicism which they borrowed from the Greeks were basically ways of life rather than speculative systems (13:248). To the extent that either of them had a metaphysical basis, the former harked back to Democritus and the latter to Heraclitus (13:253).

In Rome, Lucretius, the author of the *De Rerum Natura*, who ranked with Epicurus himself, was the chief exponent of Epicureanism (13:237). Although accepting pleasure as the end toward which all else was subordinated, Epicureanism was not at heart a cult of sensualism. Its aim was rather the avoidance of the painful and the unpleasant in long-range terms through the cultivation of proper mental attitudes—among them, courage and temperance (13:237–239).

Stoicism made of course a much greater appeal to the Romans than did Epicureanism. With time, too, it lost much of its original austerity and became rather highly socialized. In general its ideal was the wise and reasonable individual who meets life in a rational and courageous manner. In place of deliberately striving for the attainment of happiness and the avoidance of pain, the Stoic tried to rise above them—to achieve peace of mind independently of fortune through inner strength. Since it was reasonable for him to accept whatever happened, the universe itself had to be a rational and reasonable affair (13:252–253).

In imperial times many concessions had of course to be made. The new cosmopolitan atmosphere that had gradually come to prevail was not friendly to dogmatism. With this, differences in point of view became common, and Stoicism in varied forms began to spread among the masses, whereas formerly it had been restricted almost entirely to the higher classes (13:266). In the end it became of course so thoroughly impregnated with Neo-Pythagorean and Neo-Platonic elements and with Oriental mystery cultism that it lost its integrity—not, however, before many of its noblest precepts had infiltrated Christianity (25:590–593).

Meanwhile, under the sponsorship of such leading exponents as Seneca the Younger, Epictetus the slave, and the Emperor Marcus Aurelius, Stoicism matured into an ethical philosophy of the highest order, placing among other things tremendous emphasis upon such precepts as the brotherhood of man, the dignity and worth of man, and human compassion and tolerance. Never before had man achieved an ethical code so lofty and so noble. Its disintegration was as tragic as that of the Empire itself.

Roman Science and Mathematics

The Romans showed as little interest in pure science and mathematics as they did in abstract philosophy. It is again rather futile to accuse them of lack of ability. The fact of the matter is that they chose from the outset other potential facets for cultural elaboration—so much that they were not even disposed to borrow to an appreciable degree in these areas. What they did borrow they put to use, elaborating it in keeping with their peculiar utilitarian genius. Any purported scientific treatises, such as Pliny's Natural History and Seneca's Natural Questions, displayed, in comparison with the Greeks, a shocking naiveté (25:764–765; 11:307–311). And along with it they showed an avid predilection for such cults as astrology.

On the other hand, they evidenced a striking capacity to put to practical use some of the things they borrowed. They made no contribution to medicine—Galen was a Greek. However, they went far toward setting up an effective public health program and sanitation facilities. Their engineering exploits went vastly beyond those of the Greeks (25:764–765). And they were anything but amateurs in agriculture and animal husbandry!

BIBLIOGRAPHY

See Chapter 8

CHAPTER VIII

Education in Ancient Rome

Education in Ancient Rome

FOR a variety of reasons the story of the rise and development of education in ancient Rome lacks much of the thrill and romance of its counterpart in ancient Greece. In a sense the diference between the two is almost as striking as that between the Laws of the Twelve Tables and the immortal Homeric poems. To begin with, the Greeks had painstakingly to elaborate a borrowed alphabet before they could give serious thought to literate education; the Romans received their alphabet almost readymade through the Etruscans. In their school tradition, the Greeks set out with a thoroughly novel aim of education—the training of citizens; the Romans, although not entirely oblivious to citizenship obligations, were primarily concerned with the more primitive concept of the disciplined member of the family. Greek boys got their inspiration from Homer; Roman boys from the prosaic Twelve Tables. Roman boys long received their education chiefly in the family; Greek boys primarily in the community. The Roman boys' training, apart from family influences, was largely focused upon literacy; that of the Greek upon a well-rounded versatile personality.

When schools finally did appear, only that for the elementary level was essentially indigenous—and its aim was fixed upon literacy. The secondary school (school of the grammaticus) was a borrowed foreign language school dominated by Hellenistic literary aims—the Latin grammar school did not appear until the first century B.C. The school of the rhetor, likewise at first a foreign language school, did not appear until imperial times when the need for oratorical skills had largely disappeared. All this stands in striking contrast to the natural burgeoning of Greek schools out of pertinent social backgrounds.

The Roman Alphabet

As already noted, the Romans received their alphabet through Etruscan sources. The latter appear to have borrowed two separate versions of it from the Chalcidian Greek colony at Cumae. The Romans borrowed the earlier of these either during the late seventh or early sixth century B.C. Subsequently, they introduced, in the course of several centuries, certain modifications which adapted it more closely to the needs of their language. The original Roman alphabet had twenty-one letters; the final one, twenty-three. The oldest inscriptions go back to this period (16:520–526; 27:32–40).

In the oldest inscription on the Praenestine fibula the Romans wrote from right to left—as did the Etruscans and the Italic peoples. Shortly thereafter, however, they permanently adopted the direction from left to right (27:38). Early writing accessories of the Romans were ink and a slit metal reed. At first they wrote upon leaves, bark, and waxed wooden tablets. Later, leather, linen-paper, and parchment came into use (11:73). For school purposes there was of course the ubiquitous wax writing tablet, and its accompanying stylus (14:248).

The Rise of Formal Education

Any decision regarding the rise of formal education in Rome depends, as it did in Greece and other countries, upon our definition of the term. If by the rise of formal education we mean the beginning of the regular school tradition, then —although there may have been a few schools as early as 500 B.C.—it could not, as Butts observes, have been before the third century B.C. (7:115). Roman tradition was as unfavorable to the institutionalization of education as it was favorable to its administration in the family.

If, on the other hand, we mean by the rise of formal education the provision of facilities for the training of specialists—especially scribes and accountants—to assist in the administration of the economic surplus, we are justified in assuming that formal education began with the teaching of writing and the keeping of accounts. The early acquisition of the alphabet by the Romans furnishes of course incontrovertible evidence that they had need of an effective medium for the keeping of records and accounts. The practical Romans would never have borrowed and painstakingly adapted an alphabet without need of it. And the uses to which they were to put it were certainly anything but literary, for the birth of literature was centuries removed (15:76–77).

The history of Roman education, to the extent that it is restricted to the development of the regular school tradition, falls roughly into four stages—the native Roman period, extending to the middle of the third century B.C.; the period of transition to Hellenistic ideals and practices, extending to about the middle of the first century B.C.; the period during which the new Hellenized education reached its full maturity and came to represent the norm of practice, extending to the latter part of the second century A.D.; and finally, a period of decline, extending to the end of the Empire (21:160–161; 30:503). We shall restrict our discussion to the first three of these.

Native Roman Education

Although there may have been an occasional early *ludus*, or private elementary school, native Roman education was carried on almost exclusively in the household under the direction of the *paterfamilias* (5:62). There were no state regulations of any kind—custom buttressed by ancient Roman morale sufficed to insure that the father would shoulder his responsibilities seriously. Apart from the multifarious religious and patriotic observances and the daily routine of living in which the young played the roles of apprentices, the content of native education was extremely limited, embodying little more than the minima of reading, writing, and counting. The number system was so cumbersome that operations beyond addition and subtraction had to be acquired from specialists. The Laws of the Twelve Tables had of course to be memorized—even beyond the native period of Cicero's time (9:96). Beyond this, there was little in the way of literature. Music was conspicuous by its absence. And physical exercises were mainly martial in character and purpose. Such an education was obviously designed to perpetuate the existing order without modification (26:522–523).

The Hellenization of Roman Education

Although the Romans had not been remotely immune to Greek influences emanating from Magna Graecia during the native period, the conquest of Rome by Greek culture did not get under way in earnest until after the fall of Tarentum in 272 B.C. On this occasion the Romans began to bring Greek slaves to Rome. Some of these were highly educated and served as teachers in the households of the wealthy. One of the most notable of them was Livius Andronicus who later translated the Odyssey into Latin Saturnian verse. This was to serve as a textbook for several centuries. By way of recognition for this service Andronicus received his freedom (5:64). He remained in Rome and was generally active as teacher and literary leader to the time of his death in 203 B.C. (30: 572). The poet and dramatist, Naevius (ca. 264–194 B.C.) was likewise active during the latter part of this century. And ironically enough, toward the close of the century, Cato the Elder brought Ennius (ca. 239–169 B.C.) to Rome. He was subsequently to replace the rude Saturnian Latin verse with the flexible hexameter of the Greek epic (30:572).

As Boyd points out, the prevalence of teachers of Greek (grammatici) has led some to assume that the grammar school had already come into existence at this time. There is, however, as he stresses, not a shred of solid evidence in support of this. The so-called grammatici of this period were nothing more or less than private teachers in the households of important families (5:65). The work of these teachers was none the less thoroughly effective.

After the opening of the second century B.C., the influx of Hellenism gained such momentum that the complete Hellenization of Roman culture became inevitable despite stubborn resistance on the part of the defenders of the old order. With the close of the Second Punic War, the Greeks themselves came in great numbers and were prepared to teach the Romans no end of skills and disciplines. And the art of Greece was of course bodily transported to Rome (26:953–954). So subtle had been the spread of the language itself that when the Stoic philosopher, Crates of Mallos, lectured in Rome in Greek about 169 B.C. he appears to have been perfectly understood without the aid of an interpreter (9:111; 30:572). And by the middle of the century there was, as Boyd observes, a very widespread appreciation of Greek literature among upper class Romans (5:65).

The Hellenization movement, as Trever stresses, involved much more than the dissemination of the Greek language and literature. In contrast with the narrow vocationalism of the Romans, it fostered broad literary and intellectual interests, and encouraged critical thought and discussion. The result was, among the upper classes of course, the emergence of a new and vastly more symmetrical type of Roman personality, representing at its best a happy blend between the old Roman and the new Hellenistic. Among the second century representatives of this type were Scipio Africanus the Elder (ca. 237–183 B.C.), Titus Flaminius (ca. 230–174 B.C.), Aemilius Paulus (229–160 B.C.), and Scipio Aemilianus (185–129 B.C.). The latter became the center of the famous Scipionic Circle which included not only the foremost Roman generals, statesmen, and orators, but also such noted outsiders as Polybius the historian and Panaetius the Stoic philosopher (25:144).

As already noted, the old order was by no means reconciled to the Hellenization of Roman culture. Cato the Censor (234–149 B.C.) was especially vehement in his denunciation of all things Greek. He had been a great orator of the old style and was the author of a Manual on Oratory (19:334). Nevertheless, he turned to the study of Greek in his old age (9:101). Even the attempt to develop Latin schools of rhetoric was opposed by the conservatives. As late as 161 B.C. the senate went so far as to expel "the *rhetores Latini* along with the philosophers," but, as Trever adds, "the law was a dead letter" (25:144).

The opposition of the old order was of course by no means wholly without foundation. The blending of old cultures into new syntheses is at best hazardous and difficult, especially so without powerful overall motivation and direction. The wholesome influences emanating from the Scipionic Circle affected in the very nature of the case only a limited stratum of the population. Much that came with Hellenism was trash, and much that was sound in native Roman culture went overboard. The results of this were in many respects extremely unfortunate. As Trever stresses, in place of sound intellectual orientation, and the moral strength implicit in Stoicism, there emerged by degrees a shallow oversophistication and a rampant individualism. Creativeness made way for pedantry and artificial display. Educationally, this manifested itself especially in the over-emphasis upon rhetoric and oratory as ends in themselves (25:145).

The Ludus of the Litterator

The development of schools—elementary, grammar, and rhetorical—during the transition period has to be largely inferred from indirect evidence. As Boyd points out, even such a specific reference to the establishment of a grammar school as that of Spurius Carvilius during the mid-third century B.C. has no real facts to back it up (5:64). Actually, the elementary school, the *ludus* of the *litterator*, appears long to have been the only *bona fide* school in Rome. It received boys, and in some cases girls as well, at six or seven and kept them until twelve or thirteen. Its chief concern was to teach them reading, writing, and counting. In certain cases, before the grammar school took definite form, it may also have given some instruction in literature (5:66). As Hellenization progressed, it adopted certain Greek customs, among them that of the paedogogus as a companion and guardian of the pupil (9:104). Its methodology we may by-pass. It was at best—in the earlier stages at least—primitive (14:246–252). During the first century of our era the *ludus* enjoyed wide popularity, and it endured of course to the end of the Empire (30:578).

The School of the Grammaticus

About all that can be safely said regarding the development of the schools on the two succeeding levels—those of the *grammaticus* and of the *rhetor*—is that the former was firmly established, both in its Greek and its Latin versions, by the mid-first century B.C., and that the latter, although under way at this time, probably did not reach its peak until the first century A.D. In the earlier stages, there appears to have been some overlapping between the two, the curriculum of the former often including a certain amount of rhetorical training and that of the latter reaching down into grammar and literature.

In general, however, the legitimate province of the grammaticus was basically grammar and literature. In addition, he was expected to teach certain supplementary subjects, among them geometry, astronomy, geography, natural science, history, mythology, and music—as a rule probably in rather elementary and applied fashion (10:59; 14:257–258; 21:171; 19:350).

The grammaticus normally received boys at about twelve or thirteen and kept them until they assumed the *toga virilis* at about sixteen (10:60). The first grammar schools were of course Greek. However, as early as the first century B.C. Lucius Aelius Stilo is said to have set up a Latin grammar school, and by degrees thereafter boys began to patronize both types of schools (10:59; 7:116). There is widespread agreement among authorities that the teaching in these schools was thorough and efficient, especially so in grammar, composition, and literature. At first Greek literature naturally predominated, but as Latin literature grew in quantity it came to assume an increasingly important place. In the Latin grammar schools of the imperial period Virgil actually very largely replaced Homer (10:59).

The Rhetorical School

Upon the completion of the grammar school curriculum the Roman youth, who entertained ambitions for a public career, entered one of the rhetorical schools. These, too, were at first strictly Greek, but during the first century B.C. comparable Latin institutions began to appear. As a matter of fact Greek teachers of rhetoric had been active during the latter part of the preceding century as evidenced by the action of the senate in 161 B.C. (25:144). Despite the popularity of the Latin rhetorical schools, it was difficult to eradicate the notion that they were not the equal of the Greek. Even as late as 92 B.C. a decree was issued against Latin teachers of rhetoric (30:585).

Instruction in the rhetorical schools was of course designed to train public speakers of the highest order. Oratory was, as Moore observes, a powerful instrument of government in the days of the Republic, and when the Republic passed, and with it much of the need of civic oratory, the Romans retained it as an end in itself (19:340; 30:605). Indeed, the trained orator became synonymous with the educated Roman. Moreover, they elaborated the art of training the orator to a point that has never been equalled or surpassed. The details of the ideals and practices which governed the training of the orator are of necessity beyond the scope of this discussion.

However, it should be noted that the chief spokesmen on the subject—especially Cicero in his De Oratore and Quintilian in his Institutio Oratoria—called for much more than the finished and fluent speaker and the connoisseur in literature. The orator was to be broadly trained in the liberal arts, and in philosophy, jurisprudence, and history (25:288). Also, he was to have keen insight into, and broad experience with, life. Finally, he was to be a good man—a man with a deep sense of moral responsibility (9:125, 135).

The Roman Ideal of the Educated Man

Despite all this, the Roman ideal of the educated man, as embodied in the orator, was basically a shallow affair—all the more so because it represented the only ideal of the educated man they managed to develop. Had they conceived of the orator as one of several types of professionally trained men, the case might be different. By his very nature the orator's supreme function was to persuade—to incite to action (1:215–216). The fact that he was an individual of high moral responsibility and good intention did not remotely guarantee that he had the social insight and wisdom to lend his weight to the promotion of the issues and measures that were most urgently needed by Roman society. In contemporary perspective, a comparable course of action would be to place the control of the political, economic, and social problems of a great commonwealth into the hands of a group of well-intentioned, technically trained lawyers who were utterly lacking in social science orientation.

The fatal predicament of the Romans—as of the Greeks before them—was of course that they had no real notion of social science. In discussing some of the factors that contributed to the decay of classical culture, Turner aptly says: "The weakness of classical culture had origin in the Greek mode of thinking, of which both Hellenistic and Latin literature, philosophy, and science were expressions.

"When Greek, Hellenistic, and Latin learning is viewed as a whole, it is seen to have been a vast body of speculations, opinions, and guesses—some brilliant and some absurd. But behind it, diverse as were its forms, was a constant effort to know *unchanging reality*—the 'elements,' the 'truth,' the 'moral law,' the 'absolute.' This effort, it should be realized, promoted the formulation of systems of thought which explained the universe, defined the moral law, and sought first principles. But it did not promote a continuous expansion of factual information about man and his world. The Greeks and their successors never dealt with the finite world. They developed no means of accurately measuring quantities of matter, produced no mathematical calculus for describing matter in motion, and initiated no systematic investigation of natural phenomena. In fact, they never understood that the doing of these things was a part of intellectual activity. Logic, the only intellectual instrument they shaped besides allegory, is an instrument suitable for testing the coherence of predictions but not useful in assembling and evaluating factual information. The mode of thinking which failed in these respects was consistent in that it nurtured the attitude that labor is degrading, the conviction that arithmetic is an egalitarian science, the idea that mechanics is a low and vile art, and the dogma that contact with matter is spiritually corrupting. The social science of the Greeks and Romans also failed to achieve any analysis of economic or political phenomena that were useful in formulating policies; in fact the Greek thinkers considered such effort unworthy, and the Romans were less attentive to such phenomena than the Greeks. The great production of the classical mind in the field of social thought was Roman law, i.e., a body of social controls which enforced policies that were not justified by the economic conditions prevailing in the empire. This statement means that the policies failed to serve the interests they were meant to serve. The triumph of rhetoric in literary expression and education was merely another form of the failure to deal with concrete experience.

"The intellectual effort which directed men's minds toward unchanging reality left them helpless in a social order that changed in spite of them. Men, for whom the word 'invention' meant only the discovery of verbal conceits in literature, were hardly the ones to find solutions for their problems in either technological or institutional innovations. Classical learning attempted to teach men how to act, not how to produce or construct, and when successful in this effort it produced closed minds, which, if change occurred, were necessarily blind" (26:1022–1023).

Education in the Early Empire

The system of grammatical and rhetorical training which was approaching its maturity with the close of the first century B.C. continued unabated through the first two centuries of our era. Then it went into gradual decline along with the decay of the Empire. Under imperial conditions it became of course largely divorced from life. Oratory ceased to be an important instrument of government. Apart from the role which it continued to play in legal practice, it became, therefore, increasingly a decorative and ornamental accomplishment. Along with this, came a general decline in seriousness of outlook and purpose. Even before the end of Julio-Claudian times, themes for declamation and disputation had become noticeably shallow and trite. By way of contrast, verbiage and gesture had become much more subtle and ingenious (25:456).

Roman emperors, from the Julio-Claudians through the Antonines, were on the whole favorably disposed toward education—to a considerable extent no doubt because the emperors themselves were for the most part well-educated men. When Augustus found it necessary to ban foreigners from Rome he expressly exempted teachers, and he was incidentally the founder of the first public library in Rome (5:78). And, as Moore observes, even the weakest of his immediate followers were not without some interest in education and learning (19:367).

The most significant departure came of course with Vespasian (69–79). His endowment of Greek and Latin chairs of rhetoric in Rome established a policy that was to be continued and extended by subsequent emperors. He also established a great public library in the Temple of Peace which Hadrian was subsequently to organize into the Athenaeum— the only Roman university (5:78; 10:61).

With Hadrian (117–138), Antoninus Pius (138–161), and Marcus Aurelius (161–180), the encouragement of education became more deliberate and systematic. In consequence, as Boyd observes, "a great system of education, as broadspread and as well-ordered as the Empire itself" emerged by degrees (5:80). The Museum in Alexandria was reactivated, and Athens once more became the leading center of learning. In the provinces, municipalities were required to establish and maintain schools. Endowments, special privileges for teachers, and subsidies for economically handicapped students became rather common (5:80–81).

Meanwhile, the wealthier Romans continued of course—as they long had—to supplement their rhetorical and philosophical education by study and travel abroad (8:462–463).

Regarding Roman educational theorists very little need be said. The two outstanding theorists were of course Cicero and

Quintilian. Cicero wrote his *De Oratore* at the height of his
intellectual maturity in 55 B.C. (25:294), and Quintilian's *Institutio Oratoria* was published in A.D. 93 (25:606). Cicero
confines himself almost entirely to a discussion of his ideal
of the orator and the type of education he should receive. As
might be expected, he finds himself very much at odds with
the more superficial features of rhetorical training, but there
is no doubt in his mind about the appropriateness of rhetorical education for Romans. The same thing is true of Quintilian who discusses the methodological aspects of such training in greater detail. Having once become oriented toward
this end, the Romans could neither sense nor conceive of any
alternative. Quintilian also devotes some attention to childhood and elementary education. However, his proposals can
scarcely be said to go beyond sound common sense (5:69–73;
9:124–142; 25:456, 605–607).

BIBLIOGRAPHY

1. Bailey, Cyril (Editor), The Legacy of Rome. Oxford: The Clarendon Press, 1923.
2. Barnes, Harry E., The History of Western Civilization, Volume I.
   New York: Harcourt, Brace and Company, 1935.
3. Benedict, Ruth, Patterns of Culture. Boston: Houghton Mifflin
   Company, 1934.
4. Boak, A. E. R., A History of Rome to 565 A.D. New York: The
   Macmillan Company, 1929.
5. Boyd, William, The History of Western Education. London: Adam
   and Charles Black, 1947.
6. Breasted, James H., The Conquest of Civilization. New York: Harper and Brothers, 1938.
7. Butts, R. Freeman, A Cultural History of Education. New York:
   McGraw-Hill Book Company, 1947.
8. Cary, Max, A History of Rome. London: Macmillan and Company,
   1935.
9. Dobson, J. F., Ancient Education and Its Meaning to Us. New
   York: Longmans, Green and Company, 1932.
10. Duggan, Stephen, A Student's Textbook in the History of Educa-
    tion. New York: Appleton-Century-Crofts, 1948.
11. Durant, Will, Caesar and Christ. New York: Simon and Schuster,
    1944.

12. Fell, R. A. L., Etruria and Rome. Cambridge: The University Press, 1924.

13. Fuller, B. A. G., A History of Philosophy. New York: Henry Holt and Company, 1945.

14. Graves, Frank P., A History of Education—Before the Middle Ages. New York: The Macmillan Company, 1914.

15. Kenyon, F. G., Books and Readers in Ancient Greece and Rome. Oxford: The Clarendon Press, 1932.

16. Kroeber, A. L., Anthropology, New Edition. New York: Harcourt, Brace and Company, 1948.

17. Kroeber, A. L., Configurations of Culture Growth. Berkeley and Los Angeles: The University of California Press, 1944.

18. Langer, William L., (Editor), An Encyclopedia of World History. Boston: Houghton Mifflin Company, 1948.

19. Moore, Ernest C., The Story of Instruction—The Beginnings. New York: The Macmillan Company, 1936.

20. Moore, F. G., The Roman's World. New York: Columbia University Press, 1936.

21. Mulhern, James, A History of Education. New York: The Ronald Press, 1946.

22. Randall-MacIver, David, Italy Before the Romans. Oxford: The Clarendon Press, 1928.

23. Smith, Charles E. and Case, Lynn M., A Short History of Western Civilization. Boston: D. C. Heath and Company, 1948.

24. Starr, Chester G. Jr., The Emergence of Rome as Ruler of the Western World. Ithaca: Cornell University Press, 1950.

25. Trever, Albert A., History of Ancient Civilization, Volume II, The Roman World. New York: Harcourt, Brace and Company, 1939.

26. Turner, Ralph, The Great Cultural Traditions, Volumes I and II. New York: McGraw-Hill Book Company, 1941.

27. Ullman, B. L., Ancient Writing and Its Influence. New York: Longmans, Green and Company, 1932.

28. Wallbank, T. W. and Taylor, A. M., Civilization—Past and Present, Volume I. New York: Scott, Foresman and Company, 1949.

29. Webster, Hutton, History of Civilization—Ancient and Medieval. Boston: D. C. Heath and Company, 1947.

30. Woody, Thomas, Life and Education in Early Societies. New York: The Macmillan Company, 1949.

CHAPTER IX

The Rise of Hebrew Culture

AS Hitti shows at some length, "the Hebrews were the fourth major Semitic people—after the Amorites, Canaanites, and Aramaeans—to settle in Syria" (24:176). Although the connotation of the term Semitic is strictly linguistic in scientific usage, Hitti feels that the close resemblance of Semitic peoples in such matters as physical features, psychological traits, and cultural patterns implies additional bonds —that is, bonds transcending the closely related languages spoken by these peoples. Since the Arabian peninsula appears to have been the original home of all of these peoples, he strongly suspects that at least some of the ancestors of all of them must at some time or other have spoken the same language and occupied a common locale (24:61–62). This would in the very nature of the case have conditioned a measure of racial and cultural continuity.

Migrations and Invasions

Historians and Old Testament scholars now generally concede that the Hebrew conquest of Canaan was anything but the adroit and united affair portrayed in the chief Biblical narrative in the Book of Joshua (24:Ch. XIII; 35:Ch. I; 44: Ch. I; 46:Ch. III; 51:Ch. VII; 53:Ch. VIII; 54:Ch. VII; 57: Ch. X). Actually, there appear to have been several invasions separated by long drawn out time intervals, and the invaders were obviously not remotely a unified people (51:206). Unification came slowly and was as a matter of fact never fully achieved (44:7–9).

197

The Biblical accounts of the peaceful patriarchal migrations are so tied up with myth and legend that it is extremely difficult to distinguish between fact and fancy. Actually, as Meek shows in some detail, the term Habiru, denoting a wandering nomadic type, is rather conspicuous in both cuneiform and Egyptian texts. This does not of course remotely authenticate Abraham and his descendants as historic personages. However, it does establish the patriarchal type as contemporary with Hammurabi in the mid-eighteenth century B.C. (35:6–16).

Since the patriarchal age was also the age of the Hyksos invasions of Egypt, Meek strongly suspects that some of the Hebrews may have been carried into Egypt and befriended by the Hyksos. After the expulsion of the latter, about 1560 B.C., they appear to have returned to Palestine (35:16–18).

The Hebrews that left Egypt with the Exodus had presumably migrated there by degrees beginning about 1400 B.C. (51:206). However, the whole question of their sojourn in Egypt and the Exodus is so involved in myth and legend that valid generalizations are extremely hazardous. About all that can be said with a reasonable degree of assurance is that the number involved was very small—restricted, as Meek observes, to only a few of the southern group (35:29–31); that the Pharaoh of the oppression appears to have been Rameses II (ca. 1301–1234 B.C.); that the Exodus—whatever its extent and nature may have been—occurred late in the thirteenth century B.C. (35:35; 10:256); and that the emigrants, along with other desert tribes, may have spent some time wandering about the Sinai peninsula while they were being initiated into the Yahweh cult and organized into a confederacy by their tribal leader, Moses (51:206; 35:35–37). Although there is, as Sachar observes, not a shred of evidence in support of the historicity of Moses, most critics are disposed to accept him as at base an historic person (46:16–18).

Beyond the legendary patriarchal migrations there appear

to have been two major Hebrew invasions of Palestine—one from the east across the Jordan in the course of the Tel el-Amarna age beginning about 1400 B.C. (36:21–25), and the other from the south to the north into the territory subsequently known as Judah some two centuries later (35:38–42; 51:207; 54:331–333). The crucial event associated with the first of these invasions was the capture of Jericho by Joshua. Archeological evidence shows that this occurred before 1400 B.C., and that Shechem and Bethel fell somewhat later (35: 23–25). The participating tribes appear to have been loosely organized at first, but in due time Joshua organized some of them into a confederacy at Shechem. According to tradition he made a covenant and set up a simple code of laws for them. This northern confederacy, as Meek observes, constituted the nucleus of what later came to be known as Israel (35:25–26; 46:24; 51:206; 54:331–332).

The second of these invasions—the invasion from the south northward—brought with it Judah and related tribes. These were the tribes whom Moses had foregathered in the Arabian peninsula—the tribes whom he had organized into a confederacy and initiated into the Yahweh cult. As Joshua before him, he had made a covenant and set up a code of laws for them (35:35–36). About 1200 B.C. these tribes began to push into southern Palestine and to continue northward until they had in their possession most of the region south of Jerusalem and east of Philistia (35:38–42; 46:24; 51:207–208). This confederacy constituted the nucleus of what subsequently came to be known as Judah.

It remains to be noted that the account of the Hebrew invasion of Palestine, as we have sketched it above, differs from the older traditional account which continues to have its distinguished adherents. By-passing details as much as possible, the traditional account assumes that Moses rather than Joshua came first in point of time, and that the interval between the Exodus and the capture of Jericho was—apart from the generation during which the tribes wandered in the Sinai peninsula—relatively short. According to Hitti, for example, the Exodus occurred about 1290 B.C. and the desert nomads reached the Transjordan about 1250 B.C. Jericho presumably fell shortly thereafter, although the conquest as a whole and the parcelling out of the land to the several tribes extended over the "last quarter of the twelfth and the first three quarters of the eleventh centuries"—the period coinciding with that of the Judges (24:180).

Meek's evidence in support of the priority of Joshua is thoroughly convincing (35:35–44). Moreover, as he points out, further, the widely different time settings thus ascribed to Israel and Judah respectively go far toward accounting for the cultural differences between them, the former benefiting in the very nature of the case by earlier and longer drawn out contacts with the culturally superior Canaanites. And as Meek puts it: "The settlement of the two groups at different periods and under different leaders, and with different cultural and religious attainments, would also account best for the continued friction between them when they did come together.—Only for a brief period were they ever united and then not very closely.—As two peoples they began, as two peoples they insisted on living, even to the bitter end" (35: 46–47).

Settlement

In the wake of invasions came settlement, and this, too, had to be fought for. The invaders were rude nomads and peasants. The Canaanites whom they sought to displace, had an urbanized cultural tradition that went back some fifteen hundred years—a tradition that was heavily indebted to Egypt and Babylonia. In the face of strongly fortified cities and iron chariots, the military advance of the Hebrews was slow and the Canaanitish cities long retained their independence. Meanwhile, the Hebrews dwelt in villages and in the countryside, intermarried with the Canaanites, and absorbed much of their culture (54:333–337). It was not until the early part of the twelfth century B.C.—shortly after the end of the second invasion—that the Hebrews had subjugated the Canaanites of the central hill country. And by that time they had the Philistines on their hands (51:208).

Actually, the Hebrew subjugation of the Canaanites was not so much a matter of their extermination as of their absorption, bodily and culturally. Intermarriage was commonplace, and as Hitti shows in some detail, there was very little that the conquerors did not take over from the conquered—their very language, together with the alphabet and the art of writing; the whole range of agricultural practices, along with the associated religious fertility cults and rites; art and architecture, both secular and religious; music and musical instruments; poetry and songs; crafts and industries; and views of life and of after-life (24:203–207).

The age during which the Hebrews settled Canaan is generally known as the period of the Judges. There was at this time no well-organized over-all governmental machinery. The tribes acted for the most part independently, cooperating only in extreme emergencies. Affairs within the tribes were taken care of by leaders, called Judges. These arose more or less spontaneously in time of need. Only on rare occasions, as in the case of Deborah and Barak, did such leadership become intertribal in scope. The Hebrews loved freedom and were loath to place their primitive clan democracy in jeopardy (24:180; 53:86; 54:334–337; 56:46–52).

The Philistines

The Philistine menace finally forced them to unite. The Philistines, one of several so-called Peoples of the Sea, had attempted to invade Egypt early in the twelfth century B.C. Rameses III repulsed them, but allowed them to settle permanently along the South Syrian coast. They hailed from the Aegean islands, including Crete, and carried the elements of Minoan culture. Upon conquering several Canaanite cities and adding some of their own, they took over the gods of the Canaanites along with much of their language and culture. In political and military organization they were superior to both the Hebrews and the Canaanites. The same thing was true of their armor and their industrial implements, largely because they virtually monopolized the mining and smelting of iron.

As a result, the Hebrews found themselves increasingly in danger of complete subjugation. By the beginning of the eleventh century B.C. they were being driven to the hill country; by the middle of the century the Philistines captured Shiloh, the famous sanctuary, and carried off the sacred Ark of the Covenant; and somewhat later they had established garrisons in the hill country itself (24:180–185; 43:48–52; 51: 208; 53:86–87; 56:54–56).

Establishment of the Monarchy

The Biblical accounts of the establishment of the monarchy are conflicting, and scholars differ in their interpretation of them. However, there seems to be no doubt but that Saul (ca. 1028–1013 B.C.) was called to the kingship to wage war against the Philistines, that his early spectacular successes were followed by defeat and suicide, and that he was subject to psychic disturbances. It seems probable, however, that at least some of the unfavorable characterizations of him may represent fabrications of later Judaean chroniclers who wished to belittle him in the interest of his successor (46:31– 34; 47:35; 48:89; 51:209; 56:57–60).

The Reign of David

David (ca. 1013–973), who was to place the new monarchy upon secure foundations, is both a legendary hero and an his-

THE RISE OF HEBREW CULTURE

torical character. As Swain observes, the most probable of the legendary stories associated with him would seem to be the one that pictures him as a "brigand chieftain, with head-quarters in a cave at Adullam, who rented out his men to Saul or to the Philistines as occasion offered" (51:209). His strong claim to historicity rests upon the fact that the account given of him in II Samuel, Chapters 9–20, written sometime during the ninth century B.C., is generally regarded as one of the finest and most authentic historical records produced by the ancient Orient (53:87).

During the early years when Saul's son, Ishbaal, ruled the north at Mahamaim David served as king of Judah at Hebron. Upon the death of Ishbaal, the northern tribes swore allegiance to David and he became king of Israel as well (43:61–62; 56:66–67). In rapid succession thereafter he subdued the Philistines to the point where they ceased to be of any consequence, completed the conquest of the Canaanites, annexed Edom, Moab, and Ammon, and restricted the Aramaeans to northern Syria (24:187–188; 53:87).

Sometime after the establishment of the united kingdom, David captured Jerusalem from the native Jebusites and set it up as his capital. Here he erected a royal palace with the customary Oriental harem, and a national sanctuary for Yahweh in which he housed the Ark that had been neglected after its recovery from Philistia (43:63; 56:67).

Although David's government was highly centralized—he himself serving as king, judge, and general—its organization took on increasing complexity as varied subordinates were placed in charge of new external and internal functions and relationships (43:65–68; 46:36).

Despite his notable and lasting achievements, David's career as king ended tragically. He degenerated by degrees to the level of a petty Oriental despot and abandoned whatever standards of justice and decency he may have cherished earlier. As a result, there was little in the way of moral transgression that could not be charged against him. And with it all he was the constant target of plots and intrigues (43:68).

The Reign of Solomon

Solomon (ca. 973–933 B.C.) succeeded David as the result of a palace intrigue. Through a series of executions he assured himself against further challenges of the succession (43:68–69; 46:38; 56:70). Tradition does not depict his personality as vividly as it does that of David, and it is more difficult to decide where legend ends and history begins (43:69–70). Nevertheless, certain personal characteristics stand out boldly: There is the Oriental monarch with a penchant for luxury, elegance, and a large harem; the able organizer and administrator in respect to both domestic and foreign affairs; the promoter of large-scale commercial and industrial projects; the relentless exactor of forced labor and taxes; and the great builder.

Solomon made no attempt to extend his territory. He turned instead to problems of consolidation and improvement. He divided the country into twelve administrative districts with a royal governor in charge of each. Since this cut across tribal lines it tended to place national welfare above tribal loyalties (53:88). With other states he made no end of treaties and alliances designed to promote cooperation and strengthen security. As Sachar aptly puts it, even "his harem was a register of the multiplicity of his friendships" (46:41).

As an ardent promoter of commercial and industrial enterprises he controlled trade routes, fortified key cities, erected storehouses, constructed new roads, and promoted extensive mining and smelting operations. Large-scale trade was carried on through merchants attached to him. He even went so far as to build and operate, with the aid of King Hiram, a fleet of ships for Red Sea trade (24:185–190; 46:41; 54:339).

Solomon's most notable achievements as builder were of course the royal palace and the temple. The former required thirteen years to construct and the latter seven. The materials and the skilled craftsmen were supplied by King Hiram of Tyre. Unfortunately, the expenses incurred in these building operations and the maintenance of an elaborate court bore heavily upon the people in terms of both forced labor and taxation. It was this that was to split the monarchy upon Solomon's death (24:189–191; 46:39–42).

The Divided Kingdoms

Upon Solomon's death, his son Rehoboam was named as successor at Jerusalem. However, before he could actually succeed to the kingship the nomination had to be confirmed by the national assembly meeting at Shechem. When this body met it was in a serious mood and demanded a definite statement of policy regarding the future of taxation. Goaded on by unwise counselors, the sixteen year old youth replied in a manner that cost him the support of the ten northern tribes. This gave rise to what is generally known as the Divided Kingdoms—Israel and Judah. Rehoboam became king of Judah and Jeroboam king of Israel. The latter, a onetime government official under Solomon, had been living in Egypt to avoid execution on charges of rebellious activities (3:139–140; 24:191; 46:43–45; 43:73–74; 48:91; 51:211; 56:76).

The breach between the two kingdoms endured to the end. And there was intermittent warfare between them. As already noted there were fundamental differences between them. Israel's territory was fully three times as extensive and much more fertile. Her cultural tradition was older and therefore farther removed from nomadic antecedents. She was economically and politically more mature, and better equipped for warfare. This meant of course that she was internationally more active and aggressive—a fact that incidentally led to her earlier demise (3:143; 39:352–353; 46:55–56; 53:89).

Although each kingdom had its able rulers and its protracted periods of stable government, intrigue and revolution were constantly in the offing. Accordingly, the political history of the kingdoms is neither unique nor interesting. It is in fact a rather sordid story that shows the Hebrews to have been no different from other ancient peoples. Altogether Israel endured slightly over two centuries, and Judah approximately three and a third. Each had nineteen kings, those of Israel falling into nineteen dynasties, seven of which were overthrown by violence, while those of Judah all remained in the line of the house of David (24:191–192; 46:43–44; 51:212).

An extended account of these kingdoms together with their rulers is beyond the scope of this discussion. Suffice it to call attention to some of the outstanding kings, and then to note in somewhat greater detail some of the problems that confronted the Hebrews of the Divided Kingdoms. These were of course predominantly political, economic and social, and religious. The political problems concerned their relationships with other peoples—relationships which were ultimately to lead to their undoing. The economic and social problems revolved about the accumulation and distribution of wealth resulting from industrialization and urbanization. The religious problems fall into two categories—those having to do with the struggle between Yahwism and Baalism, and those associated with the rise and dissemination of ethical prophetism.

Rulers of the Divided Kingdoms

As Swain observes, only four or five rulers of the northern kingdom merit special mention. Of these, Omri (885–874 B.C.) moved the capital from Shechem to Samaria and attracted considerable attention abroad. His son, Ahab (874–852 B.C.), —although with his Tyrian wife, Jezebel, thoroughly detested by the Biblical writers—turned out to be Israel's greatest king (3:153). Jehu, who exterminated the house of Ahab in one of the most brutal series of murders on record, founded a dynasty that endured for approximately a century. Israel

THE RISE OF HEBREW CULTURE

fared badly during the reigns of Jehu and his two sons. With the accession of Jeroboam II (785–745 B.C.) it regained much of its prosperity and prestige. Then followed a final quarter century of anarchy during which only one of the remaining kings escaped assassination (3:192–199; 43:93–98; 51:212–213).

There was nothing spectacular about the kings of Judah. They enjoyed, however, on the whole, a much greater degree of stability than those of Israel. As Wellhausen points out, on the rare occasions when a king was murdered by the subjects, the people ran down the assassins and placed a member of the house of David on the throne (58:477–478). Among the earlier kings, Asa (914–874 B.C.) and Jehoshaphat (874–849 B.C.)—contemporaries of Omri and Ahab in Israel—proved themselves exceptionally competent rulers (3:154). Uzziah or Azariah—a contemporary of Jeroboam II in Israel—likewise manifested a high degree of ability (3:184). And we cannot of course overlook Hezekiah (720–692 B.C.) with his penchant for foreign entanglements and his puritanical leanings (3:213–216). Economically and politically, his son, Manasseh (692–638 B.C.), appears to have been by far the abler. However, he was much too indulgent toward non-Yahweh religious cults to escape the odium of the pious Hebrew historians (46:58). Josiah (637–607 B.C.), the exponent of Deuteronomism, was obviously a ruler of very superior caliber.

Political Problems of the Divided Kingdoms

It is generally conceded that the Hebrew conquest of Palestine was greatly facilitated by the political conditions prevailing in the ancient world at that time. The Egyptian Empire had gone into decline, and Assyria, although Tiglath-Pileser I had made raids as far west as the Mediterranean late in the twelfth century B.C., was not to become formidable until after the middle of the eighth century when Tiglath-Pileser III created the Empire. Israel's serious involvement with Assyria began at this time. Largely because its kings persisted in forming hostile alliances with other states, the relationship terminated abruptly and tragically under Sargon II in 722 B.C., with the destruction of Samaria and the deportation of thousands of its population (53:96). This ended the existence of the northern kingdom, and the ten tribes as a separate entity disappeared. They were absorbed by the general population among which they happened to have settled. In northern Palestine they intermingled with the colonists brought in by Assyria to form the Samaritans (24: 196).

Due to the fact that Judah outlasted Israel by a century and a third, it not only bore the full brunt of Assyria's aggression but had in addition to face its imperial successors—the Neo-Babylonians. Indeed, Judah began under aggression and went down under it. The kingdom had scarcely become established under Rehoboam when Shishonk, an Egyptian Pharaoh, seized Jerusalem and despoiled the temple and the palace of their ornaments and treasures (24:198). However, despite no end of challenging and provocative situations, down to the fall of Israel, little Judah had shown a remarkable capacity for non-intervention and downright submission. And initially at least, Hezekiah seemed to be bent upon a continuation of this policy—a policy incidently strongly approved by Isaiah. Before long, however, patriotic pressure from within and solicitation from without induced him to join a league that was plotting against Assyria. As far as Judah was concerned this led to the siege of Jerusalem by Sennacherib in 701 B.C. Although the Assyrians withdrew for some reason without taking the city, Hezekiah lost much of his territory and wealth and became a vassal of Sennacherib (24: 199–200; 46:56–58; 53:97).

During the first three quarters of the seventh century B.C. Judah remained submissive to Assyria. However, when Neo-

Babylonia won its independence from Assyria in 625 B.C., and the latter was headed for extinction, foreign involvements promptly re-appeared. Josiah, famous for his religious reforms, apparently hoped to reunite Samaria and Judah into an independent Hebrew kingdom. When, with the fall of Nineveh in 612 B.C., Egypt attempted once more to extend its control into north Syria, he fought against the latter and was killed at Meggido. Thereafter, Judah's policy varied. Josiah's immediate successors, Jehoiakim and Jehoiachin, supported Egypt. Zedekiah, the last king, was initially loyal to Nebuchadrezzar, but internal pressure presently forced him to seek independence, presumably with Egyptian aid. This spelled the end of Judah. Nebuchadrezzar laid siege to Jerusalem and captured it in 586 B.C. Estimates regarding the proportion of the population carried into exile vary greatly (24:200–202; 46:59–60; 51:214–215).

As in the case of other peoples, settled life brought industrialization and urbanization to the Hebrew kingdoms. Although the territory of the two kingdoms was limited to about seven thousand square miles, the number of settlements that could be classified as towns came to be no less than four hundred (4:60). As centers of industry and commerce, and the gathering places of the rich and the poor, these urban communities began to reflect an economic and social differentiation that was strikingly at variance with primitive clan democracy. There were not only the rich and the poor, but the rich were growing richer and the poor poorer. Economic and social inequalities were further aggravated by the effects of war and catastrophe upon land ownership. The peasants especially were unable to weather these crises and their land drifted increasingly into the hands of the wealthy. The result was an ever-growing landless proletariat. Since industry and commerce were unable to absorb this, the bulk of it became poorly paid agricultural laborers (3:185–188; 4:56–59; 54:348–350).

Economic and Social Problems of the Divided Kingdoms

At first the Hebrews were rather helpless in the presence of the growing economic and social inequalities. The landless proletariat and the urban poor, along with those who still had vivid memories of earlier clan practices, pled for reform. But there was no one to sponsor it in practice. Such administrative and legal machinery as existed was in the hands of the privileged. These, as Sachar aptly puts it, "were models of technical goodness. They held their heads high in righteousness. They did nothing that was not within the limits of the law. They were fervid patriots, quick to uphold national honor, ever ready to defend the sanctity of property rights and social stability. They adhered strictly to all the ritualistic demands of religion. Theirs were the fattest sacrifices, theirs the most generous tributes of thanksgiving and free-will offering; theirs the sweetest words to the bowing priests. Who could challenge these pillars of respectability, except social radicals, rebels who demanded more than legality, who refused to weigh actions in the conventional scales, who sought to introduce a gentle spirit of equity into the rigid legalism of the period?" (46:64). The social radicals and the rebels were of course the prophets.

The religious problems of the Divided Kingdoms fell into two categories—one having to do with the struggle between Yahwism and Baalism, and the other with the rise and dissemination of ethical prophetism.

The Struggle Between Yahwism and Baalism

As noted earlier, according to tradition the Hebrew tribes who had left Egypt with the Exodus—along with other tribes who had foregathered in the Sinai peninsula were organized into a confederacy and initiated into the Yahweh cult by their tribal leader, Moses. Neither the Old Testament nor the Biblical scholars are fully agreed regarding the origin of Yahweh.

However, it seems reasonable to conclude, as Meek does after a painstaking examination of available data, that Yahweh was first known as a storm god in Arabia, that he was in time adopted by Judah as its tribal god, that he thereupon became the god of the southern confederacy of which Judah was the core, and that he became the god of all the Hebrews in the time of David when Judah dominated all the tribes (35:111–118).

The fact that the northern tribes did not to any extent embrace Yahwism prior to the time of David raises the question of the nature of their original religious cult. Meek considers this question at some length and comes to the conclusion that it was the cult of the bull-god or Baalism—not, however, the Baalism of the Canaanites, but rather a cult carried into Canaan by a Hebrew tribe of bull-worshipers, very probably by Joseph the leading tribe of the north. The priests of this cult were the Aaronites, and it must have been, as Meek puts it, "in the name of this god that Joshua made the covenant at Shechem and established the beginning of the northern amphictyony. As this confederacy established its sway in the north, bull worship became the dominant cult among the Israelite tribes, as Yahwism did in the south—" (35:132–140).

With the establishment of the monarchy, Yahwism became the state religion and Yahweh the national God. While this did not lead to the suppression of other cults, it did send them temporarily into eclipse (35:146). With the subsequent secession of Israel, Jeroboam promptly re-established the bull-cult as the official religion of the north. This automatically lowered Yahweh to the position of a minor deity. The Aaronites replaced the Levites as the state priesthood, and the bull-cult was set up at Bethel and Dan. However, just as the triumph of Yahwism under the monarchy did not completely suppress Baalism, so now the return of Baalism did not completely suppress Yahwism. It was to continue as a private cult. "Intolerance in religion," says Meek, "was not a characteristic of ancient peoples, and was only introduced into Israel by the prophets" (35:169).

The clash between Yahwism and Baalism was in large part due to the fact that the two cults were associated with different levels of social and economic development. The base of Yahwism was nomadic and pastoral. Within the clan and the tribe mutual responsibility, mutual aid, and substantial equality obtained. Individual hazard was small. And there was the one desert god. By way of contrast, the base of Baalism was agricultural, urban, and commercial. The Canaanites had long ago replaced clan democracy with primitive capitalism. Land had become a commercial commodity. There was marked economic and social inequality. And there were of course the obliging regional Baals.

Actually, the champions of the Yahweh cult were quite unaware of the influence of these economic backgrounds. Instead, they associated the clan democracy and the social justice, to which they were irrevocably committed, with Yahweh worship. By the same token, they associated social injustice with the worship of the Baals.

The Rise of Prophetism

Those who were most inordinately hostile to Baalism were to supply the nucleus of the prophetic group. The activities of Elijah and Elisha serve to illustrate this. The former, it will be recalled, journeyed from Gilead east of the Jordan river to Samaria to protest Ahab's seizure of Naboth's vineyard, while the latter was largely responsible for instigating the bloody Jehu revolution. Both were zealous advocates of social justice, and both were bitter opponents of Baalism. Under the Jehu regime Baalism fared badly, with regrettably no corresponding upsurge in social justice (31:29–33).

Actually, Baalism was anything but gone. It was to reassert itself again and again. Meanwhile, the prophets began to transform the austere desert Yahweh into a God more nearly in harmony with contemporary civilization (35:171). This task was to be accomplished primarily during the eighth, seventh, and sixth centuries B.C. The great eighth century prophetic spokesmen were Amos (fl. ca. 760), Hosea (fl. ca. 750), Micah (ca. 740–700), and Isaiah (ca. 724–680). These were followed by Jeremiah (ca. 625–586), Ezekiel (fl. ca. 600–570), and the Second Isaiah (fl. ca. 550) in the seventh and sixth centuries.

"Out of the mire of Hebrew political life," says Sachar, "the prophets rose like strange exotic blossoms. Their work is as surely the contribution to civilization of ancient Israel as Hellenistic art is the Greek contribution, and imperial law and government the Roman. Extraordinarily complex spirits they were: supreme individualists, yet preaching restraint and conformity to law; intensely patriotic, yet upbraiding the nation and threatening it with destruction; innately religious, yet despising the forms that religion took. They smote the idea of a national god and a narrow patriotism, often making military and diplomatic action impossible by their uncompromising attitude. They laboured to substitute plain, moral requirements for elaborate ceremonial and formal creed. They were the stern guardians of individual and national conduct, the living Hebrew conscience, the poets of statesmanship. And they were completely fearless in pursuing their self-appointed mission, bearing abuse with sublime patience, defying kings and priests and populace alike, eternal rebels" (46:61).

Viewed as natural phenomena, the prophets were above everything else the champions of social justice in their day. This made them of course no less champions of Yahweh, for as Turner puts it "the identification of Yahweh's law with a just society was the truly original element in prophetic thought" (54:354). The notion of social justice was obviously a carry-over from the days when clan and tribal democracy had prevailed. With Yahwism and social justice essentially synonymous, social injustice had of necessity to be attributed to men. It was the result of sin—and the prophets were continuously protesting against sin, and predicting the punishment thereof.

Unfortunately, the pre-Exilic prophets, with the possible exception of Isaiah, failed to conceive of realistic revolutionary programs against social injustice. Instead, as Turner observes, they contented themselves with a few palliative gestures, and advocated a return to a primitive economic and social order. On the other hand, "as 'religious visionaries' they reached supreme heights: the synthesis of Yahwism with social idealism. Thus from the primitive Hebrew *nabi* sprang seers—in every instance men of the people—who, by projecting a deep sense of suffering in supernatural terms, gave ethical attributes to deity. From the evils which the people felt ought not to exist the prophets developed a conception of justice that ought to exist; as Hebrews it was inevitable that they should define justice as the reign of Yahweh's law. The prophets' sublime conception of Yahweh was merely the focus of their social vision" (54:355).

The Rise of Monotheism

A further contribution of the prophets was monotheism. This concept, as Meek shows at some length, was elaborated slowly over a long period of time. In Mosaic times monolatry prevailed. That is, Yahweh had the united allegiance of the tribes constituting the confederacy. With the monarchy under David and Solomon, he had become the national god of the Hebrew state, and no one remotely conceived of him as the god of any other people. However, the prevalence of the Baals shows that he was by no means the only god worshiped by the Hebrew people.

The new type of prophet, the *nabi*, that began to appear in Saul's time, was to become one of the chief forces in the promotion of monotheism. This type was characterized by a spirit of intolerance that was unusual in the ancient world. It conceived of Yahweh as a jealous god demanding the exclusive loyalty of his worshipers. Hence, it was uncompromisingly hostile to all alien cults. Its orientation was generally so much to the past that it stood consistently in opposition to innovations. It reached its climax in the revolution of Jehu who attempted to eliminate all competitors of Yahweh. For a time at least it reestablished Yahwism in the north. As a result, two hostile kingdoms had for the first time in history the same state god.

This, as Meek stresses, represented an extremely important step in advance. "The establishment of Yahweh as the god of two distinct nations like Judah and Israel, and the recognition that he could use an alien people like the Assyrians as an instrument of punishment against his own people when they failed him, eventually led the prophets to see in Yahweh a god of the world, a god universal" (35:225). While Amos and other eighth century prophets appear to have been the first to regard Yahweh as the god of other peoples, they failed to deny the existence of other gods. The first Isaiah, however, went so far as to look upon them as inconsequential. "This," as Meek puts it, "was theoretical monotheism, which very quickly blossomed into the practical, thoroughgoing monotheism of Jeremiah and Second Isaiah, who declared in most emphatic terms that Yahweh alone was God and all so-called gods had no real existence—" (35:226).

"The Hebrew prophets," says Meek, "began as champions of Yahweh. That led them to oppose all alien cults, and bit by bit that led them to the position that Yahweh alone was God. With them monolatry blossomed into monotheism, nationalism into universalism, and religion became a matter of the heart and of righteous living rather than mere ritualistic practice. With them developed a new interpretation of god, a new interpretation of man, and a new interpretation of religion. With them origins ceased and the fruitage of ages of intensest religious experience was given to mankind in those mighty oracles which still remain the wonder and admiration of the world" (35:228).

The Deuteronomic Reformation

The long reign of Manasseh (692–638 B.C.), although politically stable and economically prosperous, proved to be a period of reaction for prophetism. Yahweh worship was not abandoned, but there flourished along with it any number of local and foreign practices that stood in opposition to it (43: 116–119). The prophets themselves had found it necessary to work underground. And there must have been revolutionary plotting (31:45). In any event, when upon Manasseh's death and the assassination of his son, the eight year old Josiah succeeded to the throne, the prophets once more asserted themselves, and the events which followed—commonly known as the Deuteronomic Reformation—must have been the work of the prophetic party.

The reformation began in 621 B.C. when Hilkiah the high priest reported the accidental discovery of an old law book in the temple. This crystallized the reforms which the prophetic party was anxious to effect. In the interest of prestige, the code, which now comprises portions of the Book of Deuteronomy, was ascribed to Moses, but it had obviously been written by the prophets while they were underground. It was, as Sachar puts it, "based upon the old Mosaic tradition, recast and amplified and steeped thoroughly in the prophetic spirit. The social, political, and religious ordinances so much abused and violated were plainly recited. The Hebrews were constantly reminded that they were a holy people, separate, unique, with a high standard of conduct" (46:72).

When it was read the code made a tremendous impression upon Josiah, the prophetess Hildah, and the people, and, as Pfeiffer observes, they clearly regarded it as the word of Yahweh. Moreover, Josiah promptly set it up as the law of the nation and began to enforce it (41:52). The temple was cleared of the altars and symbols of foreign gods; local sanctuaries were destroyed and their priests attached to the temple in Jerusalem were removed; and definite steps were taken to correct serious economic and social evils (34:106; 54:356–357). However, the reformed monarchy was short-lived. Within a dozen years Josiah fell in battle, and thereupon, although the code remained in effect, the usual reaction set in. Moreover, Judah was rapidly approaching its final doom (3:239–248).

Nevertheless, the Deuteronomic reform was an event of the utmost significance in Hebrew cultural history. The adoption of the code as the written constitution of the state signalled the birth of the Hebrew Scriptures. "For the first time in the history of mankind," says Pfeiffer, "a book was canonized as sacred scripture" (41:52). Strangely enough, the code was the creature of the prophets rather than of the priests or law-makers. Oddly, too, it was in the end to lead to the undoing of the prophets "by substituting a book for inspired speech, as the ultimate divine authority" (41:55).

The Exile

With the destruction of Jerusalem in 586 B.C., Judah became a Babylonian colony. Only the most important families were carried into exile to join those who had preceded them in 597. The rest remained to carry on at Mizpah under an able native governor by the name of Gedaliah. When the latter was murdered a few years later some of the others, fearing reprisals, fled to Egypt. However, Judah was by no means depopulated. In fact the largest proportion of the Hebrew people lived in Palestine; a somewhat smaller proportion in Egypt; and the smallest in Babylonia (3:252–254; 46:78).

During the forty-three years that Nebuchadrezzar ruled Babylon the lot of the exiles appears to have been very tolerable. They lived in small groups, and as long as they paid their taxes and obeyed the laws of the land, they were free to regulate their own lives. Within limits they appear to have prospered, and positions of responsibility were not beyond their reach. Babylonian life was decidedly stimulating, and there was danger that the aliens might be completely carried away by it. And actually, a considerable proportion of them were assimilated in varying degrees. The more pronounced nationalists, however, refused to give in, and effected instead various adjustments that enabled them to continue their worship of Yahweh. In this they were greatly aided and abetted by the priest-prophet Ezekiel who held before them the goal of the commonwealth governed by ritual law and assured them of ultimate restoration.

There is evidence, further, of much literary activity during this period. Among other things, the histories of the kingdoms and the messages of the great prophets appear to have been redacted and re-interpreted. It was during this time, too, that the synagogue came into being. Initially, the exiles appear to have gathered in homes on the Sabbath to hear the traditional prayers and to study the books and the lore brought with them. Presently a special community building known as the synagogue came to be set up for this purpose. In time this became a characteristic feature of Hebrew or Jewish communities everywhere (3:252–266; 31:55–60; 46:78–81).

The Restoration

Beginning with the Persian period in 532 B.C., and for half a millennium thereafter, Hebrew history is very meagerly documented. "The centuries following the restoration of the Jews to Palestine," says Baron, "are among the least well known in Jewish history. Sources for the period between Nehemiah and the Maccabean revolt are so limited and of such slight historical value that even the essential lines of development appear ambiguous. While we have some glimpses of Palestinian life, almost nothing is known of the Jewries of the Diaspora. The sparse and scattered references to the Jewish masses left behind in Babylonia prove little more than that there was an unbroken continuity until the Jews reappear in history in large and well organized settlements about the beginning of the Christian era. Egyptian Jewry, outside the Elephantine colony, remains a sealed tomb until after the conquest of Alexander the Great" (4, Volume I:128).

The traditional accounts of the restoration, as set forth in the Books of Ezra and Nehemiah, are now seriously questioned by critical scholars. They are not too sure that Cyrus issued the decree attributed to him, and they suspect strongly that only a very small number of exiles may have returned to Jerusalem. The restoration of Jerusalem may thus have devolved largely upon the Palestinians themselves. This would not of course have precluded some assistance from Babylon as evidenced, for example, by the contributions of Nehemiah (46:84).

The second temple was completed in 516 B.C. It was to serve as the center of restored worship for half a millennium. Little is known of subsequent events, prior to the arrival of Nehemiah after the middle of the fifth century. The latter not only rebuilt the walls of Jerusalem but assisted in the introduction of significant reforms. There is no agreement regarding the role played by Ezra, who apparently followed rather than preceded Nehemiah. He is, however, inextricably tied up with the rise of the scribe class, and the legalistic and puritanical upsurge beginning with the fifth century. The latter, says Sachar, took the form of "a steady reaction against religious laxness, a reaction sponsored by the scribes, who were becoming ever more influential. The scribes, forerunners of the Pharisees, were the interpreters of the law, the leaders in the synagogues. They were closer to the heart of the people than the priests. Zealous in their belief that the law of God must be strictly observed and that Israel must remain a separate people, they fought every attempt at compromise. It was due to them that, after the fifth century, Israel threw itself into complete dependence on the Torah (the Mosaic law) as the guide of life."

The law, which had been orally preserved for generations, was now carefully brought together and consecrated as the foundation of Jewish civil and religious life.—All existence was centered in the law. The Jews became the people of the book. The early Hebrews had created the Bible out of their lives; their descendants created their lives out of the Bible (46:88).

Hellenism and Judaism

Among the successful contenders for power following the death of Alexander the Great in 323 B.C. were Ptolemy Lagi and Seleucus. The former made himself master of Egypt, while the latter by degrees gained control of western Asia and most of Alexander's eastern Asiatic empire. Palestine's position between these two empires was not a happy one. Initially under Egyptian control, it was buffeted back and forth for a time, and then passed under Seleucid rule in 198 B.C. (3:297–298; 38, Volume II:187, 202; 46:99–100).

But, as Sachar stresses, for the Jews the rise of these empires and the control of Palestine were minor considerations as long as they did not jeopardize their religion (46:99–100). Actually, the cultural changes that came in the wake of them —especially the phenomenal spread of Hellenism—threatened to overwhelm Judaism. Both Egypt and the Seleucid empire had become thoroughly Hellenized. Palestine likewise had become impregnated with Hellenism, and it was of course completely surrounded by Greek cities. Under these circumstances Judah could not be expected to hold out indefinitely.

The contrast between Judaism and Hellenism was too striking to be reconciled in the case of given individuals. "The

Hebrew," says Sachar, "stressed reliance upon an omnipotent God and conformity to a divinely sanctioned moral law; he was essentially serious, restrained, willing to recognize his finite limitations. To seek God was the ultimate wisdom, to follow His precepts the ultimate virtue. The Greek accepted no revelation as ultimate; he strove to penetrate to the core of his conceptions, analysing the bases of his knowledge. He was blessed with a delicate, subtle reason and with a keen desire to use it, to probe with it, to open the very heart of reality. The Hebrew was inclined to mysticism; he accepted the moral law and would not go beyond it. The Greek bowed to no law but that of complete self-expression. He loved beauty and art, the outdoor life, and every aspect of nature which appealed to his aesthetic sensibilities. Where the Hebrew asked: 'What must I do?' the Greek asked 'Why must I do it?'—the Uppermost idea with the Greek was to see things as they really are; the uppermost idea with the Hebrew was conduct and obedience" (46:100).

By the beginning of the second century B.C. Hellenism had penetrated Judah sufficiently to constitute a serious threat to the integrity of Judaism. Since the two cults were not reconcilable in the case of given individuals, the population split into factions, with the Hasidim or Puritans and the Letzim or Hellenists at the extremes. On the whole those on the upper economic and social levels allied themselves with the Hellenists and those on the lower levels with the Puritans. The conflict reached its climax unexpectedly with the accession of Antiochus IV to the Syrian throne in 175 B.C. By-passing details, this brilliant but erratic monarch undertook to impose Hellenism upon the Jews by force and thereby incited a revolt that was to prevent the dissolution of Judaism.

The Maccabaean Revolt

While the events leading up to the so-called Maccabaean Revolt were getting under way, many inhabitants fled from

Jerusalem into the mountains and prepared for resistance. Leadership was to be supplied them by the aged priest, Mattathias, and his five sons, the Maccabees. The priest, before fleeing to the mountains with his sons, had slain a renegade Jew and an officer while sacrificing upon a pagan altar. The story of the Maccabaean brothers and their descendants, also known as the Hasmonaeans, cannot be detailed here. Suffice it to note some of their major achievements. By 164 B.C. Judas, after cleaning and rededicating the temple, had regained religious freedom (38, Volume II:232–233; 46:104). By 142 B.C. Simon won political independence for Judah, and the office of High-priest became hereditary in the Hasmonaean family (38, Volume II; 262–263). This left Simon free to declare himself king, but he failed to do so and devoted himself instead to the upbuilding of the country (46: 105). His son, John Hyrcanus, who succeeded him in 134 B.C., went the limit and declared himself king. And strangely enough, he employed force in converting other peoples to Judaism (38, Volume II:273; 31:83). His son, Aristobulus, who succeeded him in 104 B.C., further extended the boundaries of the country and generally adhered to his policies (38, Volume II:273; 46:105).

The Hasmonaeans had now obviously outgrown their original purpose. They had arisen to salvage Judaism; now they were increasingly jeopardizing it. The immediate result was a pronounced factionalism. The Sadducees, representing the upper economic and social levels—the elements that had been generally friendly to Hellenism,—favored the aggressive imperialistic policy of the Hasmonaeans. The Pharisees, representing the middle classes and those primarily concerned with the observance of the law and the maintenance of ritual and moral purity, rose increasingly in opposition to the Hasmonaeans. Under Alexander Jannaeus, the successor of Aristobulus, civil war actually flared up (46:105–106; 31:80–84). When Jannaeus died in 75 B.C. he was succeeded to the

throne by his wife, Alexandra, who in turn appointed her
son, Hyrcanus, to the office of High-priest. This momentarily
placed the Pharisees in control—regrettably only to exact
vengeance. Upon Alexandra's death in 69 B.C. her two sons,
Hyrcanus and Aristobulus, fought for the succession, the
former being supported by the Pharisees and the latter by
the Sadducees. After a period of intrigue and assassination,
both parties appealed to Pompey for aid. The latter settled
the issue in 63 B.C. by capturing Jerusalem and reducing
Judea to a Roman province under Hyrcanus (38, Volume II:
299–303; 46:106–107; 31:84–86).

Rome and Judaea

The relationship between Rome and the Jews was at best
turbulent and tragic. It began in sordid fashion in 63 B.C.,
when Pompey's legions in storming the temple slew some
twelve thousand Jews who would not defend themselves on
the Sabbath, and only at intervals did it rise above it thereafter (3:328; 38, Volume II:301–303; 46:107).

In 39 B.C. Anthony and Octavius asked the senate to confirm Herod as king of Judaea. The latter, half Jew and half
Idumaean, was the son of the noted Antipater upon whom
Rome had bestowed citizenship. Before Herod could assume
the kingship he had, however, to dispose of the last Hasmonaean claimant, Antigonus, who had set himself up as
king with the aid of the Parthians. With this accomplished
by 37 B.C., he ruled until his death in 4 B.C.

Unbiased historians generally rate Herod as one of the
world's great rulers. He brought prosperity and peace to
Palestine as Augustus did to Rome. He was a great builder
and an enthusiastic patron of the arts. The temple in Jerusalem not only surpassed the one attributed to Solomon, but
came to be regarded as one of the wonders of the Augustan
age. Unfortunately—apparently for reasons quite beyond his
control—the Jews refused to accept him. They despised him

for his alien racial heritage, for his firmness and generosity, and above all, for his love and encouragement of Hellenism. In the end the frustration induced by prolonged Jewish hostility and by serious household intrigues appear to have warped his temperament and undermined his sanity (16:531; 38, Volume II: 350–372; 46:114–115).

With the death of Herod the end of the Jewish state drew near. Herod's kingdom was divided between his three sons. Archelaus, the eldest, who lacked his father's good qualities, received Judaea, Samaria, and some Idumaean territory. He began his reign by slaughtering three thousand people in the temple court. And thereafter, until A.D. 6, when he was banished to Gaul, revolts and massacres were the order of the day. Rome now replaced the kingship with procurators directly responsible to the emperor. However, it soon became apparent that these, too,—rather irrespective of their merits—were quite incapable of maintaining order. "Under all procurators, good and bad alike," says Sachar, "there were clashes and the land seethed with rebellion" (46:117). With its patience exhausted, Rome resorted to extreme measures—only, however, to encounter more fanatical resistance. "The Romans," says Sachar, "were frankly bewildered. They had dealt with many turbulent peoples, but with none so contrary —so insanely intractable" (46:117).

The great national rebellion finally broke out in A.D. 66 with the capture of the fortress at Nasada and the slaying of the Roman garrisons, and it was to continue for four years. We shall by-pass the details of the campaigns that finally crushed the uprising, noting merely that they were carried on under the able command of Vespasian and his son Titus. As Sachar stresses, "the fall of the temple and the dissolution of the State destroyed all of the outward symbols by which the religious and national life of the people had been regulated," but "fortunately Judaism was not dependent for existence on a sanctuary and sacrifices. The life-blood of the nation was the law and the traditions which had grown up about it. The truest defenders of the faith were now, not the desperate Zealots who sacrificed themselves with sublime stupidity, but the scribes and sages who devoted their lives to teaching the masses the meaning of the ancient heritage. Such was Johanan ben Zakkai, who established an academy at Jabneh at the very moment that the physical State was being destroyed" (46:120).

There followed now nearly a half century of peace. Then, in A.D. 115, while Trajan was away from Rome subduing the Parthians, a series of rebellions flared up in Mesopotamia, Egypt, Cyrene, and Cyprus. These had apparently been instigated by an irreconcilable fanatical minority that was always ready to rebel when Rome showed any signs of weakness. Suffice it to note that these uprisings were sufficiently formidable to call for drastic action and strong reprisals (46: 121).

Trajan's successor, Hadrian, adopted a peaceful policy toward subject peoples, and many were initially disposed to look upon him as another Cyrus. However, toward the end of his reign he issued two edicts which promptly drove Judaea into revolt. One of these called for the rebuilding of Jerusalem as a secular city; the other was designed to stamp out physical mutilation including circumcision. The leaders in the revolt were the noted rabbi Akiba and the young warrior Bar Koba. The uprising, finally put down by Severus, entailed more casualties than that of A.D. 70. Judaea was abandoned as the name of the province, and the Jews were forbidden to enter Jerusalem again (46:122–123).

The Dispersion

Despite the vast numbers slaughtered from time to time and the hordes carried into slavery, the Jews showed a remarkable capacity for biological survival. The real dispersion beginning with the Babylonian captivity carried them by degrees through the whole Mediterranean world, and as they spread they multiplied. "By A.D. 70," says Durant, "there were thousands of Jews in Seleucia on the Tigris, and in other Parthian cities; they were numerous in Arabia, and crossed thence into Ethiopia; they abounded in Syria and Phoenicia; they had large colonies in Tarsus, Antioch, Miletus, Ephesus, Sardis, Smyrna; they were only less numerous in Delos, Corinth, Athens, Philippi, Patrae, Thessalonica. In the west there were Jewish communities in Carthage, Syracuse, Puteoli, Capua, Pompeii, Rome, even in Horace's native Venusia. All in all we may reckon 7,000,000 Jews in the Empire—some seven per cent of the population—" (16:545–546). Turner suspects that during the second Christian century one out of every ten persons—seven out of seventy million in the Roman Empire—may have been a Jew and that another million may have been living in Mesopotamia (54:705).

Cultural Contributions

As is generally known, the cultural contributions of the Hebrew people were almost wholly restricted to literature and religion. And literature, as it has come down to us, in the form of the Old Testament, was so largely in the service of religion that it scarcely existed in its own right. Why should the Hebrews have failed to make contributions in such areas as science, philosophy, and the arts? Clearly not because of lack of capacity. Actually, there were two very good reasons—the second more cogent than the first. To begin with, from the time that they entered Palestine the Hebrews found themselves constantly in the midst of peoples who were culturally more advanced. As a result, they had abundant opportunity to borrow—and as a matter of fact they borrowed freely of whatever they had need. However, the primary deterrent from creative endeavor in certain areas was their orientation. They failed to do creative work in science and philosophy because they had developed no interests in these areas. They looked to authority and revelation for knowledge and guidance, not to experimentation and reason. Only in such of their works as Job and Ecclesiastes are there indications of trends toward a rational orientation. Along with lack of interest in science and philosophy went, as Bertholet observes, an extreme practical realism—a dependence upon the sensuous that largely precluded abstraction and generalization. The very terms for such concepts as eternity and transitoriness were lacking. With this, extensive recourse to metaphor and allegory was inevitable (5:304–306).

In the case of the arts there was of course the comprehensive proscription against the carving of images (Ex. XX, 4). Such a commandment, says Bertholet, would have been inconceivable among a people with a well-developed sense of the plastic arts (5:306).

It was thus, as already noted, in the sphere of religion that the Hebrews manifested their creative genius. In this sphere they surpassed all other peoples in originality and independence, and in the lofty conceptions which they ultimately reached. At the outset their religion was closely comparable to that of other nomadic peoples. It was, as Meek observes, a "polydaemonistic and poytheistic" affair—with no end of spirits to direct human endeavor (35:91). With much travail, they rose in time to monolatry—the exclusive worship of one god without denying the existence of others. The Supreme achievement—the belief in one universal God who is as much interested in one people as another—came more slowly (35: 222–228; 41:470–480; 51:238–241).

The Old Testament

Since the Old Testament is the literary monument of this unique religious development we must briefly note some of its salient features. It was written over a long period of time— a period comprising more than a millennium—from about 1200 to 100 B.C. It represents all that has survived of the

Hebrew literature written before the age of Alexander (36: 25; 41:20). The content roughly falls into such categories as songs, law codes, narratives, oracles, prayers, and wisdom. The oldest materials—some of them transmitted orally and others written down individually in advance of their incorporation in the several books—appear to have been war songs, proverbs, riddles, fables, and prophetic oracles. Then came stories and law codes. And before long the priestly chroniclers began to weave them together into larger units (6: XII–XIV; 41:21–24; 54:708). Such recombination, along with revision, was to go on indefinitely. As a result, most of the books of the Old Testament are highly composite. While this is of course most true of the books embodied in the Pentateuch, none of the others appear to have escaped repeated revision (27:55–65; 51:221).

The Pentateuch deals with human origins and the history of the Hebrew people to the death of Moses. Until modern Biblical scholarship showed it to be the product of numerous authors and repeated revisions it was supposed to have been written by Moses. All available evidence now points to beginnings such as are enumerated above. The earliest compilations, and the sources on which they were based, are lost, but there are identifiable, within the existing books, the works of earlier authors. These are customarily referred to as sources or documents, and are labeled by the symbols J, E, D, and P. The J and E documents originated about 850 B.C., the former in Judah and the latter in Israel. The narratives cover much the same ground, but differ significantly in style. They derive their labels from the names they use for the deity—Yahweh and Elohim, respectively. Late in the eighth century B.C., the J and E documents were combined and elaborated into a new narrative—a narrative with a pronounced prophetic orientation. This document bears the label JE.

Another document embodied in the Pentateuch is known as D. It comprises most of the Book of Deuteronomy. Since this is largely made up of the Deuteronomic Code of Laws, it has a style uniquely its own. It was drawn up late in the seventh century. The final document, known as the Priestly Code, is labeled P. It is a formal and very erudite post-Exilic codification of ritual laws. The final compilation of these several documents to form the Pentateuch appears to have been effected about 400 B.C. (41:187).

The above sketch of the formation of the Pentateuch is generally known as the Graf-Wellhausen hypothesis. It has been criticized, but, as Rowley stresses, the critics have to date failed to substitute a theory that explains so many facts so well (45:46). Moreover, as Swain puts it, "the fundamental contention of the higher critics, namely, that the Pentateuch reached substantially its present form only at the end rather than at the beginning of ancient Hebrew history, is now denied by no competent scholars" (51:222; 45:Chapter II; 41:Chapter V, VI, and IX).

The formation of the remaining books of the Old Testament is beyond the scope of this discussion. Suffice it to stress once more that all of them are in varying degrees composite, and to note in passing that the motive that impelled the redactors, especially the historians, was not so much the desire for sounder factual bases for generalization as it was the desire for greater consistency between generalizations and beliefs. The Hebrew historians, says Swain, "wished to make history fit a pattern, and in general their pattern was a theological one. Thus the compiler of the Book of Judges made his history follow one simple formula: the Hebrews worshiped Yahweh and were happy; they fell away, worshiped foreign gods, and were punished with foreign oppressors; they repented, turned again to Yahweh, were forgiven, and prospered once more. This cycle was repeated a dozen times" (51:226–227). With a constantly changing religious orientation extending over many centuries, the past had to be repeatedly re-interpreted. As a result, revision was more or less continuous until canonization finally put a stop to it (41: Chapter IV).

Although the Council of Jamnia is supposed to have fixed the canon of the Scriptures for all time toward the close of the first century A.D., it is generally assumed that this step represented the end of a process that had been under way for several centuries. As Rowley points out, the canonization of the Law, although informal, appears to have been absolute before the end of the fourth century B.C.; that of the prophetic collections by about 200 B.C.; and that of the Writings by 111 B.C. The process underlying canonization appears to have been one of gradual growth in veneration (45:Chapter XXII; 41:Chapter IV).

The Hebrew Bible as finally canonized consists of twenty-four books arranged in three main divisions—the Torah or Law, the Prophets, and the Writings. The Law comprises the five books of our Pentateuch—Genesis, Exodus, Leviticus, Numbers, and Deuteronomy. The eight books constituting the Prophets fall into two sections—the Former Prophets with Joshua, Judges, Samuel, and Kings; and the Latter Prophets with Isaiah, Jeremiah, Ezekiel, and the Book of the Twelve. Under the Writings are embodied eleven books—Psalms, Proverbs, Job, Song of Songs, Ruth, Lamentations, Ecclesiastes, Esther, Daniel, Ezra and Nehemiah (one book), and Chronicles.

In the Septuagint, the Greek translation of the third and second centuries B.C., the books were re-grouped by subjects, and included among them were the so-called Apocrypha which the Council of Jamnia subsequently excluded from the Jewish canon.

BIBLIOGRAPHY

See Chapter 10.

CHAPTER X

Education Among the Ancient Hebrews

THE most distinctive feature of Hebrew education through the ages has unquestionably been its close integration with life. "Jewish education," says Drazin, "was never something extraneous to life or merely an instrument that served to prepare for life and that later could be discarded when its utility was exhausted. Jewish education was rather synonymous with life. It unfolded life, giving it direction and meaning" (13:12).

Along with the ancient Romans, the early Hebrews centered education almost wholly within the family, and within the family the father was of course the chief functionary. In this setting education was above everything else highly practical. "To the mass of the people," says Morris, "the concept of education, of teaching and learning as a continuous process unconnected with immediate practical needs, hardly existed in the earlier times. There was as yet no regular term to denote either learning or teaching.—It is in the Book of Deuteronomy that the primitive idea of 'guiding' or 'instructing' definitely gave place to the conception of teaching and learning in the modern sense." The notion of education "as a regular form of social activity" was to come appreciably later with the rise of the synagogue (37:8–9).

The Alphabet

With the conquest of Canaan the Hebrews by degrees took over the language and the alphabet of the Canaanites.

The prevailing speech of Palestine was the northern offshoot of the so-called western branch of Semitic. It differed only dialectally in the several regions including Phoenicia, and evolved into Hebrew in which the Scriptures came to be written (7:65–66; 24:79, 203; 28:514–515). Although they may have been indebted to other sources for the initial cues, the so-called primitive Semitic alphabet, consisting of twenty-two consonant characters, appears to have been assembled by the Phoenicians. As Kroeber observes, what there is in the way of fragmentary inscriptions points to the existence of this alphabet as early as 1200 B.C. (28:515). The earliest completely intelligible Palestinian inscription utilizing it appears to be the Calendar of Gezer with a list of farming operations arranged by months. It is dated ca. 1100–900 B.C. The famous Moabite Stone recording the historical relations between Moab and Israel is dated ca. 850 B.C. Dated somewhat later are extensive collections of potsherds, seals, and stamps. The inscription over the Pool of Siloam at Jerusalem is assigned to the reign of Hezekiah, ca. 700 B.C. The Lachish letters were written in perfect Biblical Hebrew in 586 B.C. when the Babylonian forces were in the act of storming Jerusalem (14:108–119).

Actually, the period beginning with the second millennium B.C. appears to have been one of extensive experimentation with writing in Palestine, Phoenicia, and Syria. The details of this do not concern us here. Suffice it to note that at least two separate and distinct alphabets were invented in the course of this millennium. One of these originated in the Semitic-speaking city of Ugarit on the west coast of Syria north of Phoenicia about 1500 B.C. It consists of twenty-eight characters formed by use of the cuneiform technique. As Kroeber observes, the clay texts of this North Semitic language can be read accurately. The alphabet is genuine and in no way ancestral to the Phoenician or ours (28:516–

517). The record of the Primitive Semitic or Phoenician alphabet, which was to survive and become ancestral to subsequent alphabets, is much more obscure.

This linear alphabet consisting of twenty-two consonantal characters was presumably assembled or set up by the Phoenicians at Byblus. However, there are strong indications that they may have gotten their cues from the Sinai inscriptions. The latter, discovered in 1905 by Flinders Petrie in the ancient Egyptian copper mines south of Palestine, consist of sixteen brief inscriptions presumably made by Semitic workmen employed by the Egyptians. The number of characters ranges between twenty and thirty, some of them resembling Egyptian hieroglyphs and others proto-Semitic letters. The language appears to be Semitic—a few words having actually been identified. The inscriptions have been variously dated between ca. 1850 and 1500. For a variety of reasons, not all authorities are as yet prepared to accept the characters represented in these inscriptions unconditionally as the precursors of the Primitive Semitic alphabet. However, barring new evidence to the contrary, the trend seems to be toward increasing acceptance of them (14:94–98, 140–144; 7:289; 24:110–114; 28:516; 50:48–53).

Whoever they were, the inventors of the Primitive Semitic alphabet extricated themselves from a mass of ideograms and word, syllable, and sound signs, and hit upon the idea of developing a list of signs or characters for such consonant sounds as they needed. In this they relied upon the principle of acrophony. According to this principle, as Kroeber puts it, "a simple form of a word sign" is used "as the letter for the first sound of the word" (28:517). (The Egyptians had earlier hit upon twenty-four signs of this type but without sensing their significance.) In Semitic, *aleph* and *beth* were the word symbols for *ox* and *house*, respectively. In the alphabet which the Phoenicians presumably received from the Semites, they had in addition become the signs for the initial sounds *A* and *B* (14:152–161; 24:109–113).

The alphabet developed in accordance with this principle, had come to embrace twenty-two consonant characters. These were—apart from a rather complete lack of vowel signs—quite adequate for languages of the Semitic group. As already noted in an earlier context, when this alphabet reached the Greeks it had to be extended to include vowel signs.

The lack of vowel signs naturally made learning to read a more difficult task. The so-called vowel point systems were not set up until after the middle of the first millennium A.D. (41:89–90). Biblical Hebrew remained in general use until the fourth century B.C. when Aramaic began to supplant it for vernacular purposes (41:73). For several centuries thereafter, at least to the end of the first millennium B.C., bilingualism seems to have prevailed. That is, the people continued to understand Hebrew after a fashion but used Aramaic for everyday purposes. Presently of course Hebrew was to become the language of scholars. During the time that the Mishnah was being compiled it was actually greatly extended as a living language. As we shall note later, the transition from one language to another, together with the retention of Hebrew as a sacred and scholarly language, was to complicate the problem of teaching reading still farther.

Early in the course of the second century B.C., along with the general linguistic upheaval, the old Phoenician letters which had been used in manuscripts from the beginning began to make way for the so-called "square Hebrew" characters currently in use (41:72–73).

Finally, it should be noted that the Hebrews, along with other ancient peoples, used their alphabetic characters also as numerals. They were arranged in a decimal system, and elaborated in a manner closely comparable to that of the Greeks (55, Volume I:204).

Writing and Its Uses

Despite the fact that writing reached a high level of development and served varied purposes, authorities are generally agreed that a knowledge of it was not widespread among the early Hebrews. Professional scribes appear to have been fairly common, and there are indications of families and guilds of scribes. As Driver observes, boys who were destined for such careers were apparently selected early and subjected to long and meticulous training (14:87–90; 5:312–313).

Writing served a wide variety of purposes. The Calendar of Gezer, it will be recalled, carried a list of farming operations arranged by months. The Moabite Stone, written by King Mesha of Moab, records historical relationships between Moab and Israel. The large collection of inscribed potsherds uncovered in Ahab's palace lists supplies of oil and wine along with relevant names and dates (14:108–109). Seals and stamps carrying varying amounts of legend serve to identify owners. Then there were of course inscribed weights and measures, and also mason's and potter's marks (14:113–117). The inscription over the Pool of Siloam at Jerusalem explains how the workmen excavating from opposite ends effected their junction. The famous Lachish letters carried military correspondence (14:118–119).

With the beginning of the monarchy there are indications of royal scribes and chroniclers. As Bewer stresses, these presumably kept fairly detailed records that were to be used by subsequent historians (6:43). After the downfall of the monarchy the Divided Kingdoms kept their own individual records (5:340–345). In addition, as Bewer puts it, "a parallel book of official records was prepared by the priests of the temple in Jerusalem. From the beginning they chronicled year after year the important events of the temple. And they were many, for the temple stood in the centre of the religious life of the nation; all great undertakings and especially all wars were consecrated here, trophies were brought to it, tribute was taken from it. Like the Royal Annals the records of the Temple Annals rested on contemporaneous knowledge, and they were therefore invaluable for the history and administration of the temple. But they also perished in the great conflagration that destroyed the temple and city in 586 B.C." (6:44).

From what has been said above, writing apparently served much the same purposes among the early Hebrews as it did among the other ancient societies that came within our purview.

Writing Accessories

The earliest writing thus far discovered in the West is, as Driver points out, recorded on stone. Some of it is carved upon natural rocks; some is incised upon prepared blocks; and some is scratched upon small rocks. Inscriptions upon broken pottery, known as *ostraca,* are about as old and numerous. Inscriptions on metal likewise appear very early. The scarcity of clay tablets in Palestine seems to be due almost wholly to lack of suitable clay (14:78–80).

Both leather and papyrus are ancient writing materials. Yet the Old Testament fails to associate them directly with writing. However, as Driver observes, one or the other is implied each time a Biblical writer refers to a book or a roll for only these materials could be rolled up. Actually, both leather and papyrus came into use early, the former being of course reserved for the more important documents (14:81–83).

A book, as Driver notes further, took the form of a scroll that could be rolled up. The text was written lengthwise in columns. The writer or reader began at the right and moved to the left end, winding up the scroll with his right hand as he finished each column and unwinding the other end with his left hand (14:84).

Two types of writing instruments were in use—a crude stylus with a metal point which enabled anyone acquainted with the alphabet to scratch letters on a hard surface; the other a reed pen with ink used by the professional scribe (14:84–87).

Formal Education

As in the case of most other early societies, there can be no pronouncements regarding the emergence of formal education among the Hebrews apart from a careful definition of the term. If by the emergence of formal education we mean the rise of the regular school tradition it was, as we shall note in passing, strictly a post-Exilic phenomenon; if, on the other hand, we mean the setting up of facilities for the training of specialists—among them, the priests and Levites, the Court and Temple chroniclers, and accountants,—then formal education must have been underway at the beginning of the monarchy. And to some extent possibly even earlier.

"That the priests and Levites received some kind of systematic and formal instruction," says Greenberg, "must be taken for granted. The priest had to be thoroughly acquainted not only with an elaborate and complicated sacrificial system but with the equally intricate laws of Levitical purity and physical health. The Levites had to be proficient as assistants to the priests and as members of the Temple choir. They could not possibly enter upon their duties without thorough previous instruction. The advanced age at which they started to perform their duties in the Temple, the priest at thirty and the Levite at twenty-five, probably reflects the extended period of training they had to undergo" (22:922).

Fully as urgent was the need of special training for chroniclers and scribes. Indirect evidence points to the existence of books and records even before the monarchy. And writing, as already noted, had reached an advanced stage (14:87–90). The administration of the economic surplus, too, had become sufficiently complicated to demand a trained personnel. The fact that such technical training appears to have been provided privately and by families and guilds does not remotely deprive it of its formal character (52:28).

Native Education

For our purpose we shall distinguish only two main stages in the development of Hebrew education—the Native and the Post-Exilic. The outstanding characteristic of Hebrew education during the native period was its concentration in and about the home and the family. In this and certain other respects there is a close resemblance between the ancient Hebrews and the early Romans. In each we have the patriarchal family pattern with extreme power and responsibility vested in the father, the same practical and austere orientation toward life, a similar disregard for physical and aesthetic training, and a closely comparable stress upon law as a basic element in the content of education.

While private training appears to have been available for the sons of the well-to-do Hebrews, and facilities must have existed for the training of specialists, there were no schools in the modern sense of the term during the native stage. Education was eminently practical and came initially at least largely through participation in the life of the family. In the end of course, as Swift stresses, such participation was bound to be enriched through varied communal experiences, among them the great religious and secular festivals (52:21).

With the rise and spread of literacy came the need of teaching the young to read and to write. However, apart from the facilities for the training of professional scribes and chroniclers, there are no indications of schools for this purpose. Indirect evidence supplied by the Old Testament points to a fair degree of literacy among the young in pre-Exilic times, and it leaves no doubt whatever but that the obligation of teaching reading and writing—to the extent that these skills were deemed essential—devolved upon the father (8:53–54; 52: 28–31).

Post-Exilic Education

There is little uncertainty regarding the over-all character of Jewish educational developments during the long interval beginning with the Restoration and ending with the Talmudic era. By way of contrast, the specific steps and sequences entailed in these developments are not infrequently extremely vague and obscure. Tenuous inferences abound, and there is much contradiction.

Actually, as Swift stresses, the Jews were busily engaged during much of this interval in setting up a universal and compulsory system of education as a means to their own self-preservation. "The gradual development of this policy among the Jews of Palestine," says Swift, "is the most interesting and most significant feature of the history of education from the time of the restoration of the Jewish community in the sixth century B.C. to the end of the Jewish state 70 A.D." (52:86). Putting this policy into effect demanded among other things a special teaching profession and regular institutions. That these conditions were met is abundantly attested by the subsequent existence of an able teaching profession and an adequate institutional set-up. Regarding the time and the sequence in which the conditions were met there is much more uncertainty.

The Rise of the Synagogue

Nevertheless, some things stand out rather conspicuously. One of these concerns the rise and development of the synagogue. As already noted, the exiles presumably hit upon this in Babylon and brought it back with them at the time of the Restoration. It was, as Swift puts it, destined to become "the earliest, the most wide-spread and the most enduring of all the educational institutions after the Exile. It was the first institution to offer systematic instruction to both sexes. It was the parent of the scribe college and the elementary school. Out of it arose the movement which resulted in universal education. Under its influence and that of the scribes all Jews became students of the Law; the law became the most reverenced of all studies, and the center of religious and intellectual interest" (52:90–91).

During the Exile, in the absence of the temple, the synagogue provided the exiles with an opportunity for informal worship and instruction. Upon the Restoration, it supplemented the temple cultus and flourished along with it. The legalistic developments associated with Ezra lent further emphasis upon instruction in the Law. In this setting the synagogue rose to great prominence as an educational and devotional center in post-Exilic days. "Scripture readings," says Greenberg, "gradually became a fixed feature of the gatherings on the Sabbath and on Monday and Thursday, the two market days when the peasants came into town. Reading Scripture in itself, however, could not serve the educational purpose adequately. Hence, there was added either a translation into the vernacular or a religious message based upon the passage that was read. In time, the Five Books of Moses were divided into sections, so that the whole Pentateuch might be read from beginning to end on the Sabbaths once in three years or once every year" (22:920).

The institutional development of education was intimately tied up with the synagogue. "From the very beginning," says Greenberg, "there was a very close relationship between the school and the synagogue. The synagogue premises were the meeting place of the school, and synagogue functionaries very often acted as teachers" (22:924). This was true of both elementary and secondary schools. Only in rare instances was it necessary to house these on premises apart from the synagogue (13:60–62).

The Scribe Class

Let us now, in advance of further discussion of institutional developments, turn to the scribe class—the Soferim and their successors, the Zugot and the Tannaim. The rise of this class, says Swift, "may be regarded as the beginning of a distinct teaching profession among the Hebrews" (52:32). The scribes, he points out further, looked upon "their work as a holy one: to them had been entrusted the sacred task of transmitting the laws given by Yahweh himself. Through their literary and educational activities they eventually gained almost complete control over religious thought and education. They interpreted the Law for the masses. They furnished the texts upon which instruction was based. They established elementary schools and colleges. They taught public and select groups of pupils.—On occasions of public worship they translated the Scriptures written in a tongue almost unknown to the masses in the post-Exilic period into the language of the people. In their teaching and in their lives they represented the new educational and religious ideal of the times, Judaism. Within their schools arose that oral literature which developed into the Talmud" (52:84).

As noted earlier, beginning with the fourth century B.C., the Jewish people took rather complete refuge in the Law as the guide of life. Since this is an obscure period in Jewish history not too much is known regarding the causes of these legalistic developments. Tradition associates them with Ezra the scribe who presumably came to Jerusalem in 397 B.C. to establish Judaism as formulated by the Babylonian priestly schools (38, Volume II:Chapter X). Whatever its causes, there can be no doubt regarding the reality of the legalism that is associated with the age. As such, it was sponsored and promoted by the Soferim, or scribes, to about 200 B.C.; the Zugot, or 'pairs' who headed the Sanhedrin, to about A.D. 10; and the Tannaim, or great teachers, to about A.D. 220 (13: 35–36).

Basically, this legalism rested upon the assumption that the Torah—the written Mosaic code plus its subsequent oral elaboration—supplied a complete guide for the regulation of every detail of the Jew's life. Obviously the Torah could function to this end only if the Jew knew its precepts. Hence, the Law, both written and oral, had to be interpreted and taught. This accounts for the emergence of the groups referred to above—the Soferim, the Zugot, and the Tannaim. These were all primarily interpreters and teachers. They represented the schools that carried on the scholarly work, the more popular type of interpretation and teaching being left to the synagogue.

It should be noted at this point that initially only the written Law was recognized. Acceptance of the oral tradition as equally valid and sacred came with the legalism associated with Ezra. While the interpretation of the written Law—due to its general character and the constantly changing external conditions—was a difficult matter, it bore no semblance to the complexities involved in the interpretation and application of the oral Law. The latter had been accumulating since the beginning of the Scriptures and had to be laboriously compiled and codified.

The Making of the Mishnah

The Zugot or 'pairs' played conspicuous roles in the compilation and interpretation of the oral Law. The last and most famous of them—Hillel and Shammai—founded schools sponsoring contrasting attitutes toward the interpretation of the Law, the former counseling moderation and the latter a rigorous literalism. Hillel's policy won out in the end. As a result, Jewish legal development retained a high degree of flexibility despite its apparent formalism.

Under the Tannaim the compilation and interpretation of the oral Law continued, and codification got under way. Akiba early laid down the general plan for codification. Upon his death the project was continued by Meir. Judah Hanasi, a descendant of Hillel, carried it to completion shortly after A.D. 200. The result was the renowned Mishnah. To this point the vast mass of traditional Law had been transmitted orally. And authorities are by no means certain that it was written down even now—at least in its entirety (11, Volume VIII:102; 55, Volume X:160–161).

In contrast with the Midrash, which consisted of running commentaries on the Scriptures, the Mishnah was a systematic treatise with the content arranged in six classes or orders— Seeds, Seasons, Women, Damages, Holy things, and Purities. Each order was in turn divided into Tractates, and each Tractate into chapters and paragraphs. As Margolis and Marx put it, "the aim of this work was clearly to furnish a textbook of the guidance of judges and religious teachers. Whatever had been settled in the past or in Judah's own school, by majority vote or through the preponderating influence of one in authority, was entered as a decision anonymously. The formulation was mainly taken over from Meir's Mishnah; but as a rule Judah put down in the same form an opinion reached by himself, generally with the concurrence of the patriarchal court. Thus the compilation, to a limited extent, assumed the form of a code. Dissenting opinions were carefully set down, together with the names of their sponsors. The accepted view was placed last; the opposing opinion was recorded in order to show that it had been considered but failed of acceptance. Altogether a hundred and forty-eight scholars are mentioned by name and these and the other teachers of the period from Hillel to Judah were called Tannaim, Mishnah teachers" (34: 222).

Toward the Talmud

With the oral Law compiled and codified in the form of the Mishnah, developments shifted to the discussion and interpretation of its provisions. This gave rise, in the course of the next two to three centuries, to the elaborate commentaries known as the Gemara—one developed by the Palestinian and the other by the Babylonian school. The scholars who elaborated these commentaries were known as the Amoraim. The Mishnah together with the commentaries forms the Talmud. Of this there are two recensions—the Palestinian made up of the Mishnah and the Palestinian Gemara, and the Babylonian made up of the Mishnah and the Babylonian Gemara. The former was completed about A.D. 400 and the latter about A.D. 500. For a variety of reasons the latter is both quantitatively and qualitatively superior to the former.

As Margolis and Marx observe, "The Talmud is primarily a legal commentary upon the Mishnah.—Every statement is scrutinized, every division of opinion traced to its source and principle. The discussion, as it grew in the course of generations, is faithfully reproduced, thus presenting a picture of cumulative layers of argumentation. The reader is taken into the atmosphere of the schools; he is made to witness the strenuous mental contests as proponent and opponent engage in thrusts and counter-thrusts. Constantly one is led from one subject to another, the very variety keeping the mind agile. The curt phraseology, half Hebrew and half Aramaic, yields now and then to the easy flow of the Aramaic vernacular; the legal tone is dropped, and the strain is relieved by a succession of sententious sayings and quaint tales (haggadah). Sometimes the lighter matter covers several pages and even complete chapters. As a result of the ease with which transitions are effected, the Talmud becomes a veritable encyclopaedia, in which, over and above jurisprudence, there are found imbedded theology and esoteric theosophy, moral and natural science, medicine, mathematics, astronomy, history, legend, folklore. There are two sides to the Talmud—the one rigidly legalistic and intellectual, the product of critical analysis which penetrates to the bottom of things; and the other ethical, spiritual, appealing to the emotions. Jewish life as it developed came to rest wholly on the Talmud; by it religious practice was regulated, Jewish piety in every act and in every thought molded, and Jewish mentality kept wide-awake even in the darkest periods of general stagnation" (34:245–246).

Institutional Developments

Drazin distinguishes three stages in the institutional development of the Jewish system—the founding of academies for higher learning by the Men of the Great Assembly in the period of the Soferim, the establishment of secondary schools for adolescents at the instigation of Simon ben Shetah during the first half of the second century of the period of the Zugot, and the provision of universal elementary schools by decree of Joshua ben Gamala shortly before the last days of the Second Temple (13:37–38).

The evidence supporting Drazin's generalization consists mainly of early statements quoted in the Talmud. The first two of these passages, referring presumably to higher institutions and secondary schools respectively, are admittedly vague, and have actually been variously interpreted by different authorities. However, by adducing a certain amount of additional indirect evidence, Drazin builds up a case for the rise of higher and secondary schools, respectively, that rests upon relatively secure foundations. The details of this are beyond the scope of this discussion. Suffice it to note the main features in the development of these two segments of the Jewish school system.

The Rise of Higher Institutions

In discussing the rise of higher institutions Drazin points out that the chief motivation back of them was the desire on the part of the Soferim to democratize higher learning—the desire to provide instruction for the many in place of the select few only. "Before the Jerusalem schools were estab-

ANCIENT EDUCATION

lished," he says, "it had been customary for the great masters of the Law of every generation to select an unusually gifted student, unless their own sons were such, upon whom they concentrated all their scholarly efforts. To this disciple they 'handed down' the Torah in its entirety. The chain of tradition and of higher learning was thus a selective process linked by deliberate planning. With the founding of the advanced schools, however, higher education was democratized to a certain extent and the learned leaders began to devote themselves not to one but to many disciples" (13:40–41).

Several of these higher schools apparently got under way during the period of the Soferim. Toward the close of the period they merged into one school. This endured to the time of the last 'pair' of the Zugot when it split into two rival colleges—Bet Hillel and Bet Shammai (13:40–42). These continued uninterruptedly in Jerusalem to the time of the destruction of the Temple in A.D. 70. Actually, however, Johanan ben Zakkai had secured permission from Emperor Vespasian to transfer the schools to the coastal city of Jabneh shortly before the fall of Jerusalem. Here they were reunited into one academy which functioned under Zakkai's leadership to the time of his death. Subsequently, when his disciples were scattered they established similar academies in other centers (13:49–53).

The Rise of Secondary Schools

Drazin attributes the rise of the secondary segment of the evolving Jewish school system to the fact that parental instruction had in practice failed to supply adequate preparation for the work on the higher level. "Orphaned children," he points out, "were entirely deprived of an education. Others were neglected because their fathers were too busy "earning a livelihood." In some cases at least the fathers were not sufficiently versed in the "elements of Jewish learning" to teach their sons. Finally there were those who would have

EDUCATION AMONG THE ANCIENT HEBREWS 247

been unable to pay the fees and meet the living expenses "while attending the school of higher learning in Jerusalem" even though they had managed to secure adequate preparatory training (13:43).

"With the Maccabean triumphs," as Drazin points out further, "there came a revival of the Hebrew language and of Jewish studies and observances. Many youths now eagerly desired a good Jewish education which, in the past, had been denied them. They were not far enough advanced in their studies, nor did they possess enough money to gain admission to the Jerusalem college. Nor could they find preparatory schools in which to satisfy their thirst for Jewish knowledge. Hence, the need for free secondary schools gradually arose, and in time these schools were established throughout Palestine" (13:43).

The decree calling for the establishment of such schools was issued by Simon ben Shetah, brother of Queen Salome and vice-president of the Sanhedrin, about 75 B.C. As a result, says Drazin, the Jews had for the first time in their history a two-level school system, consisting of "the Jerusalem college for advanced students and the preparatory schools which were spread throughout the lands in which the Jews lived. Elementary education was still a matter of parental care" (13:44).

The Rise of Elementary Schools

Meanwhile, the need for elementary school facilities was becoming increasingly acute. The boys were not adequately prepared for the secondary schools, and some remained quite untutored. Private schools sprang up here and there for those who could afford to patronize them. However, real relief was not achieved until about A.D. 64 when Joshua ben Gamala, the High Priest, decreed the establishment of free elementary schools for all boys. Such schools were subsequently established in all provinces where Jews resided in sufficient numbers. Strong social pressure assured them of wide-spread patronage. "This," says Drazin, "is the first instance in recorded history that we find an institution of universal and compulsory elementary education established" (13:46).

Although exceptionally well authenticated, and widely accepted, the Joshua ben Gamala tradition regarding the foundation of universal Jewish elementary education has not gone without its challenge. Morris especially has maintained that elementary education developed much more gradually than this tradition implies and that it could not have reached the advanced stage ascribed to it in Gamala's time until some centuries later (37:ch. II).

The Content of Jewish Education

Since a detailed account of Jewish education is beyond the scope of our discussion, we shall merely point to its salient features on successive levels. As Drazin points out, during the period of the Tannaim it was customary to designate elementary education as *Mikra,* secondary education as *Mishnah,* and higher education as *Talmud* or *Midrash* (13:87). Mikra had reference to reading, primarily Scriptural reading. Before he could begin with the Scriptures the boy obviously had to learn to read. This he did by the alphabetic method. His practice material was principally the Pentateuch beginning with Leviticus. Learning to read was of course seriously complicated by the necessity of translating the Hebrew text into the Aramaic, and in some regions, into Greek. Apart from reading, the boys commonly learned to write, and they may have received some training in simple numbers (13:81–87; 52:91–99).

As noted earlier, the Tannaim devoted themselves to the compilation, interpretation, and codification of the oral Law. The task was carried to completion by Judah Hanasi shortly after A.D. 200. Once it was completed, says Drazin, "this great code of law became the standard textbook for secondary education for many centuries" (13:92). But this does not, as Drazin further observes, warrant the assumption that the content of secondary education had been the same during the period of the Tannaim. The Mishnah was an evolving concern, and so was the content of secondary education.

There was, moreover, from beginning to end a clear-cut difference between the subject-matter of the Mikra and that of the Mishnah. That of the former was the written Law which could be read; that of the latter was the oral Law that had to be memorized. The latter naturally presupposed, and rested upon, the former. "When a child completed the Scriptures in the elementary school," says Drazin, "he did not stop studying the Bible. On the contrary, he proceeded to study it with more diligence and in more detail in the secondary school. That was true especially of the Pentateuch, for a new feature had been added. Whenever a certain portion that dealt with a matter of law was read in class, the teacher, orally, summarized all the details of that specific law that he knew, from tradition, and the children were required to memorize them" (13:89).

In defining the content of higher education in terms of Talmud or Midrash, Drazin points out that during the period of the Tannaim the latter implied Scriptural exposition that was actually under way, while the former referred to exposition that had been formulated and had now to be memorized in the colleges (13:98). "In the colleges," he says, "further study of the Pentateuch was diligently pursued. This time the students already familiar with the written text of the Law and with the oral traditions that pertained to each subject, were required to study the text once more and to examine and to consider the meaning of each word and letter thereof. Everything in the Divine Book was considered purposeful and meaningful. Certain hermeneutical rules were used by which the text was fully expounded.—By this method the students were able to discover that most of the oral traditions of the *Mishnah* were actually inherent in the text. Similarly, they discovered certain underlying principles through which they were able to develop new details of the laws. If these were acceptable to a majority of the college, they were added to their *Mishnah*. In time these would percolate through to the secondary schools and be added to the *Mishnah* previously taught there. For that reason, the subject matter of the *Mishnah* varied at times in the different secondary schools" (13:94).

BIBLIOGRAPHY

1. Albright, W. F., From the Stone Age to Christianity. Baltimore: The Johns Hopkins Press, 1940.
2. Albright, W. F., Archaeology and the Religion of Israel. Baltimore: The Johns Hopkins Press, 1942.
3. Bailey, A. E. and C. F. Kent, History of the Hebrew Commonwealth. New York: Charles Scribner's Sons, 1920.
4. Baron, Salo W., A Social and Religious History of the Jews, Three Volumes. New York: Columbia University Press, 1937.
5. Bertholet, Alfred, A History of Hebrew Civilization. London: G. Harrap & Company, 1926.
6. Bewer, J. A., The Literature of the Old Testament in Its Historical Development. New York: Columbia University Press, 1922.
7. Bloomfield, Leonard, Language. New York: Henry Holt and Company, 1933.
8. Boyd, William, The History of Western Education. London: Adam and Charles Black, 1947.
9. Bury, J. B., S. A. Cook, and F. E. Adcock (Editors), The Cambridge Ancient History, Volume I, Egypt and Babylonia to 1580 B.C. New York: The Macmillan Co., 1923.
10. Bury, J. B., S. A. Cook, and F. E. Adcock (Editors), The Cambridge Ancient History, Volume II, The Egyptian and Hittite Empires to 1000 B.C. New York: The Macmillan Company, 1924.
11. Chambers' Encyclopaedia, New Edition. New York: Oxford University Press, 1950.
12. Cornill, C. H., The Culture of Ancient Israel. Chicago: Open Court Publishing Company, 1914.
13. Drazin, Nathan, History of Jewish Education from 515 B.C.E. to 22 C.E. Baltimore: The Johns Hopkins Press, 1940.
14. Driver, G. R., Semitic Writing—From Pictograph to Alphabet. London: Oxford University Press, 1948.

15. Duggan, Stephen, A Student's Textbook in the History of Education. New York: Appleton-Century-Crofts, 1948.
16. Durant, Will, Caesar and Christ. New York: Simon and Schuster, 1944.
17. Encyclopaedia Britannica. Chicago: Encyclopaedia Britannica, Inc., 1950.
18. Finkelstein, Louis (Editor), The Jews—Their History, Culture, and Religion, Volumes I and II. New York: Harper and Brothers, 1949.
19. Gard, Carroll, Writing, Past and Present. New York: The A. N. Palmer Company, 1937.
20. Graham, W. C., The Prophets and Israel's Culture. Chicago: University of Chicago Press, 1934.
21. Graves, Frank P., A History of Education—Before the Middle Ages. New York: The Macmillan Company, 1914.
22. Greenberg, Simon, "Jewish Educational Institutions". Chapter 22 in The Jews—Their History, Culture and Religion, edited by Louis Finkelstein. New York: Harper and Brothers, 1949.
23. Hastings' Dictionary of the Bible. New York: Charles Scribner's Sons, 1903.
24. Hitti, P. K., History of Syria. New York: The Macmillan Company, 1951.
25. James, E. O., The Old Testament in the Light of Anthropology. New York: The Macmillan Company, 1935.
26. The Jewish Encyclopedia. New York: Funk & Wagnalls Co., 1901.
27. Kellett, E. E., A Short History of the Jews. New York: Lincoln McVeigh, The Dial Press, 1929.
28. Kroeber, A. L., Anthropology, Revised Edition. New York: Harcourt, Brace and Company, 1948.
29. Laurie, S. S., Historical Survey of Pre-Christian Education. New York: Longmans, Green and Company, 1900.
30. Leipziger, H. M., Education of the Jews. New York: Columbia University, Teachers College, 1890.
31. Landman, Solomon and Benjamin Efron, Story Without End—An Informal History of the Jewish People. New York: Henry Holt and Company, 1949.
32. Lods, Adolphe, The Prophets and the Rise of Judaism, Tr. by S. H. Hooke. New York: E. P. Dutton & Co., 1937.
33. Maller, J. B., "The Role of Education in Jewish History". Chapter 21 in The Jews—Their History, Culture and Religion, edited by Louis Finkelstein. New York: Harper and Brothers, 1949.
34. Margolis, Max L. and Alexander Marx, A History of the Jewish People. Philadelphia: The Jewish Publication Society of America, 1927.
35. Meek, Theophile J., Hebrew Origins. New York: Harper and Brothers, 1950.

36. Moore, G. F. and L. H. Brockington, The Literature of the Old Testament, Second Edition. London: Oxford University Press, 1948.

37. Morris, Nathan, The Jewish School. London: Eyre and Spottiswoode, 1937.

38. Oesterley, W. O. E. and T. H. Robinson, A History of Israel, Volumes I and II. Oxford: At the Clarendon Press, 1932.

39. Olmstead, A. T., History of Palestine and Syria. New York: Charles Scribner's Sons, 1931.

40. Peake, A. S. (Editor), The People and the Book. Oxford; At the Clarendon Press, 1925.

41. Pfeiffer, R. H., Introduction to the Old Testament. New York: Harper and Brothers, 1948.

42. Robinson, G. L., The Bearings of Archaeology on the Old Testament. New York: American Tract Society, 1941.

43. Robinson, H. Wheeler, The History of Israel. London: Duckworth, 1938.

44. Roth, Cecil, A Short History of the Jewish People. London: East and West Library, 1948.

45. Rowley, H. H., The Growth of the Old Testament. London: Hutchinson's University Library, Hutchinson House, 1950.

46. Sachar, Abram L., A History of the Jews. New York: Alfred A. Knopf, 1948.

47. Smith, Charles E. and L. M. Case. A Short History of Western Civilization. Boston: D. C. Heath and Company, 1939.

48. Smith, Charles E. and P. G. Moorhead, A Short History of the Ancient World. New York: D. Appleton-Century Co., 1939.

49. Smith, J. M. P., The Prophets and Their Times, Second Edition Revised by W. A. Irwin. Chicago: University of Chicago Press, 1941.

50. Sprengling, Martin, The Alphabet—Its Rise and Development from the Sinai Inscriptions. Oriental Institute Communications, No. 12. Chicago: The University of Chicago Press, 1931.

51. Swain, Joseph W., The Ancient World, Volume I. New York: Harper and Brothers, 1950.

52. Swift, Fletcher H., Education in Ancient Israel to 70 A.D. Chicago: Open Court Publishing Company, 1919.

53. Trever, Albert A., A History of Ancient Civilization, Volume I, The Ancient Near East and Greece. New York: Harcourt, Brace and Company, 1936.

54. Turner, Ralph, The Great Cultural Traditions, Volumes I and II. New York: McGraw-Hill Book Company, 1941.

55. The Universal Jewish Encyclopedia. New York: The Universal Jewish Encyclopedia, Inc., 1939.

56. Wardle, W. L., The History and Religion of Israel. Oxford: At the Clarendon Press, 1936.

57. Webster, Hutton, History of Civilization—Ancient and Medieval. Boston: D. C. Heath and Company, 1947.
58. Wellhausen, J., Prolegomena to the History of Israel. Edinburgh: Adam and Charles Black, 1895.
59. Woody, Thomas, Life and Education in Early Societies. New York: The Macmillan Company, 1949.

97 Wharton, Francis, History of Composition, Ancient and Modern (2d.
    Boston, D. C. Heath and Company, 1917).
98 Williamson, A., Predecessors in the History of Israel Elaboration
    (Adam and Clarke, (n.p.) 1883).
99 W — Hawes, Life — — — (n.p.) Study Sciences, New York
    The Macmillan Company, 1908).

CHAPTER XI

Education in Nonliterate Societies

ANCIENT education as characterized above took place in literate societies—societies which were in command of systems of written or oral composition, numeral notation, and measurement. In addition, these societies normally boasted fairly elaborate cultural traditions. Technical devices, such as linguistic composition, numbers, and measurement served initially primarily practical purposes. Farther along, they became means for the elaboration and extension of the cultural traditions, linguistic composition leading to literary expression and numbers and measurement becoming instruments of quantitative research. By degrees these initial ventures evolved into organized institutional programs.

However, this was but one aspect of education among these societies—the aspect of which they were in varying degrees aware. The other aspect—vastly more ancient and in some respects more influential—was the universal socialization process that operates more or less unconsciously in all societies under the influence of the prevailing culture. Education in nonliterate societies did not extend appreciably beyond this.

We have of course no authentic records of nonliterate education. This means that we are dependent upon conjecture, inference, and the study of nonliterate societies of the present and the near past. Even so, it seems desirable at this point to supplement our account of education in ancient societies with a brief characterization of educational perspectives and practices on the nonliterate level. In so doing, we shall use the term 'primitive' synonymously with 'nonliterate' and concentrate upon such crucial aspects of the situation as the child in primitive societies, family and kinship structure in primitive societies, the role of kinship in primitive life and education, scope and emphases in nonliterate education, educational practices and devices in nonliterate societies, folklore in primitive education, puberty rites in primitive societies, and the emergence of formal schools.

The Child in Primitive Societies

In spite of marked differences in standards and practices from society to society, authentic ethnological studies warrant certain generalizations regarding the status of the child in nonliterate societies. Due to the high rate of infant mortality and the widespread practice of birth-spacing, the primitive conjugal family is usually not excessively large. Abortion and infanticide occur under certain conditions, but they are usually motivated by practical considerations rather than a dislike for children (19:30–40). As a rule children are wanted and cherished. They normally have decided prestige value. Childless couples and unmarried adults are constant targets for ridicule. Cruelty to children and severe punishment of them are rare. Discipline and adult surveillance vary greatly from society to society. The same thing is true of the rate at which children are pushed toward maturity. However, whatever is being done in a given society usually makes sense when it is considered in the light of the orientation of its culture.

As might be expected, the origin and nature of the child are shrouded in mystery in the mind of primitive man. Some of the more backward groups, such as the Aranda of Australia, had not even attained a notion of physical paternity—especially in so far as this involves the role played by the father—when they were first contacted by ethnologists (21: 34). In general, there appears to be, as both Miller (19:13–20) and Pettitt (24:9–11) point out, a strong disposition to connect the child with the supernatural. Birth may represent a reincarnation as in the case of the Balinese (1:20). More often, as among the Eskimos, it appears to symbolize the return of an ancestral spirit (24:10). In either case it is a dangerous event, and evil influences must be carefully guarded against. As a result, the process is customarily enmeshed with an elaborate congeries of taboos.

Since the newborn child emanates from the spirit world, it is initially, as Pettitt puts it, if anything more strongly linked with the supernatural than the natural. It "is not simply an undeveloped human being." It "partakes of the mystery out of which" it "has come, and is in a process of transition from the superhuman to the human" (24:10). Since this process can easily be reversed, the child must be treated with great caution and marked discretion. Even an unintentional slight might prove dangerous. It is, moreover, not infrequently assumed to possess supernatural powers of apprehension. It may not only understand what is said in its presence from the moment of birth, but may even detect what is going on in the minds of those about him (24:11).

And the child may actually be dangerous. Says Corer, in speaking of the Lepchas of Sikkim: "But although in one way adults regard children as potentially small adults, they have a somewhat ambivalent attitude towards them. Children are not quite human. If they survive they will turn into proper members of society; but if they die they will turn into particularly malevolent devils—*num-een-moong.*—A child who dies before about his tenth year is treated very differently from an adult: no funeral ceremonies are held for it and the body is thrown unceremoniously into the river; but elaborate apotropaic ceremonies are performed to ward away its ghost devil. . . . The more attached a child was to his home and family, the more vigorously will his *num-een-moong* attempt to reduce the other members to the same state as itself. Consequently a child represents potential supernatural danger.

"The attitude of parents towards a child between the ages of about four and ten is therefore twofold: the child is a potential adult, but one in need of training and education to make him a socially valuable adult; at the same time the child is a potential source of supernatural danger, and as such it would be uneconomical to lavish too much affection upon it. Should the child live it will be a great source of comfort and help; should it die it would be a source of great danger; the two contingencies must be taken into account" (9:302).

In general, then, the widespread notion of child intimacy with the supernatural appears to have had significant bearings upon the reactions of primitive peoples to children. Pettitt feels that it is largely responsible for the kind of considerate treatment accorded them everywhere, and that it apparently also has gone far toward motivating precautions against malevolent spirits. And, in North America at least, it appears to be intimately tied up with the subsequent solicitation of the patronage of good spirits (24:9–10).

Family and Kinship Structure in Primitive Societies

The family is the elementary social unit in all societies. Murdock identifies three distinct types in 250 representative societies—the *nuclear family*, consisting normally of "a married man and woman with their offspring"; the *polygamous* family, consisting of "two or more nuclear families . . . having one married parent in common"; and the *extended family*, consisting of "two or more nuclear families affiliated through an extension of the parent-child relationship." Among 192 societies of Murdock's sample 47 featured the first of these family types, 53 the second, and 92 the third (22:1–2). However, another sample of 238 societies revealed that only 43 of them insisted upon strict monogamy. This means in essence that plural marriage is more prevalent than would appear at first sight (22:24).

As noted above, polygamy implies plural marriage on the part of either husband of wife. When a man is married to more than one wife contemporaneously the relationship is polygamous, and when a woman is married to more than one husband at a time it is polyandrous. The latter is so rare, however, that Murdock aptly characterizes it as an "ethnological curiosity" (22:25).

Since the nuclear family, when it does not exist by itself alone, always enters into the composition of the other types—the polygamous and the extended,—Murdock regards it as the basic functional social unit in every society. Its fundamental functions—sexual, economic, reproductive, and educational—are the same whether it exists singly or in composition with others (22:10).

The social character of the nuclear family group derives from the fact that "sets of reciprocally adjusted habitual responses" tie the "participant individuals collectively to one another, . . . the clustered relationships" being "eight in number: husband-wife, father-son, father-daughter, mother-son, mother-daughter, brother-brother, sister-sister, and brother-sister" (22:3–4).

Incest taboos offer, in Murdock's estimation, one of the most striking examples of the influence of "family structure upon individual behavior." Incest taboos, he points out, "invariably apply to every cross-sex relationship within the nuclear family save that between married spouses" (22:12). Their immediate effect is of course to restrict the nuclear family to two generations. As Murdock puts it, "they compel each child to seek in another family for a spouse with whom to establish a marital relationship. In consequence thereof, every normal adult in every human society belongs to at least two nuclear families—a *family of orientation* in which he was born and reared, and which includes his father, mother,

brothers, and sisters, and a *family of procreation* which he
established by his marriage and which includes his husband
or wife, his sons, and his daughters" (22:13).

The fact that an individual belongs to two nuclear families
gives rise to potentially extremely complex kinship systems.
With marriage occurring within an incestuous family, the
latter would be very simple calling for little more than differentiation between members and non-members and classification by age and sex (22:13, 94). Under the influence of incest
taboos, however, the two families overlap and their members
are arranged in varying "degrees of nearness or remoteness
of relationship" (22:14). Thus, "any individual in any society
has potentially seven different kinds of primary relatives,
33 of secondary relatives, 151 of tertiary relatives, and geo-
metrically increasing numbers of distant relatives of various
degrees" (22:96).

Since such a stepwise gradation can be extended indefinitely, societies have generally "found it necessary to reduce
the total number of kinship terms to manageable proportions
by applying some of them to different categories of relatives"
(22:14). As both Gillin and Gillin (7:241) and Herskovits (11:
298–299) point out, the use of a so-called *classificatory terminology* often brings together different relatives under single
categories—such as uncles, aunts, and cousins in our own system. And many primitive societies actually do make large use
of classificatory *father*, *mother*, *brother*, and *sister*, categories. On this basis there is often no distinction between father
and father's and mother's brothers, between mother and
mother's and father's sisters, between one's real brothers and
the sons of other fathers and mothers, and between one's
real sisters and the daughters of other fathers and mothers.

Beyond this, all societies affiliate an individual with a restricted group of relatives, the whole group being too cumbersome for intimate contact. This is accomplished through a
rule of descent—usually patrilineal, matrilineal, or bilateral.

Patrilineal descent affiliates an individual with the consanguineal kin group of the father, matrilineal descent with that of the mother, and bilateral descent with some of the nearest kinsmen of both parents. Unilinear descent (patrilineal and matrilineal) predominates in primitive societies (22:44). The restricted group of kinsmen with which the individual is thus affiliated not only provides intimate contacts, but defines in a large measure reciprocal privileges and obligations. "Descent," as Murdock stresses, "is not synonymous with genealogical relationship" . . . it "refers solely to a cultural principle whereby an individual is socially allocated to a specific group of consanguineal kinsmen" (22:42–43).

Since residential cohabitation in marriage is universal, and husband and wife cannot both continue to reside with their respective families of orientation, all societies have found it necessary to adopt a rule of *residence*. Murdock enumerates five of these—the *patrilocal*, requiring the bride to reside with or near the groom's kin; the *matrilocal*, requiring the groom to settle with the bride's kin; the *bilocal*, permitting the couple to reside near the family of either spouse; the *neolocal*, enabling the couple to set up its own domicile independent of parental locations; and the *avunculocal*, prescribing residence with or near a maternal uncle of the groom. In the vast majority of the societies studied by Murdock the patrilocal and matrilocal rules prevailed, the former outnumbering the latter in the ratio of more than four to one (22:16–17).

A rule of residence tends to assemble in one locality a particular group of kinsmen together with their families of procreation. If the rule is patrilocal, the kinsmen are patrilineally related; if it is matrilocal, the relationship is matrilineal. The bilocal rule in turn brings together an assortment of bilateral relatives. And, as Murdock puts it, "out of such local clusters of kinsmen may arise two major types of social group—extended families and clans" (22:17–18).

The extended family is about as continuous in time as are unilinear kin groups and the community. The main types—the patrilocal, matrilocal, and bilocal—are determined by the prevailing rule of residence. The patrilocal type consists of the "families of procreation of a man, his married sons, his sons' sons"; the matrilocal includes the "families of procreation of a woman, her daughters, and her daughter's daughters"; the bilocal type in turn "unites the nuclear family of a married couple with those of some but not all their sons—daughters, —and grandchildren of either sex" (22:34–35).

Nuclear and extended families are, in Murdock's terminology, "residential kin groups." The kinship bonds which hold the members together "are always in part affinal" (by marriage); "never exclusively consanguineal." These groups regularly include "husband and wife but not brother and sister" (22:41–42).

The extended family as a residential kin group in turn gives rise to a second type of kin group—the *consanguineal*. The bonds which hold the members of such a kin group together are, as Murdock stresses, exclusively consanguineal. They always include "both brother and sister" but, due to the fact that these normally belong to different groups, "almost never both husband and wife." Since married brothers and sisters belong to different groups and are separated by incest taboos, consanguineal kin groups cannot share common residence. Their form is primarily determined by the rule of descent (22:42).

The main forms of consanguineal kin groups are the *lineage* and the *sib* or *clan*. These are produced by either rule of unilinear descent—patrilineal or matrilineal. When the members of such a group can definitely trace their relationship to each other it is known as a *lineage*. When the genealogical relationship is assumed but cannot be definitely traced, the group is known as a *sib* or *clan*. Since descent may be either patrilineal or matrilineal, there are both patri-sibs and matri-sibs (22:47).

As a unilateral group of consanguineal relatives, the sib occupies, wherever it is found, an important place in primitive social structure. It is, as Gillin and Gillin put it, an organization into which an individual is born and from which he cannot resign. Its members commonly address each other in such terms as *brother, sister, father, mother.* Its patterns are in large part extensions of family patterns (7:237–238). Membership entails both serious obligations and large-scale privileges. "Members of a sib," says Turney-High, "avenge wrongs, afford mutual protection, feed the needy, and provide a system of poor relief, mother's pensions, and child welfare—services which are taken over by the state in our society" (31:468–469).

Since most sibs, along with other unilinear consanguineal groups, are exogamous, the members of a sib must seek mates in other sibs. This calls for rules of preferential mating. The most widely approved rule is marriage between *cross-cousins.* These are the children of brothers and sisters, both real and classificatory. Marriage between *parallel cousins*—the children of brothers or sisters—is generally prohibited. As Herskovits points out, marriage between cross-cousins does not violate incest taboos because brothers and sisters belong to different sibs; that between parallel cousins would be incestuous because siblings of one sex—brothers or sisters—belong to the same sib (11:299).

A further characteristic of sibs and other unilinear consanguineal groups is that they commonly bear the names of animals, plants, or other natural phenomena, and that they assume the existence of mystical relationships between themselves and the latter. This phenomenon, along with associated practices, is known as *totemism,* and the eponymous objects themselves as *totems.* Since the totemic objects are frequently regarded as the common ancestors of the group their integrity is generally safeguarded by taboos. Socially, totemism tends to unify a group and to give it a sense of exclusiveness (7:236).

Two additional concepts must be brought into perspective —the community and the tribe. The community or local group is, along with the nuclear family, a universal group, being usually known as a *band* under hunting conditions and as a *village* or *neighborhood* with permanent residence. Of 241 societies in Murdock's sample 39 were organized in bands, 13 in neighborhoods, and 189 in villages (22:80). The community is of course a territorial unit. It has a distinctive culture of its own, along with a strong *in-group* feeling. Its internal organization varies, depending in part at least upon the manner in which the kin groups are integrated. Not infrequently, the community itself is a kin group (22:88).

The term *tribe* is often used very loosely to designate almost any kind of a group. It has, nevertheless, a quite specific technical connotation. Turney-High defines it as "the largest kin-based social-control organization in non-literate society" —the family representing the opposite extreme (31:474). "In its simplest form," Linton characterizes it as "a group of bands (local groups) occupying contiguous territories and having a feeling of unity deriving from numerous similarities in culture, frequent friendly contacts, and a certain community of interest," and points out that its nucleus is probably "always formed through the increase and splitting of an original band" (14:231–232). For Gillin and Gillin it connotes *"any collection of preliterate local groups which occupies a common general territory, speaks a common language, and practices a common culture"* (7:287).

The Role of Kinship in Primitive Life and Education

One of the most unique features of primitive life is its involvement with kinship. "In Tikopia," says Firth, "the following are some of the spheres into which kinship enters as an articulating principle. It is the basis of association in the small residential units, the house-holds; it is the acknowledged bond between the members of the major named groups of the society; it provides the link with elders and in part with chiefs, who exercise political and religious functions for these groups and for the society as a whole; it is the overt principle regulating the ownership and suzerainty of land. Kinship provides terms for address and reference, thus giving a linguistic bridge between individuals; it is the common basis of assistance in cooking and primary economic cooperation; it stands behind a great series of duties, privileges, taboos, avoidances; it proscribes certain types of sex union and marriage; it is the basis for the assemblage of members of the society on the birth, initiation, sickness or death of anyone. Enshrined in tradition, it bulks largely in the accounts of the origin of present-day social groups and the distribution of territory among them; projected into the realm of the spirit-heavens it gives the basis for approach to ancestors and gods, and it is used as the key to the interpretation of the disordered behavior of individuals in a state of dissociation" (6:377–378).

The extreme emphasis upon kinship in primitive social life stands, as Turney-High stresses, in striking contrast to its decreasing importance in Western social life (31:461). Actually, apart from the nuclear family and a restricted group of loosely recognized kindred, it is no longer a functional element in our culture. We affiliate ourselves with individuals and groups irrespective of kinship lines.

The purposes which kinship serves in primitive societies are, as Gillin and Gillin point out, primarily practical. It is the main determiner of the categories and groups that are to participate in the cultural affairs of the societies. Indeed, in some primitive societies lack of kinship identification completely precludes social participation of any kind, so much so that even ethnologists working among them sometimes find it necessary to be adopted into native families, or in less drastic cases, at least to be assigned a definite place in the social structure (7:227).

Kinship systems in primitive societies assure the individual a high degree of social orientation and security. The various interpersonal relationships in which he automatically finds himself are well-defined. As Thompson and Joseph point out in their characterization of the Hopi system, each relationship "implies a set of obligations and privileges" along with "prescribed attitudes and behavior." Such a system, they stress, "is important because it applies to (and regulates Hopi attitudes and correlative behavior toward) not only all Hopi related by blood or marriage but also (through a series of extension mechanisms such as ceremonial adoption and initiation) to practically all interpersonal relations in the tribe, and many relationships with neighboring tribes, such as the Navaho and Zuñi. Hence, an individual is related, either through actual kinship or through an extension of it, to practically everyone else in the pueblo and also in other Hopi pueblos, and his behavior in practically all face-to-face relationships with other individuals with whom he comes in contact, except Whites of course, is prescribed and regulated accordingly" (29:36).

Says Opler, in speaking of the Apache child and his kin: "The social world to which the child is first introduced consists of a well-organized group of kin. The significant events of his life will be planned and made possible by his blood relatives. Should a person be wronged, his relatives act for him and with him: should he be accused, they shield him from vengeance. If a man dies with grievances unavenged, his relatives perpetuate his quarrel in a feud between families. It is they who have the responsibility for his death rites and who mourn for him" (23:54).

For all this the primitive pays of course a high price. He is socially oriented and secure, but he has no freedom and no opportunity for the exercise of initiative. He cannot choose his associates, and his obligations and prerogatives are meticulously determined for him. As Lowie puts it, "he is bound to render services to an individual of one class; with a member of another he may jest and take liberties; with persons of a third category he must have nothing to do except through intermediaries; and so forth" (15:80).

Since the primitive child is born into a complex structure of kinsmen and kinship regulations, one of his major problems is to learn to fit into and function in such a system. This means that he must be gradually inducted into the intricacies of the system under the direction of kinsmen.

Leighton and Kluckhohn, in discussing Navaho childhood, point out that "the main lines of communication" in this society "are between relatives." As a result, "the first and most important lessons which the child learns about human relationships are the approved ways of dealing with various classes of relatives" (13:44). He "learns early that he can expect certain relatives to follow a prescribed way of behaving toward him. He finds that his mother's brothers will scold him severely or punish him, but that he can get away with playing tricks upon them . . ." "He is taught, as he grows older, that toward all the persons whom he calls 'my sister' he must be respectful and practice certain avoidances; he must be restrained in any joking and never deal in humor of a sexual connotation; decorum must be observed in face to face speech, which in conservative families still involves the use of a special set of personal pronouns."

"Two 'brothers' or two 'sisters' (both real and classificatory) present a solid front to the rest of the world but may tease each other privately.—On the other hand, the youngster comes to expect an exchange of vulgar jokes with anyone whom he calls 'my cross cousin'.—With the father's parent there is reciprocal repartee about sex of somewhat subtler nature. With the mother's parents joking is more restrained."

"We need not follow out all the details of these patterns.—

The important thing is that there is a definite way to behave toward all persons addressed by the same kinship term. This limited set of patterns for social life, acquired in childhood, is later used to bridge excursions into the wider social environment. The ways in which a Navaho adult deals with all individuals who come into his life tend to represent modifications of these master designs for interpersonal relations" (13: 44–45).

In their characterization of the education of the Hopi child, Thompson and Joseph point out that "training in the basic disciplines—as well as initiation into the intricacies of the kinship system with its complex reciprocity patterns is the responsibility of the household group.—During childhood and youth for girls, and up to about the sixth year for boys, the learning process is chiefly in the hands of the mother and other females of the household, aided by the mother's brother when stricter discipline is needed, and also by the father and the maternal grandfather" (29:52).

Let us now note in somewhat greater detail the roles which specific kin groups and kinsmen play in the education of the primitive child. Our first concern is of course with the two family groups—the nuclear and the extended. The most unique common features of the social life of all societies is, as repeatedly stressed, the nuclear family. It is within this group that the individual in all societies "establishes his first habits of reciprocal behavior, his first interpersonal relationships." These early intra-family habits and relationships, modified and extended through subsequent learning, in turn provide patterns for other kin activities and relationships (22: 92–93).

The nuclear family, as Linton points out, operates under certain inherent limitations. It is set up anew in each generation. The personalities of the spouses are formed independently in advance of mating and must be adjusted in varying degrees. It is basically unstable in character, being constantly subject to dissolution through divorce or death. As rapidly as the children grow up, they desert it to form their own families. The family circle is so restricted that emotional energy is confined within extremely narrow limits (14:160–161). It is, nevertheless, a remarkably effective socialization agency.

By broad consent the extended family is strong where the nuclear family is weak. It has continuity in time. Since its nucleus consists of brothers and sisters, real or classificatory, there is, as Linton stresses, no occasion for the mutual adjustment of adult personalities (14:161). The stability of such a group is extraordinarily high because divorce and death disrupt it only minimally. Emotional energy is widely diffused for there are numerous fathers, mothers, brothers, and sisters. The child has little opportunity to develop fixations, and situations inducing frustration are rare.

"If from earliest childhood," says Reichard, "I live in close contact with four or five women and address them by the same term and they treat me with equal affection and care, it is unlikely that I shall regard one quite differently from the others. If I do it is not necessary that my favorite be my actual blood mother. The idea of absolute mother-love is an exaggeration of our own culture. There are many cases where a mother's sister, a foster mother, or even a neighbor is regarded more fondly by a child than his real mother. Primitive society gives no proof of the stepmother idea as a natural human characteristic. On the contrary, it shows by attitudes of different relatives toward children and toward adoption that ours and other similar attitudes are based on particular prejudices not founded on biological instincts that unite parents and children" (27:421).

In characterizing the extended family among the Apache, Opler says: "The household into which the child is born is one of a cluster of elementary families related through the maternal line. Near an older man and woman reside their unmarried sons and daughters, their married daughters and the sons-in-law, their daughters' daughters (married and un-married), and their daughters' unmarried sons. The number of separate dwellings varies according to the size of the group and the ages and marital status of the individuals in-volved.—It is with the members of this maternal extended family that the child has his earliest and most meaningful contacts. In his own household live his parents and his broth-ers and sisters.—Within easy reach are the maternal grand-parents, the mother's sisters and their husbands and children, and the mother's unmarried brothers.—The extended family from which his father has come may be located in the same vicinity." If so, "the paternal relatives will see him often and show great affection for him" (23:18–19).

"A Samoan village," according to Mead, "is made up of some thirty to forty households, each of which is presided over by a head-man called a *matai.*—These households in-clude all the individuals who live for any length of time under the authority and protection of a common *matai.* Their com-position varies from the biological family consisting of parents and children only, to the households of fifteen and twenty people who are all related to the *matai* or to his wife by blood, marriage, or adoption, but who often have no close relationship to each other.—Such a household is not neces-sarily a close residential unit, but may be scattered over the village in three or four houses" (17:39–40).

As Mead observes further, "Few children live continuously in one household, but are always testing out other possible residences. And this can be done under the guise of visits and with no suggestion of truancy. But the minute that the mild-est annoyance grows up at home, the possibility of flight moderates the discipline and alleviates the child's sense of de-pendency. No Samoan child, except the *taupo,* or the thor-oughly delinquent, ever has to deal with a feeling of being trapped. There are always relatives to whom one can flee" (17:42–43).

Farther along, in contrasting the influence of the Samoan household upon the child with that of our own, Mead says: "The close relationship between parent and child, which has such a decisive influence upon so many in our civilization,—is not found in Samoa. Children reared in households where there are a half dozen women to care for them and dry their tears, and a half dozen adult males, all of whom represent constituted authority, do not distinguish their parents so sharply as our children do. The image of the fostering, loving mother, or the admirable father, which may serve to determine affectional choices later in life, is a composite affair, composed of several aunts, cousins, older sisters and grandmothers; of chief, father, uncles, brothers and cousins. Instead of learning as its first lesson that here is a kind mother whose special and principal care is for its welfare, and a father whose authority is to be deferred to, the Samoan baby learns that its world is composed of a hierarchy of male and female adults, all of whom can be depended upon and must be deferred to" (17:209–210).

The family, as noted earlier, is a residential kin group, and as such an exceptionally effective educational agency. How about the consanguineal kin groups—especially the lineage and the sib or clan—which are not residential units? How do these influence education in primitive societies? Primarily by extending the ordered and structured social background to which the child must adjust beyond the family. In speaking of the Navaho, Leighton and Kluckhohn say: "There are many Navaho clans, and every Navaho belongs to one of them. Children automatically become members of the clan of their mother. Outside the family group of close relatives the clan is the strongest tie for the Navaho. Just as one must not marry a real sister or brother, so also one must neither marry nor engage in any flirtatious behaviour with a clan sister or brother. When two Navahos meet, each quickly asks the other of his clan in order to eliminate the danger of transgressing the rules of conduct and to assure himself of the advantages of a possible clan bond" (13:6).

And farther along they add: "Until the child is five or six he spends most of his time at home. Then he begins to be taken more often to the trading store and to ceremonials and other gatherings. So far as possible, new people are placed within the kinship system. Behavior patterns toward clan (and linked-clan) relatives are the same in principle but attenuated in practice. However, when a child meets an older person of the same clan he immediately feels a degree of ease with and attraction toward the adult, because the clansman automatically assumes his place in the child's world, a high place in sentimental terms. The youngster expects—and receives—warmth and assurance, gifts, praise, and other rewards. The same, to a lesser degree, may be said for the 'relatives' through the father's clan.

"Toward nonrelatives reserve is the rule. They are described and referred to by residence, as 'the man who lives on the edge of the canyon' or 'the wife of the man who lives at Tall Mountain.' Or they may be fitted into the system of known positions as 'father-in-law of so and so' or 'clan kin of so and so' (naming perhaps one of the speaker's relatives by marriage)" (13:49).

Finally, certain special relations between members of kin groups influence the education of the primitive child in varying degrees. Let us first consider those between the child and the mother's brother or maternal uncle and the father's sister or paternal aunt. As is generally known, the latter may, apart from the parents, serve as the child's chief mentors. To the extent that they do, the arrangements are generally known as the *avunculate* and the *amitate* respectively. Says Reichard, in speaking of the former: "Where it is found, children may be particularly fortunate in that they have two fathers: their actual father, who plays with them, teaches them his techniques and lore, takes them hunting or visiting and is, in general, a fine adult companion; and the uncle who, because of his social and economic obligations to his sister's children, sees to it that they learn the lessons of the tribe and grow up to be responsible men and women. There is a degree of overlapping of social contacts and teachings of father and maternal uncle, especially if the latter lives near his sister's children" (27:419).

Beyond this, the relationship between grandparents and grandchildren stands out rather conspicuously. It is not, however, as highly institutionalized as the avunculate and the amitate. Firth found the relationship between grandparents and grandchildren in Tikopia much less formal than that between parents and children, and he suspects that it may in part at least serve to counteract the constraint induced by the latter (6:208). Leighton and Kluckhohn report Navaho grandparents as solicitous and indulgent toward their grandchildren, with a high degree of mutual responsibility between the two (13:102). Opler points out that among the Apache the maternal grandparents "function to a considerable degree as teachers," much of the instruction being imparted through stories. In addition they supply training in practical activities, as well as a certain amount of ceremonial knowledge (23:64).

The second category of kin relationships concerns such behaviors as avoidances and privileged familiarity or joking. While these behaviors vary widely from society to society, they are in one form or another universal. Although avoidance obtains most often between such affinal relatives as mother-in-law and son-in-law and father-in-law and daughter-in-law, it tends normally to extend to many other relationships including even those between the same and opposite sex (31:466–467). In scope, avoidance ranges all the way from a taboo upon the use of personal names to a complete severance of all social relations. In its implications it is, as Turney-High puts it, "not an expression of disdain but" rather "a mark of extreme respect" (31:465).

Privileged familiarity, exemplified in the joking relationship, obtains between various categories of relatives, most commonly between brothers-in-law and sisters-in-law and between cross-cousins of either sex. Its connotations are strongly sexual. As Reichard puts it: "Whereas avoidance frequently takes the form that matters pertaining to sex must be particularly avoided, privileged familiarity especially emphasizes the fact that sex may be joked about." Whatever the nature of this relationship—and it varies widely—the universal rule of the game "is that the persons standing in joking relationship may not become angry no matter what one may say to another" (27:446). While anthropologists differ in their interpretation of this relationship, it may well be, as Hoebel implies, that it serves as "a form of social and psychological compensation" to counterbalance "the strong restraint imposed by the respect attitudes within primitive kinship systems" (10:248).

Although the avoidance and privileged familiarity relationships obtain predominantly among adults, they begin to impinge upon the young at an early age, and they must by degrees be brought into conformity with them. Says Powdermaker, in speaking of the people of Lesu: "The real force of taboo relationship does not make itself felt until after puberty. The most important of these—are the cross-cousin relationships.—At the same time that the child learns the personal names of other relatives, he learns that personal names in this cross-cousin relationship must never be spoken, and that the term *koko*—is used instead. He sees the avoidance between the adults who stand in this relationship, and he, too, avoids his *koko*, although perhaps not quite so actively as the adults. Thus a child sees his father leave the compound when the maternal grandmother comes to visit them. Since the children spend most of their time on the outskirts of the adult world, they have full opportunity to observe patterns of behavior between taboo relatives—" (25:92).

And as Reichard puts it: "When a Manus girl is engaged, as early as the age of seven or eight, she must begin to hide her face from certain men in the village because of their relationship to her fiancé. Even if she herself is not engaged, her sisters or cousins may be, and she will have to avoid the boys to whom they are betrothed. The number of taboo relatives is so great and the requirements of avoidance so exacting that many childish pleasures must be gradually given up. A little girl's father ceases to take her with him because he does not need to avoid the men she does. The men do not retreat; if the taboo is to be kept—the girl must retire in their presence. Consequently it happens that her activities are much restricted and her pleasures curtailed until at ten or twelve there is little freedom left, and that little ceases absolutely as soon as menstruation begins" (27:444).

Whiting, speaking of the Kwoma, says when an adolescent boy "stares at a girl, her relatives classify the act as a sexual advance and react to it accordingly.—To avoid the sanctions against looking, a boy either keeps his eyes fixed on the ground or sits or stands with his back to a woman whenever he is in her presence. If he happens to be sitting facing a path down which a woman is walking, he must arise and stand with his back to it until she has passed. He may not speak to her until she has passed him; when they are both back to back he may speak to, but not look at, her. Whenever he meets adult females on a path, they turn aside and stand with their backs to the path until he has passed. He must keep his eyes on the ground and must not stop and talk to them until they are behind him. If a boy goes visiting, he must be very careful in his behavior. He may only quickly glance under the porch to note who is there and must then keep his eyes on the ground until he has found a seat facing away from the women, when he may gossip with them over their shoulders" (33:75–76).

Farther along, Whiting points out that the restrictions

which prevent the adolescent boy from philandering with the most available sexually mature women tend to set up emotional conflicts, but that Kwoma culture forestalls this rather effectively through the "socially permitted joking relationship." This, as he puts it, "consists of license to exchange insults of a sexual character, mostly mutual accusations of breaking sexual taboos, particularly those of incest" (33:94).

Scope of and Emphases in Primitive Education

As noted earlier, the scope of primitive education is restricted. This does not mean that it is superficial or that there are serious gaps in its structure. It implies rather that the transmission of the simple and homogeneous cultures of nonliterate societies entails no elaborate specialized organizational set-up. It is accomplished more or less automatically through the established routine of living. The primitive child truly learns by doing. It means, furthermore, as Pettitt stresses, that it is not a compartmentalized affair, consisting of segments that are specifically vocational, moral and religious, and physical and recreational (24:25). As primitive life is unitary, so primitive education is an integral and all embracing process, stressing now one aspect and then another but always in the context of the whole.

Says Powdermaker, in characterizing the educative process among the people of Lesu: "We find in Lesu no childhood world completely separated from the adult one, nor one with different ideals. Instead we find the children always observers or minor participants in the adult society. As soon as they are able to toddle, the children learn the line of sex division in social life. At all rites, and in social life, the boys are with the men and the little girls with their mothers.—They learn their future occupations by first observing and then gradually participating in the activity. They are interested witnesses to trading and other economic transactions, all of which are made in public. They hear the speeches in which reciprocity is the underlying note, observe how the payments are made, and know who has attained the most prestige. They listen to the speeches in which the women extol their husbands as good workers, or shame them for their laziness. Quite early they learn to do as they are told by their parents, and observe in the village life the respect for and the authority of the old men and women. They notice kinship patterns of behavior among the adults and begin to practice some of them themselves. The incest taboo is impressed upon them even in their play. During all this time they have been surrounded with affection and care from both their parents and their clan relatives.

"Because it is life they have been observing ever since they have been able to take notice, by the time these children have reached puberty they are well trained for their adult life, which now begins. They have heard the ideals and patterns of adult behavior set forth in speeches, discussions, gossip, and folk-tales, and they have seen them functioning in life. No other standards or ideals have been set before the child. He has not held before him one type of behavior in economic transactions, or some other aspect of life, only to learn later that this is not the actual practice. These Melanesian children receive a realistic type of education" (25:100–101).

And Dennis, referring to the religious aspects of Hopi child training, says: "From the time that the child is a few months of age he is taken to see all public ceremonies, whether in the streets of the village or in the kivas. During his childhood he witnesses practically every ceremony which occurs. Ceremonials, therefore, are not something into which he is suddenly inducted, but events which have been a part of his life—the most interesting and colorful part of it—since he can remember. What is true of the ceremonies as a whole, is true of those supernatural personages who are impersonated—the kachinas" (4:69).

The emphases in primitive education in turn reflect the emphases in primitive life. Thus, as Woody points out, there is universally a "rough division of labor" between the sexes in primitive societies (34:13). This means that the lives and the experiences of men and women differ accordingly. Among the Hopi, as Thompson and Joseph put it, "the little girl is born into a household group in which she is expected to grow up, marry, and even in many cases to continue to live until she dies as a member of a closely knit and powerful group of females. On the other hand, the little boy is expected to break away from the group into which he was born, beginning at the age of four or five years, for the less stable and more hazardous world of *kiva*, field and range, and to remain throughout life in a marginal position in regard to the household.

"While the roles of both sexes require endurance, industry and patience, that of the Hopi male, in contrast with the female, requires constant vigilance and a high degree of adaptability in order to cope with the natural, super-natural and social forces of the less restricted and less secure masculine world.—Apparently almost from birth the child begins to be aware of these sex-differentiated expectancies, which are constantly impressed upon him in his interpersonal relations. The efforts of the little girl are encouraged by telling her that she will grow up to be a good cook and those of the boy that he will be a swift runner. Even the gift giving *Kachinas* aid in defining the sex roles by presenting the girls with *kachina* images which are fertility symbols designed primarily to be hung up in the house and not to be used as dolls, and the boys with arrows which, although used in play, are important symbolically and are highly valued. In fact, the whole training process is oriented toward these ends" (29:53–54).

In their characterization of the differential vocational training of boys and girls among the Navaho, Leighton and Kluckhohn point out that "from about the age of eight on, children of the two sexes tend to be separated a good deal of the time. Each group is trained in certain skills by their elders of the same sex.—Girls learn to cook and to tend children under the supervision of their mothers and other women relatives. They begin to card and spin at about ten and to weave a little later.—Youngsters of both sexes get instruction and experience in animal husbandry and in planting and weeding crops. Fathers teach their sons the care of horses, agriculture, house-building, leather work, and other male skills" (13:59).

The preponderant role played by kinship in primitive social life, discussed at length above, supplies in most cases the pivotal emphasis in primitive education—the counterpart of the social studies in modern education. Closely allied with kinship, and supplying another major emphasis is, as Herskovits stresses, approved sexual behavior (11:319–322). While some primitive peoples rival the mid-Victorians in their puritanical attitudes toward sex, the vast majority are, within limits, more lenient in their attitudes toward it than we are. Nevertheless, control of sexual behavior is, as Murdock points out, in one form or another, a cultural universal. There is no society completely without it (22:2660).

However,—and this is the crux of the matter—most societies regulate sexual behavior for reasons other than those which prevail among us. Our society has a blanket proscription against all extra-marital sex relations. On the basis of his sample of 250 societies, Murdock considers it "unlikely that a general prohibition" of this kind "occurs in as many as five percent of the peoples of the earth" (22:264). The fact that we do have such a proscription conveys the impression that "sex itself" is "the obvious focus of sex regulation. Not only the man in the street but most of our serious scholars unconsciously assume that sex regulation in other societies must have the same basis—. Actually, the assumption is demonstrably false. To the overwhelming majority of the peoples of the world, the point of departure for the regulation of sex is not sexual intercourse *per se* but one or more other social phenomena with respect to which sex is important, notably marriage, kinship, social status, reproduction, and ceremonial. Instead of a generalized sex taboo, what the ethnographer and the historian usually encounter is a series of sex restrictions, permissions, and obligations in relation to these other phenomena" (22:263).

We shall touch upon only two of the social phenomena which may serve as foci for the regulation of sex—marriage and kinship. "The marital relationship is," as Murdock puts it, "a major focus of regulation.—Taboos on adultery—, though sometimes more honored in the breach than in the observance,—appear in 120 of the 148 societies—for which data are available." However, "these figures apply only to sex relations with an unrelated or distantly related person. A substantial majority of all societies—permit extramarital relations with certain affinal relatives." Moreover, marital sex regulation in these societies does not preclude "nonincestuous premarital relations" as evidenced by the fact that "premarital license prevails in 70 per cent" of the cases (22:265).

Finally, "the only type of sex regulation which is genuinely universal is that associated with kinship." This has to do primarily with "incest taboos and exogamous restrictions" (22:267). Since these were discussed at some length above we need not dwell upon them here, except to stress that training for approved sexual behavior is intimately tied up with them.

Within the limits of incest taboos and exogamous restrictions, primitive societies, with some notable exceptions, give children rather large freedom in sexual experimentation. This is in harmony with adult attitudes toward sex and, as Herskovits stresses, in no way indicative of lasciviousness or carelessness. Within this frame of reference, serious instruction by parents and relatives is not uncommon. In addition, the duties and responsibilities incident to the marital status are often impressed upon the novice in connection with puberty rites (11:321–322).

Primitive Educational Practices and Devices

A study of the techniques and devices employed by primitive man in the education of his children shows him to be anything but a crude bungler. On the whole he evinces remarkable insight into the ways of human beings. Whiting, who analyzed the socialization process among the Kwoma in considerable detail, found that the teaching techniques employed by this society conform rather closely to the principles embodied in contemporary Western learning theory. Significantly enough, the findings strongly contradicted the long cherished notion that primitive children learn primarily by undirected imitation. He says: "A Kwoma child learns but a small part of his cultural habits by free trial and error, that is, without some member of his society guiding and directing him. Were he to do so, he would learn those habits which are most rewarding to him and to him alone. This, however, is not what actually happens. He is forced to learn, not the habits which might be most rewarding to him alone, but the habits which are specified in the culture as being best. For generations before his birth his forbears have tried various ways of dealing with one another and with their environment. Those habits which were successful have persisted in the form of customs, while those which have failed have either suffered extinction or passed out of existence with the untimely death of those who tried them. For various reasons this accumulation of adaptive habits is passed on to the child. He does not simply learn to get along in the world; he is socialized. Thus an essential set of conditions for social learning is the behavior of the socializing agents" (33:177–178).

"Specifically, the various teaching techniques employed by the Kwoma fall into one or another of three categories: providing motivation through punishing, scolding, threatening, warning and inciting; providing guidance through leading, instructing, and demonstrating; and providing reward through giving, helping, and praising" (33:180—adapted).

Whiting's over all conclusion is that Kwoma teachers have a practical "knowledge of the way in which people learn," and that they use "teaching techniques which are adapted on the one hand to the principles of learning and on the other to the culture and the necessity of transmitting it." Assuming "the basic psychological unity of mankind," he sees no reason why the principles of learning should not "apply to the process of culture transmission in all societies," though specific teaching techniques may vary somewhat from society to society due to "divergent historical processes and differing environmental conditions" (33:201).

In his treatise on primitive education in North America, Pettitt discusses learning at some length, and adduces a wealth of evidence to show that it was a directed, rather than an undirected, process. He points out that the play activities of Indian boys frequently centered about the bow and arrow and those of girls about dolls, but maintains that the activities as such could scarcely have represented "spontaneous uncontrolled imitations" of older individuals since all unequivocal evidence "supports the conclusion that implements and toys were presented to the children by elders, along with instructions in their use" (24:41).

Beyond this, Pettitt characterizes in some detail a variety of incentives—among them praise and ridicule, privileges of maturity, conferring of personal names, and first-food rites—which the Indians employed in their endeavor to encourage desirable types of learning and achievement. Significantly enough, they had hit upon the principle—now firmly established—that the learner is stimulated by an environment which reacts in terms of reward and punishment, and as significantly, they had come to recognize that the former constitutes a more effective stimulus than the latter. As a result, they made large use of praise and reward. "It can be safely affirmed," says Pettitt, "that primitive pedagogy accepted as one of its unformulated axioms the efficacy of linking desired behavior with praise, preferably of a public and ceremonial character." Ridicule, as a means to stimulate the laggard, was used more sparingly and cautiously, being "generally reserved as the prerogative of specific individuals whose identity" was "determined by kinship, by occupancy of societal or public office, or by some other publicly recognized criterion" (24:50).

Closely allied with reward and punishment as incentives to learning were the privileges of maturity. These "ranged from removal of artificial restrictions which children had to observe, to the granting of special privileges in recognition of achievement." As Pettitt stresses, economic efficiency loomed large in the minds of the Indians. All tribes "exhibited anxiety concerning the acceptance of economic responsibility by their children." As a result, maturity was conceived of primarily in terms of productive economic achievement, and the privileges of maturity were conferred mainly in recognition of specific evidence of such achievement (24:54).

The use to which the Indians put personal names supplies further evidence that these tribes did not entrust the socialization of the young to undirected imitative behavior. These names did not of course "indicate familial or group connections." They were "unique for the family and social group at any given time." Broadly speaking, they fall into two categories: The essentially trivial, somewhat after the fashion of nicknames; and the other representing great personages, both contemporary and traditional. In either case they "served to stimulate learning, strengthen character, and develop the personality of the individual" (24:59). The former functioned largely by way of mild ridicule and served not only as deterrents to transgressors but also as incentives to socially approved achievements. The latter served in part prestige-reward purposes, and in part as media for the transference of personality. When naming served prestige-reward purposes, the names of distinguished persons were conferred upon individuals in the hope that they might thereby become endowed with some of their greatness (24:65–68).

The widespread practice of first-food rites—first-game, and first-fruit ceremonies for boys and girls, respectively—lends further confirmation to the North American Indians' interest in the economic proficiency of their children. Generally speaking, says Pettitt, "boys progressed through a publicly accepted sequence of hunting achievements, beginning usually with birds killed with blunt arrows, passing through a series of small animals of the 'varmint' class, and culminating in the bagging of the largest game animals—. Each animal killed had to be brought back to camp, and the young hunter could not partake of it himself, but had to sit in state while others feasted and figuratively or literally sang his praise. In a tenuous fashion this same practice extended to the first berries or roots, that a girl gathered; and occasionally, to her first efforts as a collector of firewood, and to her first attempts in handicrafts, particularly during her puberty confinement" (24:76).

As Pettitt points out further, the fundamental purpose of these rites was to stimulate "learning and achievement of the skills of maturity." In addition, they served as a means of inculcating "habits of generosity and foodsharing, especially with reference to the aged members of the culture group." In this case, too, the procedure was "essentially one of linking desired behavior with praise of a public ceremonial nature, with the removal of taboos commensurate with the degree of achievement, and with the adding of privileges in accordance with the same criterion" (24:84).

Folklore in Primitive Education

There is widespread agreement among authorities that folklore plays a conspicuous role in nonliterate education. It constitutes primitive man's only literature, and as Turner stresses, he takes the explanations and beliefs embodied in it about as seriously as does modern man his scientific theories (30:100). Actually, as Herskovits observes, folklore serves varied purposes. "Myths explain the universe and—provide a basis for ritual and belief. Tales, which are customarily distinguished from myths because of their secular character, are often regarded as an unwritten record of tribal history. They act not only as a valuable educational device, but are equally valuable in maintaining a sense of group unity and group worth. Proverbs—garnish conversation with pointed allusion. Riddles divert by serving as a test of wits" (11:414).

Although some folklore elements, especially the folk tale, are worldwide in their distribution, there are regional emphases and peculiarities. The proverb and the riddle, as Herskovits notes, are confined to the Old World. Stories of the animal trickster type are universal, but the purposes which they serve vary. In the Old World they generally take a moralizing turn, as exemplified in the Reynard cycle and Aesop's fables. In the Americas on the other hand, they are used primarily to explain varied phenomena, both natural and social. Trickster-transformer tales and culture hero myths are common, the former comprising such well known cycles as the raven and coyote stories. Within the Old World, Africa is most given to moralizing. In the South Seas region the informal fairy tale is rather prevalent (11:424-425).

However folklore may vary in character and orientation, it serves everywhere as a medium of instructing the young. Says Powdermaker in speaking of the people of Lesu: "Definite instruction is given in the telling of folk-tales and myths. Sometimes the children may learn them casually as they sit around the campfires at night with the adults, but to assure the children's real knowledge of this folk literature, there is a period lasting three or four weeks during which the adult males and females tell the children tales at night around the fire. A feast marks the completion of this period—. The tales are very much in the nature of Aesop's Fables, in that many of them point a moral. Etiquette, taboos, customs, all are illustrated in these narratives, as is the punishment for those who break taboos and customs" (25:93).

In characterizing Chaga practices in this respect, Raum places particular stress upon story telling as a means to character education. The stories, he points out, become more complicated as the children grow older, and they are increasingly directed toward the development of general principles and attitudes. The keynote running through most of them is that virtue leads to success and vice to failure.

"Such stories," he says, "are told by the grandfather on the pasture or on the grassplot in the yard; by the grandmother in the evening, when the children huddle round the fire; by the father when they accompany him to the forest; and by the mother on the way to field or market. When the grandparents recount a tale, not only the children, but any adults present, listen attentively" (26:216–217).

In speaking of discipline among the Apache, Opler points out that they depend much more upon "advice and traditional stories" than upon physical force. Tales, he stresses, are "particularly important" even though they may do no more than "rationalize usage or belief." When myths are related on long winter nights to both adults and children, the raconteur, he observes, invariably takes special pains to "point the moral" for the latter (23:34–35).

"The most important story a child hears at this time," he continues, "is that of the birth of the culture hero and his victorious encounters with the monsters. Familiarity with this account is a necessary background for much ritual. Parts of the story are dramatized in the girl's puberty rite. Ceremonial songs and many ritual touches refer to the protagonists of this legend.

"Scarcely less important is the set of stories devoted to the Mountain People, supernaturals inhabiting the interiors of sacred mountains. These Mountain People, who are impersonated by the masked dancers, are described in the legends as potential sources of supernatural power and as protectors of the tribal territory.

"Most appreciated by the young people, however, is the Coyote cycle, a series of episodes of the pranks of the trickster. Coyote violates all the social and sexual conventions of the society, and this permits the narrator to contrast 'Coyote's way' with more approved conduct.— Through the Coyote tales the child gets some hint of the imperfectibility of man and of the inevitability of moral turpitude in the world" (23: 35).

Pettitt discusses story-telling as a pedagogical device among the North American Indians at some length. He presents incontrovertible evidence of its prevalence in the different culture areas, and points out that folklore entered the educational program in two principal ways—as "literature—transmitted for its own value," and as "an authority for cultural beliefs and practices—taught in other ways" (24:154).

The folklore of this region, he stresses, comprised much more than formal myths, legends, and tales. "We cannot," he says, "speak of the part played by folklore in primitive education unless the term 'folklore' is used to mean the entire range of 'oral literature.' Important as were the myths and folk tales, as a body of literature, and as a source of quotations and allusions in everyday training and discipline, the practical stimulus to individual achievement probably was provided in equal measure by autobiographies, biographies, and dramatized historical episodes.

"The stories that a boy heard concerning the name that he bore, and new ones that he might win; the stories of how other specific individuals had achieved success in vision quests; of how men had built their reputations in the chase or on the warpath; of how girls won and held husbands or built respected reputations—few of these are sufficiently generalized to be dignified as folk tales or myths—yet they provide much of the background for the lives of primitive children" (24:159).

Puberty Rites

No feature of primitive education has attracted more attention than puberty rites. The purpose of these is presumably to initiate the young into the adult social order. And yet, as Firth puts it, "there are many aspects of initiation that do not allow it to be viewed as a simple cultural response to the need for preparation for a place in the social life of the community. The need is presumably universal, but the rites themselves are not. They have a capricious distribution. They are practiced by one tribe and not by another; in communities where they do exist the rites for women are often but a pale reflection of those of the men, or such provision may be the perquisite of the males alone. Again, some features of initiation are difficult to relate to any scheme of fundamental cultural needs; they are there as elements in the ritual, but they find no ready explanation as a contribution to the social efficiency of the maturing individual" (6:421–422).

This situation, Firth stresses, points to the need of specific studies on a broad comprehensive basis to determine the actual contributions which the rites make to the social life of communities where they exist; to note any differences in the social conditions of the communities that feature them and those that do not; and to find out as far as possible how the rites affect the individual recipient of them in contrast with the effect they have upon the group as a whole.

In examining the puberty rites in Tikopia, Firth concentrates primarily upon the first and last of these questions. Our concern is almost wholly with the last. "Initiation in Tikopia," he points out, "consists in essentials of an operation akin to circumcision; it is practiced upon young males a few at a time, and is accompanied by the distribution of huge quantities of food and gifts, regulated upon the basis of kinship to the initiates. A similar ritual, but on the economic side only, is sometimes performed for girls" (6:423).

Firth concludes that "the value of these ceremonies as a factor in primitive education cannot be denied, if by education is meant the process of adapting an individual to the community in which he is to live, inducing him to accept its discipline and norms of conduct—" (6:466). He points out that the manner in which the initiate is temporarily overwhelmed by his elders with no choice of action whatsoever, must inevitably impress upon him the power of social tradition, and that the attention and affection lavished upon him only moments later must by the same token convey to him a heightened sense of his own value and significance in the social scheme of things. Of comparable import, he adds, is the fact that the ceremony is from beginning to end in the hands of kinfolk of the initiate. "At the critical moment the mother's brother says, 'Be strong, nephew!'" (6:466–467).

The puberty rites of the Apache, characterized at length by Opler (23:82–139), stand in most respects in strong contrast to those of the Tikopia. Indeed, about the only common feature is the elaborate feasting which in both cases assumes the proportions of a major social event involving large economic outlays. The emphases upon the sexes are reversed, the Apache rites centering as emphatically about the girls as those of the Tikopia about the boys. Aside from the fact that the rites are closely timed with the first appearance of menstruation, the Apache by-pass physiological and anatomical considerations whereas with the Tikopia the anatomical operation is a crucial feature of the rites. The Apache rite imposes a minimum of stress and restriction upon the novitiate; that of the Tikopia is at best a trying ordeal.

Specifically, the Apache girl's rite is a stately and dignified ceremony closely tied up with the supernatural. Although the main events extend over only four days and nights, preparations for them may require as much as a year. There is large-scale tribal participation. The girl has an older woman who possesses supernatural knowledge as a constant attendant, and is herself regarded as a supernatural for the duration of the rites. The chief ritualist is a singer whose role "hovers on the border line between shamanism and priestcraft" (23:85). The masked dancers, who represent the mountain-dwelling supernaturals, derive their power from a shaman. They play a conspicuous role in the ritual. And the girl herself dances from time to time. In addition to the supernaturally colored features there is much social dancing and singing (23:82–88).

In concluding his extended characterization of the Apache girl's puberty rite, Opler says: "The prevailing tone of this ceremony is one of pleasure and promise. The physiological aspects of maturation are little emphasized. The behavior restrictions imposed upon the girl are not irksome, and their violation brings no really dire consequences. She is not isolated but achieves recognition as the central figure of a major social and ritual event during which she is likened to a supernatural being. Her formal introduction to the adult status is accomplished in the midst of abundance, ritual safeguards, and festivity; therefore, she has little desire to return to the status which preceded the recognition accorded her" (23:133).

The Apache boy's rite stands in marked contrast. It is really not a rite at all, but rather a matter-of-fact introduction to raiding or war expeditions. Before he may serve as a full participant in these adult pursuits, he must serve as an apprentice in connection with four of them. Such apprenticeship is, as Opler stresses, indispensable for successful raiding and warfare. The youth who has not gone through it is not welcome on expeditions. Yet he is not rushed into it prematurely—when he is sufficiently mature, 'he volunteers.' While he is serving in this capacity he is under strict regulations—most of them thoroughly justifiable,—and there are indications of shamanistic tutelage. If the boy acquits himself creditably on the four trial expeditions, he joins the fifth as a full-fledged participant" (23:134–139).

Not all North American Indian tribes reacted to puberty in the sane and dignified manner of the Apache. This is particularly true in the case of the girls. As Benedict points out the Carrier Indians of British Columbia represent the opposite extreme. Here, "the fear and horror of a girl's puberty was at its height. Her three or four years of seclusion was called 'the burying alive,' and she lived for all that time alone in the wilderness, in a hut of branches far from all beaten trails. She was a threat to any person who might so much as catch a glimpse of her, and her mere foot-step defiled a path or a river. She was covered with a great head-dress of tanned skin that shrouded her face and breasts and fell to the ground behind. Her arms and legs were loaded with sinew bands to protect her from the evil spirit with which she was filled. She was herself in danger and was a source of danger to everybody else" (2:28).

As far as the boys are concerned, the vision quest, or some equivalent, as among the Southwest Indians, usually took the place of specific puberty rites. However, since preparation for the vision quest often began in early childhood, it can scarcely, as Pettitt stresses, be regarded as a "puberty-linked phenomenon." Nevertheless, it served "to build the kind of character that the Indians admired," and so was a more or less indispensable prerequisite for adult status (24:90–92).

On the whole, the North American Indians were remarkably free from physiological and anatomical obsessions. "There was," as Thomas puts it, "no circumcision, no filing of teeth, no cutting of the body for the sake of scars." The only mutilations were those self-imposed for disciplinary purposes (28:349; 352–356). The aboriginal Australians and certain African tribes stand in strong contrast to this. Their preoccupation with anatomical mutilations is so extreme that initiation rites for boys, and occasionally for girls, are often grueling ordeals.

Finally, we must bear in mind that many primitive societies get along without puberty rites of any kind. To cite but one illustration. Du Bois, in speaking of the Alorese, says: "There are no rites of transition;—no ceremonies or restrictions associated with first menses. The only equivalents for such customs are tattooing for girls, letting the hair grow long for the boys, tooth blackening and filing for boys and girls, and these are optional" (5:139).

Emergence of Formal Education

This brings us to what are obviously the beginnings of formal schools. Such institutions clearly began to emerge in some of the more advanced nonliterate societies. Africa and Polynesia offer the most striking examples. In the former they appear to have had their source primarily in elaborations of initiation rites sponsored by secret societies. In the latter, by way of contrast, they appear to have arisen—in historically more orthodox fashion—to provide special training for privileged classes.

The *poro* and *sàndì* schools of Liberia and Sierra Leone, West Africa, characterized at some length by Watkins (32), furnish striking examples of formal educational institutions sponsored by secret societies. The former are designated for boys and the latter for girls. They are residence schools conducted on special sites in the forest. The terms extend over two to eight years for boys, and at least a year for girls. Attendance is continuous with no home leaves. The schools are presided over by officials of the highest rank and status. Boys are circumcised upon entrance, and girls must undergo clitoridectomy. Discipline is severe. Instruction is given in about everything that might be expected to function in the lives of citizens of that type of society, including in the very nature of the case tribal laws and traditions. Entrance to these schools symbolizes, as Watkins puts it, "death to the young, who must be reborn before returning to family and kin. Those who die from the strenuous life are considered simply not to have been reborn, and their mothers are expected not to weep or grieve for them." The home-coming ceremony is in keeping with all else extremely elaborate, impressive, and costly (32:672).

The Polynesian schools were, as Herskovits points out, in charge of learned priests. Their rise is, therefore, closely analogous to the emergence of the temple schools in the ancient Oriental urban centers. They "trained the young for the priesthood, and as specialists in entertainment." In some of them the curriculums were so elaborate that they might well be characterized as primitive universities (11:324–325).

BIBLIOGRAPHY

1. Bateson, Gregory and Margaret Mead, Balinese Character. New York: New York Academy of Sciences, 1942.
2. Benedict, Ruth, Patterns of Culture. Boston: Houghton Mifflin Company, 1934.
3. Butts, R. Freeman, A Cultural History of Education. New York: McGraw-Hill Book Company, 1947.
4. Dennis, Wayne, The Hopi Child. New York: D. Appleton-Century Company, 1940.
5. Du Bois, Cora, "The Alorese", pages 101–145 in the Psychological Frontiers of Society edited by Abram Kardiner. New York: Columbia University Press, 1945.
6. Firth, Raymond, We, The Tikopia. New York: American Book Company, 1936.
7. Gillin, John L. and John P. Gillin, An Introduction to Sociology. New York: The Macmillan Company, 1942.
8. Goldman, Irving, "The Ifugao of the Philippine Islands", pages 153–179 in Cooperation and Competition Among Primitive Peoples edited by Margaret Mead. New York: McGraw-Hill Book Company, 1937.

EDUCATION IN NONLITERATE SOCIETIES 293

9. Gorer, Geoffrey, Himalayan Village. London: Michael Joseph Ltd., 1938.

10. Hoebel, E. Adamson, Man in the Primitive World. New York: McGraw-Hill Book Company, 1949.

11. Herskovits, Melville J., Man and His Works. New York: Alfred A. Knopf, 1948.

12. Howells, William, The Heathen. Garden City: Doubleday & Company, 1948.

13. Leighton, Dorothea and Clyde Kluckhohn, Children of the People. Cambridge: Harvard University Press, 1947.

14. Linton, Ralph, The Study of Man. New York: D. Appleton-Century Company, 1936.

15. Lowie, Robert H., Primitive Society. New York: Horace Liveright, 1920, Black and Gold Edition, Liveright Publishing Corporation, 1947.

16. Lowie, Robert H., Social Organization. New York: Rinehart & Company, 1947.

17. Mead, Margaret, Coming of Age in Samoa. New York: William Morrow & Company, 1928.

18. Mead, Margaret, Growing Up in New Guinea. New York: Blue Ribbon Books, 1930.

19. Miller, Nathan, The Child in Primitive Society. London: Kegan Paul, Trench, Truber & Co. Ltd., 1928.

20. Mirsky, Jeanette, "The Eskimo of Greenland", pages 51–86 in Cooperation and Competition Among Primitive Peoples edited by Margaret Mead. New York: McGraw-Hill Book Company, 1937.

21. Murdock, George P., Our Primitive Contemporaries. New York: The Macmillan Company, 1935.

22. Murdock, George P., Social Structure. New York: The Macmillan Company, 1949.

23. Opler, Morris E., An Apache Life-Way, Chicago: The University of Chicago Press, 1941.

24. Pettitt, George A., Primitive Education in North America. Berkeley and Los Angeles; University of California Press, 1946.

25. Powdermaker, Hortense, Life in Lesu. New York: W. W. Norton & Company, 1933.

26. Raum, O. F., Chaga Childhood. London: Oxford University Press, 1940.

27. Reichard, Gladys A., "Social Life", pages 409–486 in General Anthropology edited by Franz Boas. Boston: D. C. Heath and Company, 1938.

28. Thomas, William I., Primitive Behavior. New York: McGraw-Hill Book Company, 1937.

29. Thompson, Laura and Alice Joseph, The Hopi Way. Chicago: University of Chicago Press, 1944.
30. Turner, Ralph, The Great Cultural Traditions, Volume I, The Ancient Cities. New York; McGraw-Hill Book Company, 1941.
31. Turney-High, Harry H., General Anthropology. New York: Thomas Y. Crowell Company, 1949.
32. Watkins, Mark H., "The West African 'Bush' School". American Journal of Sociology, XLVIII: 666–674, May, 1943.
33. Whiting, John W. M., Becoming a Kwoma. New Haven: Yale University Press, 1941.
34. Woody, Thomas, Life and Education in Early Societies. New York: The Macmillan Company, 1949.

Index

Aaronites, 211
Abraham, 198
Abydos, 22, 42
Academy, at Athens, 118–9, 142; at Hanlin (China), 78; at Jabneh, 225; founding of by Hebrews, 246
Accountants, 237; accounting, 185
Achaean, age, 92–3; league, 110; writing, 125
Achaeans vs. Cretans, 91–2; Dorian conquest of, 93
Acheulian epoch, 4
Achilles, 130
Actium, 166
Adcock, F. E., 250
Adullans, cave of, 203
Aegean, age, 96; antecedents of Greek culture, 88–92; Basin, 32; islands, 202; writing, 125
Aeolian settlers, 92, 111
Aesop's *Fables*, 284–5
Aesthetics, 120
Aetolian league, 110
Africa, 32, 97, 291
Agraulos, 137
Agriculture, beginnings, 11; Sumerian, 16, 22, 24
Ahab, 206–7, 212
Ahimsa, 56
Akbar, 59
Akiba, 225
Akkadian texts, 40
Alban Hills, 152
Albright, W. F., 250
Alexander the Great, 110–11, 119, 143
Alexandra, 111, 223
Alexandria, 111, 147–8
Alorese, 291
Alphabets, Aramaic, 234; Brahmi script, 62; Biblical Hebrew, 232,
234; characters, 37, 90, 126, 233; by Cadmus, 126; by Canaanites, 231–2; Egyptian, 29, 45–6, 233; Greek, 126–7, 151, 183; Indian, 62; Lachish Letters, 232; Minoan script, 31, 125; Phoenician and Semitic, 125–6, 151, 232–4; Roman, 184; Sumerian, 20; vowels, 234
Altekar, A. S., 64, 66–8
Ambrose I, 41
Amenhotep III, IV (Iknaton), reforms of, 42
Ammon, priesthood of, 42
Amoraim, the, 244
Amorites, 16, 197
Amos, 215
Anaximander, 115
Animals, domesticated, 11; husbandry, 14, 16, 22, 24
Annales, 178
Anthony, Mark, 165–6, 223
Antignoids, 110
Antigonus, 223
Antioch, 110–11, 147, 226
Antiochus III, 157; IV, 221
Antonine emperors, 169, 194
Antonius Pius, 169, 194
Apache, 265, 270–2, 285
Aphrodite, 95
Apocrypha, 230
Apollo, 95
Arabia, 211, 226
Arabian Peninsula, 197, 199
Aramaeans, 197, 203
Aramaic, 234, 244, 248
Aranda of Australia, 255
Archelaus, 224
Archimedes, 122, 174
Architecture, Egyptian, 26; Greek, 113–4; Roman, 176–7

295

Education in ancient Greece, 125, 148; Minoan and Greek scripts, 125; uses of writing, 125–6; adaptation and elaboration of alphabet, 125–8; numerical system, 128–9; formal training for Spartan youth, 131–3; old and new Athenian education, 132–43 (see also Athens); rise of educational theory, 144–6; highlights of Hellenistic education, 147–8

Education, ancient Hebrew, 231–50; distinctive feature of, 231; development of language, alphabet, 231–4; inscriptions, 232–3; writing uses, accessories, 235–7; formal training for court, for temple services, of chroniclers, of scribes, 237–8; home and family training, 238–9; the synagogue as a learning center, 239–40; for the scribe class, 241–5; development of academies for gifted students, 245–6; of secondary (preparatory) schools, 246–7; of universal compulsory elementary schools, 239–40, 247–8; salient features of curriculum on successive levels, 248–50

Educational highlights of ancient India, 60–8; the role of the Vedas and of religion, 60; the Brahman system contrasted with Egyptian and Mesopotamian, 61–2; growth of Brahman control, 64–5; role of monks and monasteries in Buddhist practices, 65; core of Buddhist instruction, 65; centers of higher education, 65–6; early uses of writing, 62–3; purpose of primary education, 67; scope for women, 67; roles of family, caste system and guilds in occupational education, 68

Education in ancient Rome, 183–95; contrasted with Greek, 183–4; alphabet, 183–4; need of writing skills, 185; role of paterfamilias, 186; influx of Hellenistic teachers, 186–7; dissemination of Greek language and literature, 187–8; development of schools—elementary,

grammar, rhetorical, 188–91; aims and curriculum of each, 189, 191; role and prestige of orator, 190–1; Roman ideal of educated man, 191; shortcomings of classical learning, 192–3; education in the early empire, 193–5

Educational perspectives and practices on the nonliterate level, 254–92; status of children, 255–7; role of kinship in life and education, 263–75; scope and emphasis in nonliterate training, 275–80; practices and devices, 280–4; use of folklore, 284–5; puberty rites, 287–91; beginnings of formal schooling, 291–2

Educational theorists, 194–5

Efron, Benjamin, 251

Egypt, 10, 12, 14–5; historical and cultural development, 22–8, 41–2; religion, 25; art and architecture, 26; mathematics, 27; science, 27–8; system of writing, 28, 44–5; literature, 29; scribes, status and training of, 45–7; practical orientation of Egyptians, 48; temple colleges, 47, 197, 200–01, 205, 209–10, 217, 220, 225

Egyptian alphabet, 28–9; education, 43–8; empire, 32, 41, 207; texts, 198

Elephantine colony, 219

Eliatics, 115, 118

Elijah, 212

Elisha, 212

Elohim, 228

Empedocles, 115, 138

Empires, Assyrian, 32; Athenian, 107; Chaldean, 32; Chinese, 74, 76–7; Egyptian, 32, 41; Hittite, 32; Minoan Sea, 32

Encyclopedia Britannica, 251

Enyalios, 137

Ephebic college program, 137, 147

Ephebus, 136–7

Ephesus, 93, 226

Epictetus, 181

Epicureans, 143; philosophy of, 180

Epicurus, 143; school of, 143, 180

Erech, 39

Language, teaching of, 183, 187–8, 247
Lao Tzu, 72
Latin, grammar, 90; grammar school, 183; language, 178; League, 154; learning, 192; literature, 178; prose, 178; Saturnian verse, 186; schools, 188
Latins, 151–2
Latium, 151–2
Latourette, Kenneth S., 75, 86–7
Lattimore, Owen and Eleanor, 87
Laurie, S. S., 251
Law, canuleian, 156; Hebrew, 239–44, 246–50; Torah, Hebrew guide of life, 241; Hortensian, 154, 156; Roman—*jus civile, jus divinum, jus gentium,* and *jus naturale,* 174–6; Twelve Tables, 183, 186
Law, codification and interpretation of Hebrew, 241–3, 248; teaching of, 46, 64–5, 183–4, 186
Laws, Spartan code of, 129
Learning in primitive societies, 281, 284–6; in ceremonials, rites, 276, 287–91; in play activities, 280–3; socialization, 265, 278; vocational, 283
Legalism, 75, 241
Legalists, 72–4
Leighton, Dorothea and Kluckhohn, Clyde, 266, 270–2, 277–8, 293
Leipziger, H. M., 251
Lepchas of Sikkim, 256
Lepidus, 166
Lesu, 273, 275, 285
Letzun, 221
Leucippus, 116
Levites, 211, 237
Leviticus, book of, 230
Liberal arts, 191
Liberia, 291
Libraries, imperial, 84; Buddhist, 66; at Rome, 194; Sumerian, 37–9
Li Chi, 72, 84
Licinian laws, 160
Linton, Ralph, 87, 263, 267–8, 293
Li Shih-min, 77, 83
Li Ssu, 74
Literacy, 67, 82, 85–6, 125, 134, 183, 238

Literature, Babylonian, 40; Chinese, 83–4, 72; Egyptian, 29; Greek, 113–4, 147; Hebrew, 226–7; Mesopotamian, 37; Roman, 177–80; study of, 65, 111, 133, 186–7, 189–90
Lives of Illustrious Men, 179
Lives of the Twelve Caesars and *Illustrious Men,* 180
Livius Andronicus, 117
Livy, 179
Li Yuan, 77
Lods, Adolphe, 251
Logic, teaching of, 65–6, 112, 192
Lower Paleolithic epoch, 4–5
Lowie, Robert H., 266, 293
Loyang, 70, 75
Luca, 163
Lucius Aelius Stilo, 190
Lucretius, 179–80
Ludus, 185, 189
Ludus of the Litterator, 188–9
Lun Yu, 72
Luxor, 43
Lyceum, founded by Aristotle, 119, 142–3
Lycurgus, 99

Maccabean, brothers, 222; revolt, 218, 221–3; triumph, 247
Maccabees, 222
Macedonia, rise of, 109–10; a Roman province, 157
Macedonian conquest, 138; domination, 110
MacNair, H. F., 87
Magdalenian culture, 3, 6–12
Magna Graecia, 140, 154, 186
Mahabharata, 60–3
Mahaffy, J. P., 149
Mahamaim, 203
Mahayana, 58–9
Maller, J. B., 251
Manasseh, 207, 216
Manus, 274
Marcus Aurelius, 169, 181, 194
Margolis, Max, 243–4, 251
Marius, 161
Mars, 172
Marx, Alexander, 243–4, 251
Maspero, G., 49